The Promise

The Essene Legacy
BOOK ONE

Channeled by Al Miner and Lama Sing

Second Edition 2010

Cover and book design by Susan Miner

ISBN -13 978-0-9791262-2-2
ISBN-10 0-9791262-2-3
1. Spirit writings 2. Psychics 3. Trance Channels 4. Essenes
4. Expectant Ones 5. Jesus Christ 6. The Promise
I. Miner, Al II. Title

Library of Congress Control Number: 2006937870

Printed in the United States of America

For books and products, or to write Al Miner,
visit our website: **www.lamasing.net**

This work is dedicated
to you who have come again
to help open the way for the return of the Promise.

Contents

Who Were the Essenes?

In Egypt, during the reign of the Sun King, Amenhotep IV, or Akhenaten, in an effort to quell the emergence of the belief in the One God, many factions were oppressed. Before the young king who was seeking to build this concept of one single God was deposed and assassinated, he saw to the escape of those who believed as he did. In its exodus, the group fled under cover of night into the far reaches of the desert, migrating for a number of years. They later re-grouped, forming secret enclaves in the harsh, inhospitable highlands of the wilderness, the Three Holy Mountains near the sea, in the area later known as the Holy Lands. The ways in were marked for others who heard the Call and would come, often from great distances – seers, teachers, guides and such. These became the precursors of those who would make the final preparations for the return of the Light of God.

Here they formed the community known as the Essenes and developed customs and beliefs that often differed drastically from tradition, such as the elevation of women in the community. Under the guidance of one such, there began the gathering up of outcast children ... bringing them into the group, nurturing them and raising them as though they were their own. Many of these, as adults devoted to the Essenes, were dispatched into outlying lands and villages to make the routes passable for Jesus in his travels. Thus, the Essene intent was carried northwest, north, eastward and far to the east, and even to the south, into the wastelands, forming the Essenian network through which so much was accomplished.

– Summarized from the Lama Sing Readings

Dear Reader,

It has proven a challenging, if joyous task to attempt mediating between the realms that Lama Sing inhabits and our own third dimensional one. In each instance we have made every effort to be utterly true to the sense of what Lama Sing is offering to us while honoring the vast expanse between us and their recounting of scenes that took place over 2,000 years ago in another tongue and culture. To be sure, Lama Sing was not only translating inter-dimensionally, but also, for our benefit, was relating events as they transpired in real time in a language (ancient Aramaic, for the most part) which often has no words that gracefully lend themselves to twenty-first century American English.

And so, we have tried to carefully discern when it was important to remain totally true to the exact wording (for example, to bring you more completely into the moment in time-space that is being depicted) and when to allow the thoughtful substitution of contemporary idiomatic English, in order that your being carried along by the narrative flow remains largely uninterrupted by your pausing to puzzle or even stumble over the text itself. So, although much of the archaic language and syntax has been preserved, some has been respectfully altered. Finally, the use of Maidens and Sisters refers to those twelve who were chosen as living embodiments of virtues to surround the Master, to mirror for Him that which He already is; the use of maidens and sisters designates those who prepared the way for His coming, sometimes generations before the Birth, as well as those who served Him according to their souls' intent.

The Editors

Foreword

What we have to share with you is a gift of light from the hearts of the faithful in times long past and is the gift of opportunity from these, our Channel and his mate, in times now present. Part of the intent of this work, as God would so will it, is that these works might return to the Earth once again.

Come with us, then, as we guide you to re-live experiences as they unfold in the preparation of the Way.

– Lama Sing

Prologue

𝔐aking the 𝔚ay 𝔓assable

*I*t is only shortly after the sun has set. In the distance mere fragments of the sun's light can be seen embracing the light of the Earth for the last few moments. Upon the vanishing twilight comes the beauty of an incredibly clear evening sky.

Here, there, then all about, the beauty and brilliance of the stars and celestial bodies grow in their number, as though some of these have come forward only for this great event.

There has been a celebration this day, some four generations prior to the Master's entry as the man called Jesus. It has been a gathering of respected members of the various clans of the Essenes, seven tribes in all: people whose basic philosophies, though not so divergent, are different enough to have caused division among these, the faithful.

Before the group gathered now around the campfire, Imnaz is speaking, as he was appointed to, on behalf of those who prophesy. "It is important for all to recognize that our work must begin in earnest, for the time is drawing near when the way must be made passable for Him who is to come and bring the light of passage to all people."

Sophie, representing the feminine perspectives of this group, inquires of Imnaz, "How are we to accomplish this?"

"Foremost, we must unify. The various factions must set aside their differences, that which divides, that this one work be recognized as that unto which we are now dedicated, the single purpose for all Essenes.

"We have, in this day's council, done all manner of divination, meditation, prayer, and such works as we know to be of truth and righteousness. From this time forth, we are of one mind and one purpose. All are asked to contribute talents, abilities, whatever each has to give, unto this work we are about ... the preparation of the Way. Sophie, you shall lead this effort."

A low murmur can be heard rippling throughout all present, as Sophie straightens herself just a bit, lifting her chin almost imperceptibly, unconsciously preparing for the great task ahead.

Imnaz then leads the group in prayer, whereupon the council divides into smaller groups to begin planning the logistics, the needs, and the methods, as there are but eighty-seven years in which to prepare.

In this momentous gathering, the Prophecy has been reignited. Preparations for the Master's entry have begun.

୫୦୧୫

Sophie set about bringing together the remnants who had fled the Egyptian lands, those who were the followers of the One God. Together, as those remnants, they reinforced themselves. She then sent forth emissaries to gather from the villages and distant places those who bore the Mark, whose very countenance evidenced the light of God. These Essenes then went forth and gathered children from all lands ... those who were abandoned, those who were cast aside because of dis-ease, those who had none to care for them, and even those who were given unto the Essenes by the faithful.

These lost children, so to say, became enriched within the loving embrace of the strengthening Essene community, which was centralized near the Three Holy Mountains, not far from the sea. First one generation and then another was taught the innermost secrets of Essene wisdom. All the while, emissaries were being sent to distant lands. Using their healing works, their divination methods, and other such, these Essenes gained allies, followers, and believers. Among them were those who wished to tithe to the Essenes for the wondrous gifts the Essenes had given to them.

Within two generations from the time of the great council, a network sufficient to support the movement of the Essenes further and further into distant lands had evolved. As the third generation passed, the network reached to the Far East, to the north, and to all the lands between. Quietly, and without acclaim, where they saw a need and where they were guided, they served. And where they were asked, they answered the call, always with the Light of God, and Imnaz as that pattern to be emulated.

Sophie's teachings were carried out as she sent these generations forth, ever gathering others, seeking those who bore the Mark. When her time on Earth came to its close, she brought before her those closest to her, blessed them, and gave them charge of the teachings and the prophecies.

Imnaz did likewise, gathering those closest to him who each carried a portion of the message, the teachings, and the faith. These then gathered more and more, and taught and enriched and loved those who were brought to them.

Soon it was the last generation, and time for the final stages of preparation. The tithes of those who had been blessed by the faith and dedication of the priestesses and priests of the Essene outreach would provide the means for the Essenes to prepare in all manner for that which was known to be forthcoming very soon.

One was anointed, called Anna, distinguished as one of enlightenment and known for her sight ... one who could see beyond. In the temples of those times there were many who revered her, yet others feared her and dared not challenge her, for it was known that some power was hers to command.

From within the community, Anna put forth the call: Who would be the teachers, who would counsel, who would make ready the passage of those from the distant lands?

So it was that these times came to pass.

Those Essenes who had gathered were blessed. They went forth and gathered more, and their number and their blessings grew.

They had prepared as best they knew to so do, for the nurturing, the training, and the safety of the children: the children from whom that one would be chosen to bear forth the Child; the children who would be readied to carry out the prophecy as adults; the group of children into which He would be born.

They had made the way passable for the Promise.

Chapter One

On the Morrow

The dawn is barely visible through the mist and billowing clouds. All about the encampment, those who are preparing to meet this new day are bracing themselves against the dampness and the cold. While it is yet dark, there is a luminosity reflected from the particles of moisture which form these slowly moving clouds, moving as though some great being were breathing in and out. The shelters are being opened and the occupants are moving about. Where there would normally be several great campfires for cooking and warmth, there are naught but several far smaller fires.

The young maidens gathering together immediately note a difference, subtle yet unmistakable, and look about for their mentors, their teachers, their parents, if you would. They begin to talk among themselves, the feeling of anticipation growing with each moment's passing.

Then one notices two great figures entering the small wadi where the encampment has been made. All the little maidens quickly turn to watch these two figures striding boldly towards the center of the encampment.

Two of the elders, Benjamin and Lucius, rise, then come the seers, Judy and Anna. All are very aware that the approach of these two has meaning. Greetings pass quickly among them and the two arrivals seat themselves before all around one of the small fires.

While the maidens cannot hear the words being spoken, occasionally the mist parts and they can clearly see the serious expressions upon their leaders' faces.

Suddenly, the two great men stand. Bowing to the elders who are still seated, they gesture the symbolic salutation of the inner Essene community and swiftly move off. The mist seems to mysteriously open to receive them, then swirl about behind them, cloaking their departure.

Benjamin rises and moves about to the outer periphery as Lucius does the same in the opposite direction. Soon there are several score of the sentinels, the guardians. With their staffs and their apparel draped over their shoulders, they stand listening as Benjamin quietly conveys instructions to them.

Equally as swiftly as the first two departed, do these depart, two by two, all in different directions. As the rays of a star bursting in the evening sky, so do they move out, some running up the side slopes of this little valley, others briskly walking off in other directions.

The caregivers stiffen, for they know something of great significance is occurring. Judy has moved to instruct several of them, who then swiftly begin to dismantle the shelters and gather up the belongings.

A number of the elder seers and prophets have gathered and are doing their casting and divination, a few rocking and swaying, some chanting. At some unspoken signal, all place their hands upon the shoulders of the others to form a circle, and they stand gazing down at their fire. Then, without a word they disband, melting, as did the others, into the mist.

Little Zephorah asks, "What is happening, dear sister?"

Anna's serious countenance softens with the child's question, and she and Ruth reach their arms out to embrace all the children who are about them. "We have received messages from our guardians that we are to move."

"Why, Anna?" questions Abigale. "What is the reason?"

"It is a part of the great teaching that in order to know one's truth, one must know that which opposes it, or more accurately, that which balances it."

"Why would that force us to move?" Sophia's eyes sparkle and dance.

"It is not that it *causes* us to move; it *embraces* our movement."

"But how can that be?" continues Sophia, also known as Little Sophie. "It feels like ..." She points in the directions the sentinels have gone, "like we are in danger."

Smiling, Anna seats herself for a moment, gesturing to the great number of children around her to seat themselves as well. "We shall learn much in this journey, dear children. But learning is a talent, an art, a gift in and of itself. If one focuses upon fear or what you have accurately called danger, Sophie, then this can be that which you will experience. But is not our Lord God present in all things? Can we not look into the face of that which challenges to see the gift it bears us? Here, then, must we do the same."

"But I ... I like it here," protests Stefan, "and so do they," pointing to the maidens who are giggling at his comment.

"Then hold the memory of it in your heart, for what you hold with memories of fondness becomes a foundation within you. Just as you are seated upon this good earth, so will your fondness for it serve to uphold you in your journey ahead. But come now. We must make ready."

Swiftly, everyone directs the children to do their works, for each has that unto which their hands must give, as well as their hearts, minds, and spirits.

Only a short time passes and the mist has thickened.

A young voice asks of Judy, "Why has God brought this mist? I can see almost nothing. What is the meaning of this?"

Judy looks down into Hannah's upturned face. "If you would think of this mist as God's embrace, and think of our journey as an opportunity to discover, then you will see that the mist and our journey can work together. The mist is nourishing the earth, is it not?" She bends to point to the delicate leaves of a small flower. "Look you here. See? The droplets of moisture are running to the center of it."

"Oh, I do. And the flower seems to smile."

"You see? The Spirit of God is all about us, in all things. How well you do to be able to see the smile of the flower. Now look at the mist, and tell me, does it speak to you differently now?"

Hands upon her waist, Hannah looks about. She draws in her breath deeply, nodding her head. "Yes, it does. I know it is cool and damp, and yet there is a warmth to it. I know that it is blocking my vision, and yet within its billowy beauty are those who have gone into it, whom I love."

"Ah-h. Now your sight is opened. Now you focus upon the gift, and not the illusion. But come, child. Be about your tasks. We are ready to depart."

Hannah scampers over to join the others. As is the tradition, they form themselves into a small group, and another behind that, and another and another.

The heart of the Essene Promise is gathered here in this great encampment. All that lies ahead, the very Promise itself, is embraced within these people.

Slowly, at first, they begin to move. At the rear are those who are so accomplished in their skill that should any pass along this gentle valley after this group, they could tell not that anyone had passed this way before. There are no traces of footsteps, no remnants whatsoever from this encampment. All is as it was before they arrived.

So they move, the mist enveloping them as it had the guardians before them, sheltering their movement that no outsiders would be able to see them. Occasionally there is a signal from the guardians at the outer periphery of their movement ... a bird's tune, an animal (or so it would seem to the untrained ear) calling out to find its companions or mate.

Many hours pass.

Anna winds her way back through the group towards the rear, checking the children, making an adjustment here or there in the garments or burdens they bear, touching a brow, caressing a cheek, kissing a forehead, until she has reached the rear guard of the group. Here she turns to stride at the side of Lucius. "Is there any word?"

"Yes," he nods, glancing off to the side and then back at her. "They search for us."

Anna sucks in her breath and her hand swiftly comes up to cover her heart.

For a time, no other words are spoken as they walk steadily, Lucius glancing this way and that, alert to sounds.

"How could they know?" Anna asks.

He turns to look down at her. "We are the focus of their emotion. Many of them are dedicated to eliminating us, as you well know. And they have great wealth. There are those who covet such wealth and whose tongues are freed from the Pledge by gold."

A shudder goes through her as she contemplates this. She cannot conceive of who would forsake the Promise for something of the earth.

His next comment breaks her reflection. "Come, sweet Anna. Let us offer a prayer for those who have betrayed us, for surely their hearts are heavy."

Anna, realizing the beauty and the truth in Lucius' comment, reaches over to take his strong hand in hers. As they walk, he offers a soft prayer. "We feel the embrace of your Spirit, Lord God, and we are filled with its light and love. We choose to give from our fullness to those of our group who have lost their way. And to those who see not the Promise, to them as well do we offer all that we are. Thank you for your gifts, Lord God, and for the treasure we hold in our midst. So let it be written."

"So let it be written."

After a few moments, Anna squeezes his hand and he turns to place his forehead upon the side of her head, in a gesture as would a brother to a sister.

Anna steps forward, moving swiftly, strongly, in the direction from whence she came, again passing amidst the children. There are three groups of them now, with the guardians interspersed around them and the teachers and elder maidens observing them, caring for their needs.

Suddenly there is a murmur ahead, and the group slows.

Before the elder maidens can react, the children rush forward in a great swarm, their voices hushed, but their enthusiasm and joy unmistakable.

For there, ahead, in the parting mist, is Jacob leaning against his staff, smiling, gesturing with a hand to the children, who swarm him. In spite of the silence being maintained, his laughter can be heard by all, and it is as though the mist laughs with him.

After a time with the children, he comes over to speak to Anna, Judy, Lucius, Benjamin, and the others. "I have a place for you where you can rest, for the journey ahead is long."

Without another word he turns, striding steadily, followed by the entire entourage as he makes a gentle turn downward and off to the right where the mist hovers above a bowl-shaped hollow. Through the middle runs a small brook, and the children immediately rush to it.

The elder maidens and the others begin to make their encampment, and soon the small fires glow softly.

Occasionally, the mist about the hollow swirls, and one or two guardians come striding up to the elders, their tall stout forms intimidating until one sees the gentle love in their eyes which shines over the strength and power of their presence. After a brief hushed conversation, they turn and move off again, the mist swirling about behind them.

Finally, following one of these visits from the guardians, Judy comes forward and confidently affirms, "We are safe here and sheltered. All is well. Let us prepare for our prayer and our ceremonies. And let us rejoice and thank our Lord God for the gift and blessings of this good life and all that it offers to us."

The children need no more than this to indicate that they are free to be children. They begin to laugh and take each other's hands and move about. Some are finding unique pebbles and are marveling over them in small groups. Others are exploring the brook and the little crannies in this, their new home, even if but for one evening, and so it goes with the remainder of this day.

Now comes the twilight. The mist has opened, and the evening sky, rich in its velvety darkness, seems to descend upon this encampment as though God had placed a blanket of loving embrace over His children.

In his typical fashion, Jacob is seated upon a small rock, his glistening staff canted across in front of him.

Rebekah comes up to him, her small hand caressing the back of his.

He turns to look into her shining face. "Well, maiden, how shall I call you?"

Rebekah giggles, "It is I, Jacob. Do you not know me?"

Jacob bends, his face somber, his eyes penetrating, coming closer and closer to the tiny, curled-up nose. "Hmm ... I do believe that I have seen you somewhere."

She giggles all the more. "It is I, Jacob. I am Rebekah. Knowest thou me not?"

He brings a hand to his chin, rubbing and stroking his beard, and his face begins to soften. "Rebekah ... hmm ... yes, I do seem to recall having heard that name before. But how shall I know this is true? Can you prove to me that you are Rebekah?"

Rebekah is delighted, as are the other children who, of course, immediately gather around Jacob, knowing that something delightful is at hand.

"I can prove it to you, dear Jacob." She closes her eyes and places her hands over her heart. Her head begins to sway gently, her tiny figure moving ever so slightly.

Jacob watches, his face filled with the warmth of his love for this gentle little maiden.

Rebekah begins to hum softly and the other maidens immediately add their own hum to hers, supporting her. As her body and head sway even more, both hands still over her heart, her lips part and a soft tone comes forth. Without opening her eyes, she lifts one hand from her heart and reaching out, places it over Jacob's heart, holding it there, a sweet smile upon her face as she continues to sway.

Jacob's head moves back, his face turns upward, smiling, and his eyes go closed. "Oh-h. I feel your spirit. It *is* you." A great laugh booms forth from him as he bends and sweeps up tiny Rebekah in his arms, placing her on his lap, leaning his head over hers.

She buries her head into his neck, giggling, nestling against his chest. "Have I done well, Jacob? Did you feel my spirit as I gave it to you?"

Leaning her forward that he can look into her eyes, Jacob responds softly, "None could have done better, sweet Rebekah. I know it is you. God could not have made such a beautiful uniqueness and called it by a better name."

She is now giggling profusely, reaching up to hug him around his stout neck as the other children run, laughing, to clamber over him. His staff falls to the ground and he nearly falls from the rock under their weight and number.

Off to the side, Anna and the others are smiling, very pleased and very much in love with the sweetness of the Promise which they see growing in their wards. Anna turns to look into Judy's eyes. Their eyes meet as they lean to place their foreheads against one another. Holding each other's hands, they turn back to look at the children, knowing the significance and beauty of their role.

Several of the elders walk towards Judy and Anna, who rise and bow, gesturing the Essene maidens' gesture. Together they seat themselves.

"What is our destination? Have you discerned this?" questions Judy.

"Yes, we have. We shall go to the Place of Teaching."

"Oh-h," Anna sighs aloud, placing her hand over her heart. "Then we have many days' journey."

"Yes," nods another of the elders, "but we shall use it well. We wish the teaching to carry on throughout the journey. It is important that the children learn to take from all of their life that which can be to their advantage."

"How can we awaken their truths when they are pushing their bodies to their utmost capability?" questions Judy, always seeking to understand both sides of an issue.

"Use the force of nature. Use the force of your own spirit. Use what you know."

Judy stares into this face for a prolonged period of time, probing, searching to understand as she so oft does.

The elder's gaze does not change. His eyes emanate that which is one with all of the Expectant Ones ... the love and hopefulness and the truth of the Promise.

Judy's face warms into a smile and the elder reciprocates. He crosses the short distance between them to put a hand on her shoulder, and bends to put his forehead upon hers.

Following this moment of understanding, Judy, Anna, and the other elder maidens move off to care for the children and ready them for the continuing journey.

8003

So it proceeds for many days, this goodly entourage almost always embraced by the beautiful luminosity of the mist and flanked by the guardians on the outer periphery, until the destination has finally been reached ... the location the children call the Place of Teaching.

Others have traveled here from distant lands, some for several years, each carrying with them a facet of the gem of beauty that ultimately forms the Promise. The sacred teachings at the heart of the Expectant Ones are held in reverence here.

It is Eloise who is the first to see them standing in the distance. The mist having dissipated, the late day's sun shines brightly upon them, as though they are some sort of curious statuary formed by nature itself in the midst of these rugged crags and cliffs. As they begin to move towards her, Eloise can see their faces, smiling, as they reach their hands out in the Essene gesture of friendship.

Some of the children break from their groups and begin to run, for they know what lies ahead.

Zephorah is the first to be scooped up by one of the stout forms who stands at the entry to this, the Place of Teaching. She embraces this great form as though he is one she had known always. Though in the brief span of her life's journey as Zephorah she has never touched this body before, all her eyes have to perceive is the intention of this heart, signaled to her by the traditional Essene gesture, and she knows instantly that her love will be received and returned to her by this man, known in her heart and spirit to be a brother.

He kisses her upon each cheek and her forehead, and swings her small body to and fro, and she laughs. The others with him come forward and do the same with the other children. As greetings are exchanged in the various traditions of these people, pushing his way forward, Lucius comes to stand before the one who speaks for the welcoming group. "Our hearts are filled with joy to behold you again."

"And ours, you," responds the spokesperson, Zenoab. "All is ready. We have greater than is the need and we welcome you." He and Lucius embrace mightily. They both then turn to look upon the group, weary from travel but faces bright and hearts visibly expectant.

"God has given us all a great blessing," Zenoab begins again, "because we are now together. Many have come from distant lands to give to you of their abilities, and in the times ahead as we give to one another and together make the Way open and passable, we shall rejoice. Let us join together now, one and all, in a prayer of celebration."

Zenoab gestures to the children to join hands, and circle upon circle upon circle forms, for the number of children is great. Once this is done, the guardians come to form a great outer circle, and within that, the elder maidens, the teachers, the seers, the prophets, the elders. They stand hand in hand, faces up-turned, as Anna offers the prayer.

"Let me be Thine, Lord God, that I might bring Thy light into the Earth and give it to all who are in need. Let me be Thine, Lord God, that mine heart shall open and receive the gifts that are offered unto me. Let me be Thine, Lord God, that I might know the presence of your Spirit in the words and deeds of my brothers and sisters now gathered. Let me be Thine, Lord God, that His Spirit can enter, and the light thereof remain for eternity to guide others who may have lost their way. Let all of us, Lord God, claim our oneness with Thee and celebrate the gifts of this journey and those yet ahead. We hold Thy Promise, Lord God, each of us in his or her own way. Soon we shall pass it to those who are to hold it anew to return unto the Giver. Open each of us, that this we shall do to the fullness and joy of our spirit's quest. Glory be to Thee, Lord God. We are one. Amen."

A soft clapping can be heard in the midst of the group, and that is all it takes for the others. First the children, eyes now bright and sparkling, raise their hands up, clap three times and then again. Next, they interlock their arms and turn about, looking into another's eyes before releasing that one's arm to turn and take another's.

So the celebration goes on into the twilight, as those whose joy is to give unto the needs of the body have gathered and prepared the evening meal. The remaining guardians spread out around the outer periphery, obviously at ease, having been told by the two great guardians that all is well.

A gentle loving light of oneness moves over the encampment, while those who are the keepers of this Place of Teaching move all throughout, talking, laughing, stopping to seat themselves amongst some of the children to answer their questions, some taking a child upon each knee, laughing with them and questioning them in return.

One such is listening to and answering the enthusiasm of Sophie who is perched upon one knee, and Hannah who is perched upon the other.

"How are you called, sir?" questions Sophie.

"I? I am called Joseph."

"Oh-h, that is a very good name. I have heard that name before. Are you from a tribe of Josephs?"

Joseph can barely contain himself, but does so and responds, smiling, "Are we not all one tribe?"

"Yes, but I know a number of Josephs. How shall I tell you apart?"

Joseph now throws his head back, laughs, and then turns to gaze into her eyes. "You shall know me not by my name but by what I do."

"And what is it that you do?" Hannah asks.

"I am a teacher."

"Really? A teacher of what?"

"I am a teacher of truth."

"What sort of truth?" asks Sophie.

A truth that is embodied in the Promise," responds Joseph softly.

"Are there many such?" questions Hannah.

"Oh, yes. Many. There are enough truths in the Promise, that each of you shall have one of your own."

"What shall mine be?" Sophie asks.

Joseph pauses. His eyes narrow a bit and he smiles,

"Your truth shall be what you find within and bring forth."

"Yes, but how is it called?"

"It is called by the nature of who and what you are."

"Then my truth is called Sophie, as I am called?"

Joseph laughs again and puts a hand to each of the maidens' faces. "That is well-spoken. You could say that your truth shall be Sophie. And yours, dear child ... Hannah."

Hannah reaches a hand up to touch that of Joseph's, still resting upon her cheek. "But how can my truth be my name? I do not understand, Joseph. Can you teach me this?"

"Yes," he responds with light and love in his eyes and voice. "I and others shall. But the first thing I shall teach you, both of you, is that *you* are going to teach *me*."

Sophie and Hannah look at each other for a brief moment, faces blank, and begin giggling uncontrollably, reaching out to touch one another as they do. This attracts the attention of other young maidens, who come over to see if they can find cause for laughter that they might join in as well, for it is, as you might surmise, one of their favorite things to do.

Theresa kneels alongside Hannah and reaches up to take her hand, which Hannah clutches eagerly, and to the side sits Mary now as well, upturned eyes, smiling face.

"What is of such joy here? Will you share with us?" asks Theresa.

Hannah laughs, and sits straight with her shoulders back, with Sophie quickly emulating her, "Oh-h, we are going to be great teachers."

Theresa and Mary, puzzled for a moment, turn to look at one another, and then they too begin to giggle.

"What shall you teach?" asks Mary.

Hannah responds, trying to be serious, "I am going to teach the truth called Hannah," and they all look at one another and burst into laughter again.

All the while, Joseph is sitting with the two little maidens on each knee, smiling, his hand upon their backs.

"Do I teach something, too, Hannah?" asks Theresa.

"Ask Joseph. It is he who said it."

Joseph nods, and Theresa knows she need not speak it.

Then, as things settle down somewhat, in a voice so soft it seems to embrace them in some wondrous way, they hear this from him ... "You know not yet, sweet children, that which you bear within. But it will be shown to you. You may not have a name at present for the beautiful gift that each of you shall give to Him who comes, but it is there. Believe my words. They are true. You may not have heard the song of your spirit in the fullness as you shall hear it in the days ahead, but it is there nonetheless.

"So, Hannah, yes. You shall indeed teach the truth called Hannah, for that is who you are and it is the most precious gift you have to give. You, Theresa, shall also give the gift that pours forth from your heart, and you shall know it to be good as you so do. Mary, there shall come unto you the opportunity that shall make your heart leap for joy and your mind sing with the wonder of it. And you, Sophie ... Not only shall you find that which you ask about but so much more, for within your tiny body is a great light.

"It is as that cookfire over there." Joseph gestures to its flames. "The fire within you is small but pure in this moment. We ... the other teachers and I, the elder maidens, and all those who are ever with you ... bring of our own being the fuel to nurture that fire within you into a great flame of truth. In a time ahead, when He who is spoken of comes, together, all of you, with us at your sides, shall warm Him with the flame of your spirit and truth. We shall give titles to your questions and your truth shall carry one of these, but you shall know them all. I will share with you, as you are willing to receive it, the ability to open your sight and I will do this in ways you will find both joyful and challenging."

Now the other young maidens have gathered as well, and are listening intently.

"Why must there be challenge?" questions Rebekah. "What is the purpose of such? There are times when we find this fearful and wearying. Why must we have this? Why has God made this as a part of the journey?"

"You are called Rebekah, are you not?"

Startled, she glances about. Seeing the smiles of her sisters all around her awakens a smile upon her own face. "Yes, I am called Rebekah. Do you know what it means?"

"I do," he responds softly. "You are a daughter of God, are you not?"

"Yes, I am." she smiles, straightening herself proudly.

"That is a good name, and it is appropriate for you. Will you teach it?" questions Joseph gently.

"If you will guide me," she responds with innocent sincerity. "If I am guided, I will do all that I am asked to do."

Nodding, Joseph smiles, pleased with her answer.

"Shall there be that which *I* shall do?" questions Andra.

"You shall do many things, and He who shall come will bless you for it."

"What shall be *my* truth, then?" Andra presses.

"You shall bear the truth that you find most abundant within you, and we will call it forth."

"Can you do that now?"

All the sisters giggle.

"I can."

"Well, do it then," she urges excitedly.

"Very well. Come here, then, child."

Now a bit uncertain and hesitant, Andra looks left and right as she slowly, almost laboriously, rises to her feet.

"Ah. What is it that you are feeling in this moment?"

Now standing, she looks at him, her face more solemn. "What if I fail? What if I am not worthy, Joseph? What if I cannot do that which you place before me?"

"Thank you, Andra, for teaching."

She pauses, looking down, then all about, then back to

Joseph, "I do not understand, dear Joseph. These are my questions, not teachings."

"These might be called, and rightly so, some of the greatest teachings of all. For when you ask, then can it be given. Do you not already know this?"

"Well, yes, but I am not in prayer asking of God."

"Why do you make them different? Are not a question and a prayer similar? Are you not taught to live your prayer, to be that which you ask to be?"

Looking down, Andra shuffles a foot nervously.

"Come here, sweet child." Joseph reaches out for her.

Hannah and Sophie move over a bit, so Andra can move in to sit between them, her head still down, obviously feeling some sense of failure.

Joseph places a hand upon her head, brushing her hair, touching her gently. "You wanted to learn your truth. You asked and so it is given."

"But Joseph," she protests, looking up into his smiling eyes, "this is something that comes from within me already. It does not feel like a teaching to me."

"Oh, but it is. For a teaching to have true meaning, it must bring something forward from within the student, that which would otherwise be hidden within. So it is a teaching. It has resonated within you and brought forth this result, and now we can meet it because we know it. Now I, and others, can give unto you. Had you not brought it forth, how could it be given to you? For none would know it."

Andra begins to smile as understanding transcends her doubt and sense of unworthiness.

"All of you ..." he continues lovingly, each child feeling as though he might in this moment be embracing her, "all of you shall learn that that which comes to your mind and heart in response to what you meet on the pathway of life shall be the greatest teachings of all. For these you have brought forward into this lifetime from the past, and from God Himself.

As they rise to the forefront of your hearts and minds, so can we honor them and give unto them, and they in turn can give unto others. Celebrate this always.

"When you meet the unknown, as you have in your long journey just completed, learn from it. Look for the gift in the mist and mystery of the unknown. Look for the enlightenment that is offered by the contrast called darkness. Look for the ease in the *dis*-ease ... of mind, body, heart, and spirit ... of those who shall be upon your life's journey. Expect these to call forth the greater strength from within you.

"Most of all, know yourselves as you do this. Fear not to look at who and what you are. If you see something within which you adjudge to be unworthy or which calls out to you in fear or doubt, rejoice! Those are the gifts to be opened, and within them is their counterpart. For where there is fear, there must also be faith; wherever there is doubt, there is certainty and hopefulness.

"But now, take these words and thoughts I have given to you from my heart, and go. Take the nourishment to your bodies, offer your prayers, and take your rest into the oneness of spirit with God. We shall resume again soon. But for now, I must leave you."

"Why, Joseph? Why will you leave us?" questions Hannah. "We are always being left. We want you to stay with us, Joseph."

"Perhaps the absence of a thing loved, sweet Hannah, will build the expectancy and joyful anticipation of its return to you. Perhaps what you are feeling now and what you are discovering in my answer to that, will lead you to your truth. Fear not, dear children. I shall see you on the morrow."

Joseph rises, gathers his garment, strides off into the shadows of the passageway between the two outcroppings, and is gone.

We pray the recounting of these works shall call to each of you ... a call that shall bring out the brilliance of the gift of who you are eternally, to merge with who you are in this current life. For thereafter there can be such a joy within you that all else must fall away and only the joy shall remain.

These are times of wondrous beauty. But, then, the beauty of God has always been and shall ever be.

Chapter Two

The Call

The predawn mist hangs some distance above the Earth, as though to provide a blanket of embrace. Beneath the mist, a small flame glows, reflected by this layer of moisture, so many particles that they would dazzle the beholder with their majesty. The luminosity seems to have its own consciousness, yet we know it to be the embrace of the Spirit of God.

Joseph adds a bit of fuel to the flame and a few sparks lazily curl upwards on the heat of the fire. Stirring the coals, he reaches within his robes and extracts bits of leaves from a little pouch, which he places into the container of water suspended over the fire. He glances up into the faces of those who are with him, noting the solemn presence, each one transfixed by the growing flames. "What have you seen?" he questions quietly of the one across from him.

The small fire illuminates this figure in a somewhat surrealistic way, the shifting radiance of its flames causing this or that highlight to change. His head is bound in a manner unfamiliar to the Expectant Ones, yet clearly he is known and respected by Joseph himself. "It is inconclusive, yet there is a foreboding, such that I might encourage you and the others to have a care."

Joseph stiffens as the impact of what the seer is telling him finds residence within him. "You see them following?"

The tall one with the wrapped head turns to look at his companion to his left, somewhat slighter of build, whose head is also covered not in the traditional Essene way. The band across his forehead bears a signet of some curious symbol, and is ornamented here and there by a reflective stone that captures the light of the flame and holds it in the midst of his forehead. This one turns to the taller and nods, his face blank except for a light that appears in his eyes. "We concur. There is movement of the forces seeking to stop us."

Joseph slumps forward involuntarily. His hands come together, both of them now holding the small stick with which he absentmindedly nudges the fuel into the center of the fire. There is a moment of silence, then without turning, he states, "Welcome, Jacob. You are needed."

The footsteps of Jacob can be heard more clearly now, along with his gentle laughter as he greets his brother, Joseph.

Joseph rises, smiling, and they embrace, gesturing the Essene gesture of love and commitment to the Promise. Standing with hands upon one another's shoulders, each gazes into the other's eyes for but a brief time, yet it is apparent that much has been exchanged without word or gesture. Eye-to-eye, spirit-to-spirit, the pathway is clearly open between these two beautiful souls.

Joseph looks behind Jacob. "Who is with you, Jacob?"

"I have brought several of our sisters. I believe it is appropriate, do you not?"

Joseph, smiling and nodding, holds Jacob's shoulders firmly. "I would certainly never question your judgment, dear brother."

Jacob laughs softly, then reaches a hand backwards to bring Anna forth from the shadows.

All rise to greet her ceremoniously and respectfully, gesturing in their symbolic ways, the Expectant Ones present gesturing according to their custom.

After Anna, comes Judy and then several others, who

swiftly move to take a secondary position behind the two seers and the others.

All seat themselves, and Joseph ceremoniously fills each one's bowl with the hot drink he has just prepared.

As they sit in the morning's silence, no hint of dawn yet apparent, Joseph begins quietly. "We have just been guided by our colleagues," nodding in the direction of the two seers, "to know that we are being pursued."

Judy places her hands over her heart, as do several of the maidens in the background. Their heads begin to bob ever so slightly, though not a sound comes from their silent prayer.

Anna straightens herself, pulling the folds of her garment closer to her neck as though to shut out this information, as though to ward off the sadness of such a betrayal. "It matters not whether the origin of this pursuit is Carmelite, Nazarene, or one of the other tribes. What matters is the Force that lured them from the Promise into the shadows of question such that they are fueled now by doubt itself. That which beckons them has taken command of their will. Say you this to be so?" She glances at the seers.

Both nod.

"What of the guardians and the watchers?" continues Anna. "Have we word?"

"Not as yet," Joseph replies, and he turns to look at Jacob who is sitting as though mesmerized by the flames, now much more active, fueled by Joseph's earlier nourishment.

Slowly, Jacob raises his bowl and sips his hot drink, his eyes never moving from the flame.

"What is the guidance, then?" questions Judy.

"It would be wise to gather all and bring them here," Joseph responds.

"Now?" she asks with some surprise.

"No, danger is not that near or we would have known of it. Let them rest. Their journey has been long and difficult."

"Indeed so," agrees Judy, "and one of considerable expenditure ... little sleep and far too few meals. The children are weary of body." Smiling, she adds, "But bright of spirit."

"Are there those in our presence who can call the Forces?" questions Anna.

Glancing up, his eyes surprisingly penetrating, Joseph looks to the seers.

From the glow of the fire, their faces look as though they are etched in some mysterious stone. Without a moment's pause and without glancing at one another, both nod.

Anna studies them, especially the taller one. "You have come from afar, then?"

"Distance is a relative thing, is it not? If you speak from certain perspectives, perhaps it is so ... Our journey has been relatively long. However, in the perspective of the light that you and your people hold within, and the lights which await the Promise's arrival, our journey has been brief." For the first time he smiles, ever so slightly, eyes twinkling.

Anna seems reassured to hear these particular words and she glances to the second one, who merely returns her gaze, placing a hand over his heart, nodding, bowing slightly.

Reciprocating the nod and slight bow, she continues boldly, "You can call the Forces?"

"We can."

"Call them, then, please."

Joseph leans back straightening himself again. "It is not time, Anna," he responds gently, "but when it is, I assure you we shall call upon them." He glances at the seers again.

"But, Joseph, if the Forces of Darkness know of our journey and our intent ... and this we know for certain ... why would we wait? Why would we not call forth now that which we know to call?"

"Is it not written, dear Anna, that according to the need, so God giveth? Have we a need in the moment?"

Well versed in Essene teachings and equally well versed in the Law, she smiles broadly as she answers, "Your words are of truth, as always Joseph. But I might remind you that preparation and foresight are also direct gifts from God. If we are prepared and if we have foresight, then would it not be more prudent to act and usurp a need, than to act in response to it?"

Joseph leans back, folds his hands upon his knees, and looks up, "Thank you, Lord God, for this beautiful teacher. Indeed, the hope of the Promise, in the spirits of our brave children, is in good hands with one such as she."

With Joseph's obvious intent at reverence and humor through these warm words, all look to one another and smile.

Then there is silence again. Many turn to look at Jacob, whose eyes are yet fixed upon the flames as he raises his bowl to sip again. Something in his essence seems to encourage all the others to remain silent.

Then, from the midst of the silence comes his calm voice. "There is naught which is apart from Thee, Lord God. We are Thy emissaries, those who have chosen to answer your Call. We know that as we are gathered here before this flame which warms our bodies, so too is your Spirit warming ours. We have not a thought nor concern of fear, for that which we hold within is a love so great, so pure, so powerful, that it repels fear as it casts off doubt and question. So perfect is it, that the Forces that would limit will only accelerate and strengthen that which we hold within. Each of us is that vessel into which you have placed a blessing to be held in sacredness for Him who shall come, that the message and the Promise shall be fulfilled and that the Way shall become known and passable. We come to you, all of us together, asking for your guidance. We ask it of Thee, Lord God ... Guide us now."

In the silence which follows, closing their eyes that their inner sight might be clearer and sharper, each in his or her own way is silently attuning, listening, reaching out to feel.

An indeterminate time passes, then comes the mellow voice of Jacob once again. "So do we give Thee our thanks,

Lord God, for the gifts you have just given us, for the blessings that await us in the work ahead. We thank Thee for Thy guidance." He begins to sing softly. As he does, Anna, then Judy, then the other maidens, and finally all, join in singing a simple song of hallowing the One God.

Afterwards, it is Judy who speaks. "I see them at a distance, a considerable distance to the south and east of us. Who else has seen this?"

"I, too, have seen it," responds Joseph. "They come mounted, moving swiftly. But they are to the opposite side of us, there on the great plains." He gestures behind him. Looking up to glance at the seers, he receives a nod of affirmation. "How many days would you say?"

"Two, perhaps three," responds the taller of the seers, and the other nods agreement.

"We thank Thee, Lord God, for this guidance and this information," Anna offers. "Let us now discuss what lies ahead. I believe, for instance, we should bring them all in."

"And the group previously sent to the northwest, to the area of the Great Library, and the others who were to go to the north and to the Sea? Would you have them all brought within, Anna?" questions Joseph.

"I would," she responds firmly.

"You cannot compare the movement of mounted pursuers to the movement of our people with so many children. How many of the groups' children are here?"

Jacob responds. "All are here."

"All?" queries Joseph with some surprise.

Jacob only nods, having returned his gaze to the fire, sipping slowly from his bowl.

"It could not have been otherwise," Judy explains. "We had no awareness of from whence the deception came. Whom, then, could we leave behind? Who could be sent in this direction or that?"

"You mean you brought them out of fear?" asks Joseph.

"No, for I see no darkness in any of those in our group, regardless of where they choose to place their loyalty. It is that, perhaps, they inadvertently could ..." Her voice trails off, not wanting to finish the thought.

"Very well. So be it. Then you are correct, Anna. We must shelter them all until we know what the status is of the pursuers."

"When shall it be done?" Anna probes, obviously concerned for her wards.

"We shall make the preparation." Joseph straightens himself and motions off into the shadows on his right. There, a number of others, previously unseen, quickly rise at Joseph's gesture, rush over, and kneel beside him. He quietly gives various instructions to them. They gesture their reverence to all present and quickly scurry off in various directions.

Anna's concern evident upon her face, Joseph reassures her, "All is well. We have sufficient unto the needs before us, and we shall send forth unto the others ... the shepherds and such who are the watchers on the periphery. All will be well, you shall see."

Straightening himself and looking about, Jacob laughs softly, "Of course. That was never a question!"

"What of the preparation? Does each maiden know her truth as yet?" questions Joseph, turning to Judy.

"Some do, for the most part, but they have not yet affirmed it or claimed it in the formal sense."

Anna adds, "They are so beautiful, all of them. It will be a difficult task indeed to choose from them."

"As it should be," smiles Joseph, rocking as though in some silent prayer of affirmation and thankfulness, "as it should be. Only the greatest of the gems chosen from that which is superior to all others is appropriate as that gift to be offered unto what lies ahead before the world."

"What of those who yet remain outside of our group," questions Judy, "those who doubt? We have need of them and their resources. How are we to communicate with them? And though they know it not as yet, they have need of us." There is a long pause. She places her hands over her heart, her head bows just a bit, and we can see a single tear form in the corner of one eye.

It is difficult to behold this great one, so revered, so honored, having in this moment a tearful thought. Not a tear that is in any sense judgmental, but a tear about to be wept because of the loss of those she loves. It is a tear that shall fall upon the earth never to be known again, never to be seen, save by those who behold it in this moment, and yet her spirit has released something into the world that could be considered a call.

For as Judy weeps a single tear for those who are lost, so does the Promise, in the spirit of that love and compassion which shall be born as the Teacher of Righteousness, come to comfort and embrace her. Yet in all the truth and teachings she has been given, and all that she knows, in this moment she pauses to grieve for those who are apart from the Promise.

"Be of good cheer, sister," Joseph encourages her, "for if their spirit is open and ready, they will hear the Call and know it to be aright. But, as you shall come to teach, it is they who must answer of their own free will. We have offered it. We have given it. It has been presented. It has been prophesied. It has been confirmed in answer to their own prayers again and again. Yet a part of them cannot hear nor see in the fullness of that which grows within each who is a part of the Promise. We shall pray for them oft, and if they hear our prayer they will answer and we will count them among our number. As for that which is unto the need of the work, good sister, thou knowest as do I, the needs shall be met ... with them, or without them."

Judy, looking down, breathes deeply and sighs aloud. "You are, as always, Joseph, correct. And I thank you for the gift of your strength and the beauty of your sight." She raises her face now to look upon him with eyes loving and a light of strength coming from the very core of her being such that it seems to embrace him with gratitude.

Joseph, nods, smiling.

The taller turbaned seer remarks quietly, "Some will come. We have seen it. Some will come to the understanding in the mid-stream of their indecision. Some will open their spirits to the fullest, to the completeness, and it shall be asked of them that they can participate in the fulfillment and the preparation."

"Shall there be many?" questions Anna with almost childlike hopefulness.

"A goodly number."

Realizing that this is all she is going to get from him, she smiles and nods in thankfulness.

Footsteps moving rapidly through the darkness quickly gather the attention of the entire group.

Joseph rises quickly to his feet. He can see in the dim light that it is one of the watchers, sentinels, as some would call them, positioned on the highest points of this craggy envelopment surrounding them.

Breathless, the watcher rushes up to Joseph and whispers something to him inaudible to the others.

Joseph, looking down and shaking his head, turns and seats himself again. "We have no signal to the east," he responds heavily.

"What does that mean?" questions Anna.

"We have brothers and sisters who are as outposts, you might call them. They maintain small herds and appear to be as simple shepherds, but they are our brothers and sisters who have offered themselves as sentinels. I fear, good sirs," looking to the seers, "our guidance is not as accurate as we supposed."

The tall one shakes his head in disagreement, "No, we are correct."

"Then what is the explanation you might offer? We have

lost the signal fire to the east."

The tall seer turns to his companion and an unspoken agreement is reached between them. Both turn to face the flame before them, gazing into it, and their eyes close. Ever so swiftly, first the tall one and then the other open their eyes and gaze at each other.

The tall one speaks for both, "It is for another cause, another reason. We find no violence, no disruption. We find they are still there. Something else has caused this."

"You are certain?" asks Joseph.

"Yes." He glances at his companion who also nods. "We are certain."

Looking down and picking up a stick to stir the coals again, Joseph admits softly, "I do not understand, for it is nearly sacred. They would not ever ... I cannot imagine that they would not prepare a signal."

Jacob begins humming. His humming is so foreign in this moment that it is almost as though an unruly child in the midst of a serious lesson had begun to hum aloud indicating his obvious lack of attention, interest, or reverence for the events at hand.

Then, humming even more loudly, he looks up, meeting the inquiring eyes of each of his companions. His broad face breaks into a smile, his eyes twinkle, and he begins to rock first to the left, then to the right, to the left, to the right, forward, backward, forward, backward.

It is Anna who first begins to giggle. Several of the handmaidens also giggle, for they love and revere Jacob beyond question. Judy is the last whose face breaks into a warm smile. Joseph's laughter can be heard next, and even the seers begin to smile, for they can know what is in Jacob's heart. It is faith. It is the power of a trust in God that questions not that which seems evidential, that which seems to be the circumstance. It is the flame of righteousness held in the spirit and heart of one whose love for God is without limit or question.

It is the joy that this one called Jacob, loved by all who know him, is expressing as a reminder to his companions: We are the Expectant Ones. We are Children of God. We do not need validation, for it is in the eternal flame of which we are the caretakers, that grows with each breath we take, with each moment that passes.

Joseph's words confirm this, "You are my sweet brother, Jacob. Ever does my spirit sing in answer to the song of your soul. You are a light to us all."

"I am, indeed," he responds mirthfully. "I am a light to you all. Will you partake of it?"

Each of them begins to laugh again, and then answers almost in unison, "Yes, carry on Jacob!" And he does, rocking this way and that, humming, and singing a little song.

All of them begin to emulate him, glowing in the warmth of the conviction, the certainty, of their spirit's light. The light that comes from within them, as each one casts off all doubt, as each one meets the fear of the unknown, dwarfs the flame of the fire before them. Each looks into the hearts of the others and sees the reflection of themselves borne in the light of the beautiful uniqueness of the one giving back to them, greater and greater with each moment that passes.

"Praise God!" exclaims Jacob finally to the sound of footsteps running towards the fire again.

Once more Joseph rises to greet the watcher who breathlessly stands before him, smiling.

"The fires! They are there! I do not know what has happened, but they are there, as agreed upon. It is the signal we have been watching for."

Joseph, smiling at the watcher who is obviously overcome with joy, reaches out to clasp his forearms and leans his forehead forward to touch the watcher's. "Bless you. Thank you for bearing us this joyful news."

As Joseph turns, Jacob's bellowing laughter fills the canyon walls of this sanctuary, and each one echoes Jacob.

Finally Judy raises a finger to her mouth and whispers, "Sh-h, we must be quiet. We will awaken the children!"

"Oh, no," comments Jacob. "I have often visited this sanctuary of light. You cannot hear beyond these canyon walls. Neither can this flame be seen, for their height is too great. Even in this," casting a hand up towards the luminous, reflective mist still hovering above them, "the light would not be reflected ... unless, of course, one has the sight with which to see," and he laughs again.

A voice comes from the passageway through which Jacob and the others entered.

Anna rises to greet a sister who whispers, shy in front of the others. Turning back to the group, Anna announces, "The time is upon us. Some of the children stir. The others have made ready, and we are prepared."

Jacob swiftly rises to his feet and extends his hands, reaching out to pull Anna back into their circle and gesturing to all those on the periphery to join in their circle.

They begin to dance about, singing prayers to God, offering themselves as vessels of blessing, asking that God's Spirit awaken within them the very highest and best, that the hope for the future in the hearts and minds of these small ones will be brought to see, to know, to hear; and that the flame within each will be fueled to its fullest measure, that each shall cast their light of beauty unto Him who comes.

Then, exchanging words of gratitude and thankfulness with one another, Anna, Judy, the other maidens and sisters begin to file back through the passageway. Behind them stand Joseph and Jacob. Some of those who are with Joseph have moved off as well to make additional preparation.

Jacob speaks in a soft but strong voice, "We are so very blessed, my brothers. It is the hope for the future that we will call forth, that we will protect and nurture, that we shall provide for. What an honor, what a blessing. We are indeed one in this work, is it not so," ending his comment with a stout inflection in his voice.

Each one remaining affirms his thoughts exuberantly.

Jacob then turns to the two seers and strides up to the taller one. "I thank you for joining us, for your long journey, and for the precious gifts you offer."

Turning to the second, "And you, as well. I know that He will travel to both of your lands. That is my prayer. And you, sir," speaking to the one with the band across his forehead and the pattern of gems across it, "the teachings of your people and the truths you hold we look to with great expectation, and we know that you shall contribute so very much to the work before us. I honor you." He bows, taking the man's hands, and putting his forehead against the back of them.

Turning back to the taller one, he repeats something similar, mentioning his people and their talents with divination, and castings and such, gesturing in equal honor, then swiftly turns to look upon Joseph and the others.

Joseph nods, his face becoming more serious, "We are told they are on their path. We are expectant of them."

"Good, good!" affirms Jacob. For a moment he pauses to look into the eyes of Joseph, and Joseph does likewise into his. "Do you feel a call, brother Joseph?"

"What do you mean?"

"Something I see, something growing within you. Of course, I know you. I know your faith. But there is something different I see here. It looks like ... like joyful expectancy!"

What has been given above speaks to issues which are never too distant from the presence of the Light. As darkness would envelop light and light would reach out to darkness, ultimately they shall come to know one another as brother and sister

Yet within, ever does that still small voice of truth and righteousness speak. Ever within is the flame of God's Promise found within each and every soul with no focus upon their deeds, words, accomplishments, physical beauty, or the lack of these. This is a song of spirit. It is the Call to awaken.

How can you know this to be true? The gifts of God and God's grace are all about you, ever, but only you can decide if they are in harmony with what you call truth. We encourage you whose hearts are willing to find that place within you where only Truth remains, and give it name. Identify it and call it forth. When you have so done, you will have given a gift unto God by the affirming of who and what you are. In the discovery comes the empowerment that will ever thereafter grow and come to be, as the beautiful soul called Jacob, an inspiration unto all.

Shalom, Om Shanti. The Peace of God be with thee ... He comes.

Chapter Three

By Cover of Night

Jacob, Joseph, the seers, and several others are yet gathered around the last remaining embers of the morning's fire.

Joseph finally rises to his feet. "Come, let us go and bring joy as best we can to the children and the others."

In a single, incredibly swift movement, Jacob is on his feet brushing himself off, his face beaming the smile so typical of him. He glances up to look at the seers who have also risen, and notes that the tall one has a strange look upon his face.

The other, his companion, glances at him and gestures to Jacob and Joseph with an outstretched hand.

All grow silent. Where previously there were smiles, the faces now grow serious, for it is evident that the tall seer is aware of something, something beyond the perception of the others ... something unto which he has dedicated his very life to be capable of discerning.

There is a prolonged silence. Then comes Anna through the crevice, the passageway to the outer area, her face snowy white. Simultaneously, the watcher's footsteps can be heard running towards them.

No one knows whether to turn to Anna on the left or the watcher approaching from the opposite direction.

Seeing him, Anna notes that he, too, is obviously in a state of alarm.

She stops and gestures for Joseph to tend to him.

The watcher practically throws himself at Joseph's feet, kneeling, grasping Joseph's garment and offering a prayer.

Joseph bends and touches his head, "Lad! What is it? What alarms you so?"

He looks up, his eyes watering. "The signal fires! They are gone. This time it is clear that great danger lies along the path that the children and the others are following. It is obvious that the pursuers are moving more swiftly than we had anticipated."

"No fires at all?"

"None, my lord. None."

The silence is deafening.

Joseph turns to glance at the seer, who is still standing motionless, his eyes closed.

The second seer is looking down. His hands have come up, and they have something between them that cannot be discerned, but it glistens here and there from the last flickering flames of the morning fire.

Joseph turns to Anna and gestures. She comes forward and, standing up close to him, whispers, "Two of the guardians have come to warn us. Someone comes."

"Where from?"

"There." She points towards the northwest.

"Are they certain?"

"They shall be here momentarily. We could see them moving at their utmost speed. We know something is amiss."

"But there is nothing out there. It is a vast wasteland, a desert. No one could survive there. We only placed them there to warn us in the event of an attempt to encircle us. What, then, could be alarming them?"

In that moment, the tall seer's eyes open. All look upon him with anticipation. At first his face is solemn, and then a twinkle appears in his eyes and a soft smile moves across his face. "They are not enemies, they are allies."

"But who?" questions Joseph.

"We have not met, but I know them in spirit and I know from whence they come."

Joseph reflects for a moment, then turns to look at Jacob. As they make eye contact, they remember simultaneously the stories told to them in childhood of a sacred place in the wilderness, a place of great wisdom, a place wherein only those who are chosen might venture.

It is Jacob who turns back to the seers. "Have you a name for this place, which I now have in mind?"

The seer with the object has placed his hands within his garments, where he almost always keeps them. "I can tell you, Jacob, that many great ones my colleague and I have known in past seemed to have vanished. Then, we heard rumors, so we meditated and saw clearly that they were yet in Earth. Perhaps they are at this place you now have in mind, a place where those who have found the Truth are called."

"What name might you give to this?" questions Jacob further. "There are legends among our people, among our own elders, of such a place. They call it the School of the Prophet. Elijah's realm.

"Of course!" Joseph exclaims. "It is written that it would endure, and that in order that the Message would come forth, the children of the children of these prophets, these seers and holy ones, would come forth as though they would appear from the realms of God."

Softly, the tall seer replies, "I should think that what you say is so, for your words resonate within me. Of those from that very place who are coming now, Anna, do you know of a number?"

"No. We have not seen them. We have seen only the guardians in their great haste to reach our camp. Let me call Sarah to go and meet them." She turns without awaiting an answer, disappearing through the passageway.

Joseph, looking down, places his hand upon a shoulder of

the watcher. "Go, my son, back to your post, and tell me immediately if anything changes. Go now, quickly."

The watcher leaps to his feet and runs off between the large boulders.

Joseph turns to look into the eyes of the seer. "To the other issue before us ... How do we forestall those pursuing us, following our trail?"

"One in their midst knows of this place, and he is leading them."

The heaviness in Joseph's heart is obvious as he looks now at Jacob, for both of them know the one, of their very people, of whom the tall seer speaks.

Jacob responds not nor does he show any emotion that is less than his continuous state of peace, no remorse over this betrayal from one of their own.

In that moment Anna reappears and rushes over to the group. "The guardians have arrived."

As the guardians enter, one cannot help but be affected by their appearance, for there is not only a stoutness of body along with unwavering eyes, but their faces are aglow, a glowing which comes from the righteousness of God. Their faces have this identical essence.

"What have you to tell us?" inquires Joseph.

The one to the left responds, "Several come in this direction, rapidly."

"Can you tell how many?"

"It is difficult, but we would assess two or three."

"Not a great number, then?"

"No. It is a small number. But what is curious is that they come from the wilderness and they are in direct movement towards our encampment, as though they know precisely where we are."

Smiling even more broadly now, the tall seer affirms this. "They do know. They have heard our call."

Joseph turns to the tall seer. "What call?"

"Your prayers, and the greater Call. The same Call that has brought my brother and me to your midst to serve you and to serve that which comes."

"How can they know of it? How can they come from the wilderness? Oh-h. Forgive me. It is the legend, the Prophecy." He turns to look at the guardians and then at Jacob.

Jacob simply nods, smiling, and then softly speaks, "We must place all trust in God. There is no other way. It is *the* way. And I know you all agree." He quickly glances about.

Anna, her hands folded before her, bends her head and brings her hands up in the Essene maidens' gesture.

"Go, then," Joseph directs the guardians. "Go out and meet them. Tell them we know of them, and we welcome them and the spirit they bear to our young wards."

The one guardian looks about and then at his companion behind Joseph, as though there is a moment of question. But so dedicated is he that the moment of question passes as swiftly as a bird in flight might pass overhead. Together, they place their hands over their hearts and to their foreheads, bow, turn, and with remarkable swiftness are gone.

Joseph, sighing deeply, looks about the small group. Several of the other sisters have come to join them. "How are the children?" he asks.

"Most are resting," Sarah replies. "Some have had a difficult time."

"How so?"

"They are dreaming the dreams."

"The Prophecy?" questions Joseph.

Sarah simply nods. "The little one named ..." and she blushes, "after me is most astute."

"Tell us of her dream. Come, tell us." Joseph gathers all closer to the small campfire and refuels it, as another comes from the side bearing an urn with water in it. "Have the children eaten?"

"They are in their prayer at this moment," Sarah replies,

"and then they shall be given nourishment."

"And their spirits ... Are they all well?"

"They are, indeed."

Joseph turns and bends, looking down into the flame, "Blessed art Thou, God. Thank you."

Anna clears her throat. "The children are looking for you and asking for you, sweet Joseph."

"Ah, yes," he responds, smiling.

"And, of course, Jacob, you as well. Their hearts are always gladdened to see you and to have you give song and dance with them."

"This I shall do, and if you will permit me, I shall do so immediately." He quickly rises and brushes himself off.

"But Jacob, there are many things to ... The travelers ..."

"Worry not, Joseph, I shall be particularly succinct this day. I have just the song for them. I will return when our guests arrive, but do send someone to advise me if matters change with the pursuers." Not pausing for a response to this, he merely turns and strides off.

The others resume their conversation, but only moments later they can hear the children's laughter and they know that Jacob has walked into the midst of the children, sweeping them up one by one here and there, pretending to fall down and letting them crawl over him.

Each one by the campfire smiles, for Jacob's love could create no other reaction than a smile.

More seriously now, Anna resumes, "What is to come now? What is our next course of action?"

To which the tall seer responds, "Call Judy."

Anna leaves the small circle to retrieve her sister. In moments they return, Judy seating herself by the tall seer at his gesture to so do.

He leans to look into her eyes. "You have many blessings, do you not, dear Judy?"

For a moment this seems to disarm even Judy, but she

recovers quickly, straightening herself, "God's abundance is for all. It is our choice to choose and to accept, and I believe I have accepted fully. So I answer you, yes."

"Well spoken." He smiles. "How is your sight?"

Judy is beginning to wonder why he continues to question her in this manner in the presence of the others and in the face of all these events now before them. Nonetheless, she honors the questioner, "My sight is good."

"Your spiritual sight?" he probes.

Suddenly she realizes what the seer is doing. He is inviting her to join him and his companion in some specific works they are about to perform. "I know that you can see into my being," she responds, "for I know that you, too, have many gifts and blessings. May I inquire of you, kind sir, why you ask this of me," leaning just a bit to glance at the other seer at his other side, "since I know that the two of you are more than capable of any works which lie before us?"

"We are, indeed. But we need your particular qualities."

"Can you be specific?" Glancing at the others, who look on with interest and curiosity, she sees a small smile on Joseph's face, but turns quickly back to the tall seer. "If you will speak of it to me, and if it is mine to give, I will give it."

"I was certain of that. We are in need of the quality of your spirit called the feminine."

"I am your choice, then?" She looks briefly at Anna and thinks of the many others.

"You are," he responds rather abruptly.

From that tone Judy understands that this is not open to question or debate. It is a matter already decided. "Tell me what you would have me do then, and I shall do it."

"Come here and seat yourself between us." The seer on his left moves to make a very small space.

Judy obediently rises to her feet and moves to them, being rather specific in how she places her body between them. The space is so small that she finds her body making contact with theirs on the right and left, a situation alien to those of different genders in the Essene community.

Shoulder to shoulder now, she glances at each of them. Their eyes meet hers with a serenity that resonates deep within her such that, though she is pressed between these two when there is obviously ample space that all could seat themselves comfortably, she knows it must have meaning.

Startling her, first the tall seer places his hand upon her right knee that is crossed before her, and then the other seer does the same. "Your hands ... Place them atop ours."

She does so, and immediately feels an energy coursing through her. Her eyes looking straight ahead, after a few moments, she feels both of the seers turn their hands upright, releasing her knees and now holding her hands in theirs. In her periphery, she can see that each is placing his other hand over his solar plexus, the midsection of the body. As though they were one, the two seers begin to slowly bob forward and back. "Do as we do," the tall seer directs softly.

After glancing left and right, she begins to bob.

The seer on the left begins a soft singsong sort of chant. "Move with the words."

They continue slowly moving forward and back.

She cannot understand the words, for the seer speaks in a tongue she has not heard.

Then there is an abrupt stop.

"Do not stop your movement."

They rock slowly, rhythmically now, as though they are all one, shoulder to shoulder.

Suddenly she hears the sweetest tone. She turns her head ever so slightly to see that the tall seer's face is aglow. His mouth is closed, save for a small circular opening in its center, through which the most incredibly pure beautiful tone can be heard. She can see his eyes. They are closed, but his eyelids are fluttering, and the tone continues. *How long*, she thinks, *can he hold that tone.* Yet, it continues.

Slowly it fades and then, to her left, the other seer picks it up as though it were some object. She glances at him. The tone is remarkably similar. Had she not known, she would think certainly this is the same voice.

"Carry the tone next," the tall seer instructs her.

Looking straight ahead, closing her eyes, trying to emblazon the tone in her body, mind, and spirit. *It is so pure, so perfect*, she thinks.

To her unspoken question, the tall seer responds, "Let the tone come forth from your spirit. Let it be in balance to ours."

She wants to ask questions. She wants to say, *How do I do that?* But the energies growing around the three are such that she feels electrified, mesmerized, as though they are lifting up somehow. But she opens not her eyes.

She can hear the other seer's tone slowly fading, and she knows hers must now come forth. Drawing in the deepest breath she can, she works her mouth as she saw them do, forming a circle with the center of it. Thinking of their tone, to her amazement, she hears a tone coming forth from her. She is in awe of it. While she is noted to have a beautiful voice and is oft asked to sing the prayer, never before has she heard from herself such a pure unwavering tone, and what startles her even more is that there is no effort. In fact, if she were fully conscious, she would question, *Am I even breathing as this sound comes from me?*

Before she can think another thought, a loud sound comes from the horizon, the sound of thunder. It so startles her that she almost breaks her tone, but she can feel an instant pressure on her right and left from the seers and knows she must not.

She then hears the two seers begin their sound again, but before they do, the tall seer whispers, "Do not stop. Continue." And he begins his tone.

The thunder repeats itself, over there on the horizon, and

then over here.

Joseph turns to look, as does Anna. Great, dark clouds are growing in the pre-dawn light, rolling, swirling. Now lightning can be seen. It is inconceivable, for such an event is so rare only a handful have seen such in a lifetime.

The clouds thicken, as though the tones coming from Judy and the two seers are calling it from the heavens above. On and on, the seers' tones become louder and louder, Judy's doing the same. The tones echo in this small canyon, the thunder continuing with great bolts of lightning hurtling to strike the earth below again and again.

No one knows how much time has passed, for the event is so mesmerizing that all those in the outer encampment have gathered on the top of a small mount. The children are clinging to the sisters with them. The brothers, and even the guardians who remain in the camp, are standing awestruck. Again and again the lightning crashes against the rolling, dark, angry-looking clouds.

Suddenly Judy feels a pressure on her right and left, and the seers' tones stop, so she stops her own, though amazingly, she does not know how she does so. For a moment, she is sitting, her mouth still pursed, a round opening in its center, but naught is coming forth. Then she realizes the seers are holding her hands. She can feel another strange current of energy flowing, coursing all throughout, and realizes she must not open her eyes. Next she feels a gentle pressure as each of the seers places his other hand over hers. Slowly, she can feel their shoulders move her right and left, right and left, right and left. And she hears the tall seer begin to sing a prayer of thankfulness unto God.

Very quickly, Joseph, Anna, and the others who have now gathered, begin to join in. In the corner of her eye, Judy can feel a tear. She tries to fight it back but cannot. She feels it roll down across her cheek to the corner of her mouth, and then another from the other eye. Soon tears are falling aplenty from the great teacher called Judy.

When the seers are finished, both of them begin to rub her hands and squeeze them, speaking to her softly, gently, words inaudible but to her. "Well done, good sister. You have done well. Your spirit is true and clear. Look, open your eyes and look. See what God has wrought."

Slowly she opens her eyes and all can hear her gasp as she looks to the distant horizon where the pursuers are known to be. It is as though the earth and the sky have been joined together in the flashes and loud, ominous sounds.

The seers rise. The tall one smoothly lifts Judy, turning her about to face him. Taking both her hands in his, he leans forward to put his forehead upon hers. "It is true what they say about you. You are a Daughter of God." With that, he straightens up, his eyes shining an inner light which he casts lovingly upon Judy. Without another word he turns and disappears in the direction as had the watcher.

The other seer then makes his people's gestures of reverence. His parting words to Judy are, "May you ever carry the Light of God, and may your teachings awaken the hearts and minds of those who will bear the gifts to the Promise, which awaits us all." He moves off soundlessly, as though he flies over the earth without touching it, along the passageway through which his companion has already departed.

There is a moment of silence around the fire, as the distant rumbling and flashing continue.

Slowly Joseph turns, and we can see Jacob striding through the passageway.

With a broad smile, he comes up to the others. "We do have the power, don't we?" and he throws his head back in his great laugh. He nods in the direction of the storm. "That should hold them for a time. If they can see any trail at all after all of that ... that is, those among them who are not fleeing in terror from the suddenness of that horrific squall. It will take them days to even remember where they are, much less where they were going." Then, more softly, "Praise God, and praise our two blessed guests. They are, indeed, our brothers in the Truth of God."

He pauses for a moment and then boldly steps across the short distance between him and Judy, placing his hands upon her shoulders. "I know you were a part of this."

"How could you know that, Jacob?" she smiles, with a bit of a tease. "You weren't even here."

"Ah, but my spirit was here." He laughs again.

No more can be spoken, for the two guardians now emerge. Following behind them are three figures, curious in appearance and dress, remarkably clean for travelers, especially travelers who have come across the wilderness of the great desert.

It is Joseph who comes forward first, extending his hands in the customary gesture of welcome. "I am called Joseph. This is my brother, Jacob, and here are our sisters, Judy and Anna. You have, of course, met our brothers, whom we call guardians."

Around his forehead, the one in the center has a band with patterns brightly woven upon it, made of hundreds of tiny beads that glisten and shine.

The one to his left has something suspended around his neck, an amulet or signet. It, too, has a luster, with similar colors, yet the pattern is different and carved. The band that holds it about his neck is similar to the band around the forehead of the one in the center.

The one on the right of the center figure also has something suspended from his neck, but it appears to be a container, a small bag of some sort. It, too, is adorned with tiny beads, woven together to form it, the beads being the common aspect among the three of them, even though each one wears his in a different position.

The center figure steps forward, "I greet you, Joseph. Thank you for your welcome hospitality."

Others have appeared from behind various boulders to bring hot tea and a bit of nourishment, biscuits and such, as Joseph gestures, "Won't you sit here by the fire?"

The three then move to seat themselves facing the others.

Sipping the tea and then placing the container on the earth beside him, the center figure speaks, "I am called Elob. We have come to guide you. We know of your situation." He turns to look at Judy. "I see your light. You have been a part of this work?" he asks quietly, motioning to the storm in the distance.

To the surprise of Anna, Joseph, and especially Jacob, who arches his eyebrows and purses his lips, Judy blushes. "I am but an instrument. The others, and the Spirit of God, doeth the work, as I am sure you know, sir."

"I do know." Elob smiles and looks about. "Now, let us attend to the matters at hand, if we might."

All have now taken positions cross-legged around the small fire, and Jacob straightens himself.

"We have come to offer you sanctuary. We have the means to meet your needs and the needs of those who bear the gifts of truth."

"Of whom do you speak?" questions Anna.

Elob smiles, knowing this is a bit of a test. "The children, of course ... in particular the candidates, the little maidens."

Anna nods, smiling, Elob having confirmed that which is in her heart.

"We wish you to make ready."

"To do what?"

"To travel with us. We have come to lead you to our place of sanctuary."

"What sort of sanctuary?"

"It is a place wherein the truth of God can be shared, that those things that are a part of God's Promise unto all will endure, a gift that we openly now give to you and your people. For you see, it has been prophesied to us, and we have seen the truth of the prophecy, for that is our life's work. Please, call your seers."

Startled at this intimate knowledge of the Essene people, Anna glances at Joseph who, with only a moment's pause, turns and gestures to one of the workers, who runs off.

Moments later, the seers return. The three guests rise, bowing and gesturing curiously to them, who simply smile.

What the others gathered do not know is that these travelers know the secret gestures of these two seers, which the seers know would be impossible under normal circumstances, since only the initiates of their people are given the sacred signs. Now the seers gesture in response, based upon their ancient teachings, the mysteries handed down.

The tall seer speaks, "We have seen you. You are of the School of the Prophets, are you not?"

Elob nods, smiles, and bows.

"Please seat yourselves," offers the seer, as he and his companion do likewise. "How has your journey been?"

"A very wonderful one."

Judy and Anna look at one another with amazement, for how can one say that a journey through the vast unknown desert and wastelands was a wonderful one? Their eyes have met and they now smile at each other as they recognize they have had the same thought. It lifts them up, for surely only those who are blessed by God could traverse such a land and survive, much less call it a wonderful journey.

Elob turns back to Joseph, his eyes remarkable. One would think that their entire life and being are open to Elob's sight. "Please," he begins, "make preparations and make them swiftly. All that is unto your need will be provided."

"But how will the children make such a journey? Where is this place you speak of?" Anna urges.

"A place wherein you will all be safe. And we have gifts of truth for your wards. We wish to give them assistance in their journey to bear the gifts they are to give unto Him ...

who comes."

Judy gasps as does Anna, as they recognize the intimacy this one has with the Essene purpose.

Jacob simply smiles and nods.

Joseph is reflective, for the mere words *He comes* mesmerize him, but a smile comes quickly. "We place our trust in you, for we know the Prophecy. We have heard the legends. Even as children, Jacob and I heard of the Prophecy, heard of you, and heard of this place of which you speak. Anna, as he has offered, we shall follow. Please, ready the children."

Anna nods and rises swiftly to her feet, as does Judy.

Joseph turns and gestures off into the corners and the passageways, and many of the workers come forward. "Go and help them. Gather up all of the containers and come here to the spring and fill them, taking only what is needed."

"How will we know this?" questions one.

"Pick it up," smiles Joseph. "If it is heavy and burdensome, leave it. Take that which is unto the need of the children and the others." He glances over at Elob, "And good, warm garments," Elob is nodding, "and blankets," and Elob nods again. "Only these things."

"But Joseph, what of all of the ..."

"Take them into the caves and cover them with stone. Perhaps one day we shall come and retrieve them."

The worker is shaking, for the things Joseph is telling him to cover are sacred and have been preserved by various tribes of Expectant Ones, each in their own way, for many generations. Some, no one knows from whence they came. Some bear strange markings said to be of those who live along the great river's passageway towards the interior, called the Nile. He strikes his chest and bows to Joseph, "What you say, we shall do." He gestures to his companions, and they hurry through the passageway and off to tend to the bidding.

Joseph is obviously impacted by the commands he has given, for in his heart he has considerable reverence for certain of these items that he has ordered to be left behind.

"Do not concern," offers Elob, "for your greatest treasures and all your people's legacy lie not in these things you are leaving behind, but within the children."

This seems to strengthen Joseph, and he smiles and nods. "Kind teacher, please take some nourishment. Would you like to rest? I know not the duration of your journey, but surely it must have been great."

Elob smiles and reaches to accept some of the foodstuffs now being offered to him, as do his companions.

The thought of the children traveling again for days longer, having just traveled under dire circumstances and such hardships, weighs heavily Joseph.

Elob speaks to Joseph's unspoken thought, "We tell you, all is well. The way is made passable. The Word of God is with the children; God will make the way passable for them, and you will see. As we move, as we journey, their spirits will brighten with the purity of the Spirit of God they shall find in each step of the way."

The sun is beginning to move down below the horizon, and Joseph questions of Elob, "You wish us to begin now? How shall we see in this darkness?"

"We will see for you," he responds softly.

Elob's two companions speak for the first time. "God gives us eyes with which to see. The light of the sun is not the source of that which enables us to see."

Joseph is awestruck by the majesty and certainty of these three. His eyes linger upon them only a moment or two longer, and he turns to Anna who has returned, followed by the children now streaming before them. "Assemble them now. We depart."

Her head turns with a start and Joseph simply smiles, as he knows Anna's question is the same one he has just voiced. He gestures the Essene gesture of love, resting his fingertips on his forehead, and he looks up and points to the evening twilight sky.

Anna knows this means that God guides. She smiles, evidencing excitement, "Come, come children. We go to a wonderful place. Look, you. The stars come wishing us to see them. Come," and they begin to move, "let us name them."

Editha giggles. "I do not know enough names to name them all."

Hannah, too giggles. "Then let us name them after things that are about us."

"Like what?" asks Mary.

"You know, uh, like this flower, and that rock, and this grasshopper." All of them are giggling now and Hannah laughs at her own suggestions.

Judy comes over to them. "But first, must we not sing a song of thankfulness unto God?"

"Oh, yes, we must," affirms Editha. "May I start it?"

Little Sarah steps up beside Editha. "May I start it with you?"

Editha reaches an arm around her and the two hop along the path following the others, and they begin to sing in the sweet voices of young children ...

Oh, sweet God, how we rejoice in your presence.
Thank you for the waters of Earth.
Thank you for the plants that grow.
Thank you for the birds in flight,
And thank you for the embrace of night.

Looking up, they begin pointing out the stars.

"That one, I shall call *Turtle*," laughs Sophie, as she is called, for she likes to emulate her namesake.

"It does not look like a turtle to me," Editha giggles. "I think it looks like a gem."

"I, too, think it a gem," responds Mary, "but ... It sort of reminds me of a turtle, too," and they all giggle delightedly.

Seen from above, theirs is a long procession. At the terminus of the line, the great guardians are pulling devices behind them. They are wide, stout branches to which have been tied sinewy trailing objects, obscuring the footprints such that none could see that another has been here.

At the forefront, Elob is speaking, "Send forth those of your people to bring back the other children."

Joseph stiffens as he walks along, "But, how will they know ... How will they find us?"

Elob smiles, turning to his companions, and all three nod. "They know of this place to which we travel, true?"

"Yes, all know of it. It is a part of a sacred covenant."

"Then tell them to gather there if the way is clear. If not, and the pursuers have found this place, then tell them we shall find them in the north, near the City of Knowledge."

Understanding, Joseph nods.

"The shepherds have a place to the southeast of the City of Knowledge. They are your brothers and sisters, these shepherds. True?"

Surprised that this secret knowledge is known to Elob and his people, but then realizing that of course it would be, Joseph answers, "Yes."

"Then perhaps it is best that we do not place them in the position of making the decision. Have them gather there, in their place near the City. I will have my people go there and bring them back to our land."

Joseph calls several of the workers and three of the guardians, and quietly issues instructions to them. "Go to the other tribes. Bring the children, as well as the seers, the prophets, and all those who are one with the Promise. Tell them the time is upon us. They must come now."

"Tell them also this ..." adds Elob, "disperse those who remain, for the vengeance rises. The opposing forces know that the Light comes. Your people must disperse. None can remain in their places as they are now."

Joseph is struck by this instruction, for some of the Essene tribes are not in agreement with him and his people.

The tall seer steps forward. "Tell them that it is the teaching of Sophie, the Great Teacher. They must now ask of their seers and prophets, *Is this the time?* And they will see it. He then turns to the center guardian, reaches within his garment and pulls out a sizeable pouch. "Here. Within this pouch are those things that will help them know from whence I speak my words. Give one, and only one, to the elder of each tribe. He will recognize it."

The guardian accepts the pouch, bows, and nods.

"Send them, now," urges Elob.

With a gesture from Joseph, they go off into the darkness, alone, in differing directions.

Joseph's heart flutters with the joy and anticipation of what he believes lies ahead. *Who can these three be, who walk several paces in front of him and his people? From whence do they come,* he ponders, watching them as they stride, moving surely, with incredible grace.

He turns to look at Anna, who has caught up with him. "How are the children doing?"

"Remarkably. It is as though we have camped for days. They seem to be ... well, as he said," nodding towards Elob, "renewed."

Joseph covers his face with his hands.

Anna places a hand upon his shoulder, "I know, my sweet brother. All these years, all the generations before us, all the prophecies and teachings, and it is here. It is now. These children will bear the gifts ... the gifts of truth that will fortify and reawaken all that He is."

Joseph sighs deeply. "It is almost more than one can conceive of. Here am I leading our people behind three total strangers into the desert in the dark of night."

"I know. It is, indeed, so curious."

Anna's words so touch Joseph that the two of them begin

to laugh. "I can feel it, all of this, in the core of my being. And the incredible storm that they called ... How is Judy faring after all that?"

"Well, let us just say she has discovered something new," and Anna laughs again.

"I should say so. I was there. I saw it. I saw them do it, and I know I will tell that tale many times. Yet as we walk along here I have a hard time believing what my eyes saw."

"Ah, yes. But your faith is great."

Joseph straightens himself and smiles, "I don't know where I'm going. I know not who these people are that I am following. But I do know this ... The Spirit of God is embracing us, and them. And I hear the Call. Do you not? I hear the Call of His Promise."

Think now for a time about sweet Joseph, Anna, Judy, Jacob, and all the many others moving in the dark of night into an unknown land ... a land about which it is told that none return. Yet here, followed by their most precious gifts and treasures, their children, they move forward in faith.

Our prayer for you, each of you, is that what we have given here might serve as a loving reminder to you of your own faith. That if you dwell upon your faith and the bringing forth of your spirit, and you hear a sweetness that grows into a remarkable call, then you are His.

We call you now ... for He comes again.

Chapter Four

After the Storm

Elsewhere, a captain slows his regiment, as he does periodically that the steeds not be overexerted. Riding during this more leisurely moment beside two who are not his soldiers, he turns to one. "Tell me, Noab, why is it that you have separated from your people and are guiding us to them?"

The directness of this question unsettles Noab for a moment, and he reviews in his mind the events that led up to this betrayal, as it might clearly be called. He glances at the captain, whose steely gaze penetrates deep into his being. "I tried to reason with them. Both of us did. I am one of the seers, elders if you prefer. I did not see in accordance with the actions they followed against our recommendations. Therefore, believing unto the One God and the guidance we are given, the others of us have taken this pathway because we believe it to be the correct one, and only because we have been assured by you that no harm will befall them ... that they are only to be dispersed. Those are your orders, are they not, Captain?"

Without any facial expression, the captain responds coldly, "That is what I have been given."

"Are they your orders?"

"As I said, that is my understanding of what I am to do."

"Forgive me, Captain, but you seem a bit evasive. Would you be more forthright?"

"In the field, it is my decision. Their decision as politicians in their grand surroundings ... They do not know what it is like out here in the conflicts with your people. Political logic and directives often cannot be met. Even they, were they to be here in my place heading out to do this work, would have to realize that circumstances dictate the action, not distant orders based on politics or whatever else."

Noab stiffens, "But you intend them no harm, true?"

"I have heard of a certain group within your number ... I do not know how you call them, but I understand they are willing to preserve their order, *your* order if you will," smirking, taunting him, "to the death. Now I ask *you* a direct question, Noab. Is that true?"

Looking straight ahead, Noab slumps a bit forward as the heaviness of the realization of what is being said comes to him. He steals a glance at his companion and thinks he sees the glistening of a tear.

"Tell him the truth," the companion responds. "Truth is our only ally, as we have been taught from childhood."

Noab turns to the captain, "It is possible ... No, perhaps it is true. I cannot answer with certainty, for they will ultimately follow the leaders. They are called guardians, and they will defend our people, without concern for their own lives."

"What is their number?" the captain grills.

"That I do not know, for in truth I cannot recall how long it has been since I have been involved in the inner circle councils. They have known for some time that we," gesturing to his companion, "do not agree. They stated to us, gently mind you, that in order for the Light to be all they believe it must be, all must support the Promise, as they call it, or not be involved."

"What, in fact, is this thing you call *the Promise*? I have heard of it, whispered here and there."

Drawing in a deep breath and straightening himself, Noab, looks straight ahead at the line of the horizon barely visible in the predawn light. "The Messiah."

"What ... *messiah?*" he spews, with obvious mockery.

"The King who will come and free our people."

He throws his head back and laughs. "More idle prophecies. You people live based on idle fairy tales, silly legends. You find some meaning in every pebble, every leaf that is turned this way or that."

Noab frowns as he looks at the captain, who continues to laugh. "I understand why you might think that. But if you had seen and lived what we have, you would know better than to think these are but fairy tales."

"Well, then, if that is so, here I am. Prove it to me."

"I believe that I could do that, in fact, Captain, were we to have time to pause and dismount. I believe that I could show you things that you would not find within your logical mind. There are many powers, many powerful elementals that are ever present."

"Like what? Look around. You can make out a few objects here and there. Make one of them come to life, or tell me something I don't know. Choose whatever you would like with which to prove these powers to me. Show me now. Or are your powers so limited, your God so distant, that they only work under certain circumstances and your control?" He throws his head back and laughs again, causing many of those who are following behind, rank after rank, to look at one another, questioning whether or not their captain has begun to imbibe again, as he has a habit of doing on their sorties.

"It is of no concern to us," Noab responds softly, "for when the time comes, and it is still distant, you will know the truth of what we speak."

"And ... uh ... just when might this time be?" the captain mocks, leaning to peer into Noab's eyes.

"Not when *they* think, and that is the whole point. They are going to disrupt everything. There are those of us who believe ... who *know* the time is more distant. It shall not occur as they proclaim it shall. When He comes, He will be all-powerful. He will *appear*. He won't be born of a *body!* He will manifest in a wall of light and take form. This we have seen. He will ride a flaming chariot from the heavens, which will open for Him. And all will know Him to be the King."

For a moment or two, the captain simply looks at Noab, somewhat surprised at the depth and power of his belief as he recounts this.

"So you see, Captain," turning to look at him squarely, "this could ruin everything ... their plan, their inclusion of the females and their participation in the unholy rites and works. They sing, they dance, they do all manner of things which are, according to our ancient teachings, blasphemy."

The captain makes a sort of guttural sound. "Well, I see that within your people there are obviously very strongly differing views. Witness the fact that you are, after all, Noab, betraying your own people. And you, too," leaning over to look at Noab's companion.

"Abiding by one's guidance and truth is not betrayal," counters Noab. "But no more of this. I would have your word that no one is harmed."

"I cannot give it," the captain replies sprightly.

"Then grant me at least this ... none but the guardians. They will be the only ones who will actively oppose, if they are not told by our leaders to stand down. I can understand, then, that if you encounter them, you must best them. But I want your word that nothing will happen to the others. They are passive; they are not as the guardians."

Glancing this way and that, and turning to look back at his large entourage following behind, the captain again settles in on his steed and looks at Noab. "I will grant you that. If they do not gather a weapon and become aggressive, they will be spared. To be succinct, our orders are to disband them. We will take them in small groups to the outer reaches and deposit them there with instructions not to gather again. If that order is violated, then I pledge to you ... *all* will meet their God."

The latter statement chills Noab, but he shrugs it off. "I will see to it that they do not re-gather. There is no need. The Messiah will come as I gave it. We have both seen it, and we know our sight is true."

"Well, then, so be it. Now, enough idleness. No more chatter here. It is time to resume our advance." The captain raises his hand, gestures, and directs his steed forward in a ground-consuming canter.

So they move, the hoof-beats rumbling upon the earth. Noab and his companion, unaccustomed to riding any such creature, continually shift their bodies to compensate for the pain of being mounted so long and now moving at this pace.

"How long before we reach where you say they are?" the captain calls out.

"At this speed, I should think midday, early afternoon at the latest."

"Good, then we will continue. But if some miracle comes to mind between now and then, do perform it." He throws his head back, laughing mightily again as he speeds off.

They move swiftly, stirring great clouds of dust.

Then the captain sees it. He raises his hand to slow the group to a walk again. "What is that ahead? Do you see it?"

Noab, looking up into the sky, gasps. Rolling towards them is a great swirling line of dark and gray billowing mass.

"What can that be?" the captain asks again, now almost at a stop.

The great legion behind him nearly collides with one another to avoid running into the captain. Many move off to the sides, as they would in a battle line, that they, too, can see this ominous thundering cloud of swelling mass moving towards them with incredible speed. A loud crash sounds with a flash of light, and several of the horses rear, the soldiers struggling to keep them under control.

Noab sits, mouth agape, his face paling. His companion has begun to pray aloud as the mass rumbles on with stunning velocity. From within the rolling clouds comes an eerie, steely-colored glow that lights the surroundings between the flashes of light ... to the left, to the right, above, beneath, within, as the clouds continue their ominous roll towards this group.

Many of the soldiers have begun to cry out with shouts of, "Captain! Captain! We must retreat now! What is this evil that approaches us!"

"Hold your places!" commands the captain. "It is naught but a small storm."

Then comes the wind, a wind unlike any here have ever seen or heard, for it begins with a moaning.

"Dear Lord God," Noab cries out, turning, shouting to his companion, "it is God. Have we wronged?"

The moaning grows, as do the winds, which are not blowing in a normal way but as though someone were exhaling a colossal breath straight at them.

As they cover their faces against the stinging sand, the rumbling is deafening, the flashes now brighter and brighter.

In the rear of the garrison, some have turned to gallop away, the captain angrily shouting at them, but they can hear not over the din of the moaning.

The horses, fearful, agitated, are also bolting. Having fallen from their steeds that are galloping off in a frenzy, some of the soldiers are scrambling to their feet, arms outstretched, screaming for their colleagues to gather them up. Off they go, some two astride a mount, others fiercely galloping away, casting a glance back over their shoulder and crying out. It is difficult to distinguish which is louder, the cries of the many soldiers or the eerie moan of the strange wind. The ground is shaking, trembling.

The captain shouts angrily at Noab, "I am going to re-group my men. Stay here. Obviously you have something to deal with, do you not?" This time his laugh, as he digs his heels into his steed to gallop after his men, is not so mighty.

Noab's companion has dismounted. His steed has run off and he is kneeling upon the ground, face in his hands, sobbing. "Forgive me, Lord God. I believed I was right, forgive me."

"What are you doing?" shouts Noab. "Here, mount up behind me. We yet have a chance to beat this storm."

"No, I now know that ours is the wrong path, the wrong choice, and I await God's intention for me. I ask only to be forgiven. If I am, I shall join them and support the Promise."

"Fool! Perhaps it is, indeed, the wrath of God coming, but perhaps it is because we have not put forth sufficient effort to convince them our vision is the true one."

Noab's companion looks up at him, hands down at his sides, "Noab, I tell you, we are wrong. This is the voice of God. Listen!"

Struggling to control his steed that is bolting this way and that, Noab hears it, and he stiffens. In that moment his steed surges upwards. Because he is stiffened, he cannot react and he falls, slamming his face into the dust of the ground. When he recovers and lifts himself up to look at his companion, there is a surrealism about Noab's appearance. Half his face is the reddish-brown color of the earth beneath them, lighter in color, making him look as though he is half one being and half another ... half of one world and half another.

Seeing this evidential message from God, his companion gasps. "It is true! Now I know it is true. We have divided ourselves. Rather than being as one, believing unto the greater number, we have claimed the earthly half of ourselves, abandoning that which is sacred." Pointing to Noab's face, "Even the earth speaks this message with clarity."

Noab reaches his hand to his face and tries to brush off the earth, dampened by moisture carried in the winds. Looking up again at the dark, ominous cloud almost upon them, he falls to the earth. One cannot tell whether he has collapsed or has intentionally thrown himself upon it, but we hear him moaning in between prayers. "Lord God, it is I, Noab, your servant. If I have wronged Thee, then I stand before Thee to be judged. But if not, I call upon you to send away this which is not of Thee, that we might continue to bear Thy message to our people."

The swirling, thunderous cloud now races over them, catching up with the soldiers. They are strewn about, the rain soaking them. Some are thrown from their mounts. Others, injured, are crying in the swirling hulk of this darkness and thunder and lightning and rain.

We hear one cry out, "O God of these people, we do not intend to wrong Thee. Please release Thy wrath from us."

But there is no one to hear him.

ℰᴑᴃ

An eerie calm follows the monstrous storm.

Beneath the soil and sand is a silhouette indicative of two figures lying beneath a shallow covering. Accustomed as they are to some types of storms, they have attempted to cover themselves and make a secure place in which they might endure. Only one figure begins to move. It is Noab.

Coughing, wiping away the sand and dirt, he struggles to his knees, looks up, and sees the eeriness of this predawn sky. Still in somewhat of a daze, he glances down at the form beside him, and then, having broken free from the spell of this ordeal, frantically begins to uncover his companion.

When he finally manages to roll him over, Noab knows he is alone.

Wiping the soil from his companion's face, he cradles his head in one arm and places his hand over his companion's heart. Still coughing, choking, he offers a prayer for his friend's spirit in the tradition of the Essenes and gently lays him down. Finally, he places his companion's hands in the Essene posture of one who is departing this life, covers him with the companion's own garment, and stands, looking about, bewildered. The strange remaining glow is not night nor dawn. It is something else.

He bends to one knee, then brings the other one to the ground, and lifts his palms up. "I thank you, Lord God, for sparing me, according to the prayer I offered unto you. Guide my companion to Thy embrace. Bring him unto your goodness. Forgive him for turning against Thy guidance in the hour of darkness, but know his heart to be pure. In Thy Name, I commend his spirit unto Thee. Amen."

Standing again, brushing himself, he looks off in the distance and can see some figures. One, he discerns to be the captain, and with him a considerably smaller number of the soldiers. Some have regained mounts; others are afoot. He can hear the captain shouting commands.

Time passes, and the captain comes to where Noab is now seated, "I suppose you would have me think that storm to be something more than a freak of nature?"

"It was."

"Well then, have you abandoned your belief? Do you think they sent it?"

"I am quite certain that somehow they have manifested it. It has given them a considerable amount of additional time. I do not know what their plan is, but I am certain now that they know we pursue them."

"How can you be certain?"

"Because of things you would not understand. I know the power, and that was an expression of the power of God called upon through their faith and those with them. I know the energy of their strong faith. I have never seen anything like it and I pray I never shall again. Still, I remain firm in my belief, in that as I have been guided."

"Where is your companion?"

"He is gone to be with God."

"Well then, do you plan to continue to lead us?"

Noab simply gazes at the captain for a moment, and then turns to look at the horizon, still strangely aglow. Feeling a need for some small bit of time alone, he responds, "I am certain, Captain, that some reorganization is in order for your garrison. True?"

The captain turns on his mount to look back and sees his disheveled troop behind. "Perhaps for once you are correct, Noab. We shall take time to reorganize, but when I come back, you had best be ready. Do you understand?"

"I will be here."

The captain reels his mount and gallops off, barking orders here and there to his bedraggled troop, stretched out in a long disorganized line.

Noab turns to look at the horizon and kneels. "Lord God, it is I, Noab. I believe in that as I have seen. Thou knowest this. But I pray, as well, if I have in some way failed or erred, I pray of you, let truth and righteousness, according to Thy Word, prevail." He bows his head, holds his hands across himself, and begins to rock slowly, as he singsongs the little prayers, so holy, so sacred to the Essenes.

ℰↃﾤ

It is a closely-knit file, the children holding hands, or several across with arms linked. The way is not too difficult, but it is arduous because the soil is loose, and footing is often difficult. To the forefront are the three from the School of the Prophets. To the rear and on the periphery, as is the tradition, are the guardians, ever watchful.

Some time has passed upon their journey, and, finally, the three to the front stop and turn to look back at the long file of Expectant Ones.

Elob speaks something to one of his two companions, who moves ahead briskly. He then turns and speaks to the other, who heads towards the rear of the group.

Moving through the line up to where Elob stands awaiting the return of his companion come Jacob, Anna, Joseph, Judy, to receive further instruction, followed by several other sisters, teachers. Others surround and continually and light-heartedly support the weary children.

Elob answers their unspoken question. "It is time for a rest for the children."

"Oh, praise God. They are so tired, and they thirst and hunger."

"We have, of course, anticipated this. My brother has gone ahead to prepare for that."

"Prepare?" questions Joseph glancing at Jacob who is, as is so typical of him, looking about, a serenity and peacefulness ever evident upon his countenance.

"How much ahead?" Anna inquires.

"Just beyond that rise," gestures Elob.

"Oh-h." With relief, she turns to go back to speak to those who are tending the children.

Some of the children are seated, their knees pulled up and their foreheads resting upon them. Others are looking about, noting the brilliance of the stars in the clarity of the wasteland sky.

Fingers of light have begun on the horizon, their lumi-nosity making the starkness of where they are journeying all the more intimidating, as is evident upon the faces of some of the adults as well as some of the children.

Anna forces a smile, and with brightness announces, "Soon, just a bit further, there shall be food and rest."

Several of the children clap and giggle.

Glancing up, she sees a small gesture from Elob. His companion who had gone to the rear of the group now moves briskly past her, smiling and nodding to her as he does, whis-pering, "Tell them all is well. Just ahead is all that is needed."

She summons the children to their feet, encouraging, supporting, and Judy does the same.

A single, mellow tone can now be heard, coming from

somewhere up ahead. The children begin to giggle, for they know only too well the beginning of a very special song from their beloved Jacob. Soon, his song fills the air with the richness and clarity of his voice. Each one thinks, *Surely Jacob is beside me, for I hear him so clearly.* All along the procession each hears Jacob as though he were at their side.

As the group rises up over the summit and comes down into a small bowl-like depression, just sizeable enough to hold their company, the children grow excited as they see one of those from the School of the Prophets standing in the midst of a small group of others who are dressed like these three. There, beside him, they see the large urns and bundles, which they know must contain foodstuffs.

Anna encourages them, "Go ahead, children. Go," thankfulness evident upon her face.

The children are each given unto their need and greater, and nourishment and fluids are then passed about to all the others. Joseph stands and leads the entire group in a prayer of gratitude, acceptance, and thankfulness unto God.

It is an inspiring sight to behold. These children, many of them having traveled so far, some frail but strong of spirit, the light in their eyes equal to any of the greatest of Essenes.

Positioned about on the perimeter are the guardians, like great beings of light. Never is there a counter comment from them or one of complaint, but always within their eyes and their very being a faith of incredible strength and absolute dedication unto the preservation of their wards. The maidens struggle to climb up to bring each of them food and water.

Joseph and Jacob, Anna, Judy, and many of the others are now seated near the three who have come from the School of the Prophets. They introduce the Essenes who are before them to their colleagues, seven in all.

With obvious gratitude, Joseph asks of one of the seven, "How did you get all these provisions here? Even with the seven of you, I cannot see how you would manage to bring such a large burden here, so far into the wilderness."

"It is as you and your own people so often say, is it not ... If one believes, then all is possible. And what are a few urns and bundles to the Lord God?" He smiles broadly and the others smile with him. "So, you see, we believe as you. Perhaps even more than you in some ways."

Joseph is puzzled for he believes that the faith of his people has no equal. "I should like to learn more of this," he responds sincerely.

Jacob is occasionally closing his eyes, moving his head left and right. Anna and Judy are attempting to rest, though they are also intensely focused upon what is being said.

"You will see," the one responds to Joseph, "that we are guided to share that which we have to share and to give to you all that is ours to give. Do not think that we have come to you to take control or to lead you apart from that which you hear within. Ever know that ours is the intention to support each of you, all of you, in that which guides you from within.

"For what I might see as truth may be found in you, or one of the others, in a different way. That, we have learned, is the intent of God ... that the beauty lies in the uniqueness, and that uniqueness is in the interpretation of the perceiver. Thus, dear Joseph, we are one with you, and all equal. The least and the greatest are the equal before God.

"It is a process of helping one another to awaken and see, and to know that the uniqueness bears the true gem unto the crown and glory of God. But we seek to learn much through your spirits and we pray of you, please share with us, as we now offer completely to share with you."

Quickly Joseph turns to look at Judy, who is contemplating this, for there are many sacred teachings within the Expectant Ones' background. Many of the rituals and ceremonies are to be shared only with those who are among the elders, or the inner circle, or those who are to bear their portion of the gifts to the awakening of the Promise.

Noting this, Anna turns to Jacob, whose eyes are now open.

He is seated erectly, not stiffly, but proudly. "I shall answer if permitted."

He receives a nod from Joseph. Judy also nods, a hint of smile, perhaps a bit of a relief evident upon her face.

Anna looks from one to the other and then smiles. "Please. Speak for us, dear brother."

"We know that you are sent to us by the One God," Jacob begins, "just as you know this, dear friends. We look upon you even at this point as our brethren. We know that you can see, and we know that you know truth. We do not know the depth of your perception of it, and perhaps you have seen that which we have not. But we accept your gifts, those which you have already given, for we know you have saved our group. And we accept that which you intend, as well.

"We shall ask for guidance that we might know if it is appropriate to share that which we consider sacred and holy, our covenant with God. We will then surely share all that we are guided to. But because we know that you understand, know that if we are bound by sacred oath that this or that may not be revealed because of certain requirements of our faith, we must uphold this."

Elob is smiling, and in the momentary silence he nods and leans forward to bow, gesturing strangely, but obviously in some gesture of honor. "As my brother has spoken, we would honor you and how you see, according to that which you are guided to know and do. There is no need, as you well know, dear Jacob, for concern or to justify what you have stated. We would encourage you ever to honor that which you consider holy and sacred, knowing full well that we shall do the same. Nonetheless, it is possible that we have looked over the horizon a bit further than you and your seers," gesturing to the tall seer and his companion, "and have stepped forward in answer to that. We would also like to say that we saw that you called upon the power and that the Spirit of God in the elements of the earth rose up to answer it. We honor you for your work, dear seers. And you, as well, Judy."

There is a hint of a flush across Judy's face, seen in the light of the new day.

"For now, let us we give shelter to your people, especially the children. We have temporary structures in bundles which we can begin erecting, for soon it will be quite warm. The children can rest under the shelter of these and will be remarkably comfortable, as shall you. We shall rest during the day and travel as the sun begins its journey to rest, that in the event there are those who are boldly striving to locate us, they cannot see any clouds of our movement nor any glistening of anything that one might carry to reflect the sun's rays. Now, let us set up our encampment. You will be safe here, and we have more food and water for the evening meal.

"Rest you all well. My two colleagues and I must now depart for a time but we will return before the sun begins its journey unto its day's rest to resume our travel with you. That you might know whereof we now depart, we must go to a place apart from the groups, where we shall perform our works as we know them, which will preserve and protect and guide. Perhaps one day you might choose to join us in such works, but for now we leave you our blessings. Our spirits of course remain with you and thus we will know your status.

"If any need arises, we will know of it. Concern not. Call your guardians in, that they too might take rest. There is no need for them to stand watch. We will see to that." He gestures, smiles, and turns swiftly, followed by his two companions, and they rapidly disappear over the horizon of the surrounding dune.

Anna is the first to speak. "Thank you, Jacob. Your words to Elob were well spoken. Judy, shall we prepare? Let us gather the maidens and set up the children's structures first. Jacob, will you gather the guardians?"

"No small task," he chuckles. "But I know they will listen and understand."

As we rise up here and look down upon the circle of sizable dunes, there is an incredible stirring within, as we behold this sight ... the Light of God ignited by the massive power of faith. For within the encirclement is this group of faithful children of God. All that they are, all that they have, is offered to preserve and bring forth the manifestation of the Promise of God.

May it be with each of you, as you read our re-counting, that you can move into these experiences; and as you do so, that you can know the nature of such a faith ... willing to set aside that which tempts in order to claim that which is eternal.

Chapter Five

The Way Is Made Passable

Under the luminosity of millions of stars the group journeys. Leading the way are the seven from the School of the Prophets, resembling the head of an arrow penetrating into the unknown. Close behind them are Elob, Jacob, and Joseph, followed by the remainder, numbering one hundred fifty-eight in total. All are exhausted. Some of the children are stumbling and the elder adults labor with every step.

Now striding very swiftly towards the front come Anna and Judy, their faces etched with concern. Though these two are known not to nourish such emotion, one could nonetheless ponder, *Is this fear I see?*

Noting that they are attempting to catch up, Jacob raises a hand, and those to the front of the group pause. The signal is passed all along the entourage, stretching a considerable distance, only two or three abreast.

Judy speaks first, "The children can go no further."

Joseph, glancing back over the long file of his people, turns and looks at Jacob and Elob.

Softly, Elob insists, "We must continue. We have no choice."

"Judy, Anna, tell the others to gather the children." Joseph's voice is almost stern. "Carry them if need be."

"But, Joseph, they are weary beyond measure."

Joseph's eyes soften. "I know, as do you, dear Anna, state of our people. But the Promise is at stake here. We ca not tarry."

She glances at Judy, their eyes connecting for a moment then she returns her gaze to Joseph. "Might we then all pray All of us?"

Jacob, who had seated himself, stands, brushing himself off. "I will lead this prayer, if you will all permit me?"

"Please do," responds Joseph.

Jacob follows behind Anna and Judy as they walk back to the midst of their group wherein the children are nestled, surrounded by the elders and all the others.

"Children!" calls Anna brightly. "Look who is here."

Their faces brighten through the weariness evident in their posture. They manage smiles, and a light comes from within them that can be seen in their eyes. The others form a group around the children, and in the center is Jacob.

He walks about the inner circle looking into each pair of eyes as though he is striving to impart some reservoir of strength. Then, having completed his tour of the inner circle, and having glanced at each one, he returns to the center and stands with his hands together, head bowed. All present do the same. When next his face comes up, all can see it is aglow, as if reflecting the myriad of stars in the evening sky. But these people know better. It is the very brightness of Jacob's spirit shining forth.

He lifts up his arms with palms outstretched to the heavens, rocks his head to and fro, and begins to turn around in a little circle, humming a song as he does.

The children are the first to pick it up, each one doing just as he does. The warmth and innocence of these children is contagious, and soon everyone brightens and all begin emulating Jacob.

Then he holds his hands up, clapping to this side and then the other, and we hear: "We greet you, Lord God, here from the midst of this abundance of gladness in our hearts. We sing out unto Thee from the fullness of our cups within, and offer Thee continual praise. We give thanks for all that we are and all that we have, and bless those who know not the Way, nor the brightness of Thy Spirit's presence. We offer ourselves in service to those who know not the Way. Strengthen us now, Lord God. As the journey unfolds before us, give unto us greater than might be the needs ahead. Into each heart, each mind, and each body, bring the light of Thy Spirit ... now." He stops and kneels, his hands together over his chest, his head bowed.

The hush of the evening is enhanced by all present ... listening, asking, opening to receive the blessings that sweet Jacob has petitioned of God. It is a timeless event filled with an energizing essence, the sudden crisp coolness of an evening desert breeze not impacting them at all.

Suddenly, one of the children gasps, then another, and another, for before Jacob, a light has begun to manifest.

A murmur of wonder passes throughout the group, followed by reverent silence as a beautiful collage of focused light manifests. It seems to reach out and touch each one present. Beside it, another light, and to the other side a third.

Then, from within the center light all can hear, *Be of good cheer, O Children of God, for I am with Thee. The way shall be made passable for you, that you may, in the faithfulness of your hearts, carry forth that which shall become rich with the harvest, the blessings from our Lord God. Prepare ye for that which shall be given, and as ye do so, expect to receive greater than is anticipated. We are ever with you.*

The two lights to the right and left of the central now move off into the group. *Oh-hs* and *oo-os* and *ah-hs* come forth all about as these two lights appear to expand and then embrace each one present. To witness this is to witness a timeless awakening of such brilliance that doubt cannot enter, fear can find no foothold. And the weariness fades away like leaves from a tree in their season.

Finally, their work completed, the two beings of light return to the left and right of the central figure. *So as ye call upon us, we who have gone before you, you make the way passable for us to be with you. Remember ever, especially you, sweet children, thou art never alone. As ye ask it, our Lord God grants us the right to answer. Thus, so have we done. According to thy prayer, sweet Jacob, is it given.*

The departure of the three lights is majestic. They do not dim nor dissipate as of something being here in one moment and gone the next. Rather, it is as though they disassemble into particles of light, floating lazily in and out, weaving all about like billions of tiny fireflies in an evening sky. They swirl all about, causing the children to giggle and touch themselves here and there where the particles of light have come to rest for a moment upon a shoulder or a head or a forehead or an outstretched palm. When these are gone, there is a freshness, a brilliance all about this group.

Joseph raises his hands and snaps his fingers, brings his hands together and claps, stomps one foot and then the other, and begins to dance about. Singing a boisterous song of praise unto God, turning his head this way and that, he scoops up a child here and there, dancing and singing.

So do they all rejoice, swirling about with one another as though they had rested for days and been nourished with sumptuous banquets, the children's laughter electrifying the stillness of the evening sky. One would think this joy could be heard for scores of miles in every direction.

Then comes the subtle gesture from Elob to Joseph.

Joseph nods, his eyes growing serious again, and he glances at Jacob, Anna, Judy, and several of the others. "Continue the journey," he states quietly.

Jacob nods and, smiling broadly, scoops up Kelleth and Josie as though they were light bundles of garments, and their tiny arms embrace his stout neck.

Now, any others of strength lift up a child, some carrying two, for they are small burdens, indeed.

Jacob calls out, "Sing children. Give us the gift of your song. Let us march on in the glory of God."

So they file in behind one another again, but this time, though they have journeyed for so many days that some of the little ones cannot remember when they were not in this desert, their movement is swift, their steps bright, and the sweet song of the children's voices is like an embrace by the Angelic Host.

"How much further would you estimate, Elob?"

"We must be there by dawn, Jacob. We have no choice. So we must maintain a goodly pace."

"We can do this," Joseph acknowledges turning to Jacob, "thanks to you."

"Ah-h. I only called forth what each always possesses." He kisses the children in his arms.

In time, their swift movement brings them to a high place in this vast wilderness.

Elob turns and announces with a broad smile, "Only a short distance now," as he points. "See there?"

Joseph, straining to see into the darkness, at last makes out the dim outline of a surprisingly large formation of rugged, craggy outcroppings in the midst of the desert. "I had no idea these were here. They look like small mountains."

"Not quite," smiles Elob, "but they will give us shelter as they have for untold eons of time. You will find all that you need and greater, for there are those of great wisdom and kindness waiting with many gifts for you and especially for the children. But come, let us keep moving, for a storm will soon be upon us."

Joseph looks this way and that. Anywhere he looks he sees naught but the crystal clarity of the desert night sky, but he questions not.

Rising before them like giant sentinels are rugged rock formations, which can be seen more clearly now in the starlight. Seemingly within their embrace are still taller and larger outcroppings. He wonders why none of his peoples has ever seen these, or at least has never told of them.

As they enter, following passageways, weaving in and around the outcroppings, the children are exclaiming in wonder, talking with excitement about the curious shapes some of the formations make.

Then, *Thum! Thum! Thum!*

All of the Expectant Ones stop abruptly to look at one another.

Some of Elob's people pass among them stating not to be concerned, that this is a special ceremony to welcome them, as well as to call the forces of nature. A number of others are off to the side in a larger recess of this passageway, watching, smiling, waving as the weary travelers file past.

The entourage begins moving, very slowly now, and Elob is relating what is taking place to Anna, Judy, Jacob, and Joseph. "The drumming you hear is how some of our brethren summon the forces, a call to the forces of nature, which you would call the Spirit of God, wouldn't you?"

Anna nods, glancing up at the sky showing between the craggy outcroppings. She glances at Judy, remembering how she helped call the storm that stopped the pursuers and scattered them.

Judy is suddenly aware of what Anna is recalling, and turns to Elob.

Knowing her thought, he nods. "Yes ... the pursuers. They have regrouped. Those who see have related this to us."

"Will you attempt to disperse them again," glancing at the two seers who are now with this small group, "as we did?"

"Not exactly so. This time they will see it coming, and we should think after their first experience, this will forestall them. I think caution now may be the better part of their zealous pursuit of these sweet children, and all of you. No, the primary intent for the storm in this instance is that there be no trail, no tracks remaining. Those who pursue you have those among them comparable to your guardians, who forage far from the main body looking for signs. We might offer a prayer for these, for some of them will not survive."

Sorrow flashes on the faces of Anna and Judy as they imagine perishing in such a storm.

Elob shakes his head, a gentleness on his face. "It will be their choice. First they will be warned, and they will have time to retreat should they choose to so do. If they do not, then the Word of God will speak again."

The drumming is growing in intensity and frequency.

Then it begins, growing from far away like some enormous beast, beginning first with a low, whistling moan. In one moment it is as a maiden crying out; in the next, it is as though a great voice is whispering from the heavens.

Those in the group scatter to comfort and reassure the children.

"This," Elob reminds them, "is the warning of which I spoke."

The winding path has, for a short distance, taken them to higher ground, and those who have reached this position can see off in the great distance a growing mass of darkness. Within it is an eerie swirling of yellows and tans, billowing, moving very slowly but gaining steadily in speed. From the right of their field of vision, to the left from whence they came, rolls an ominous, thunderous sound.

∞⃝⃝

Tamarak, the captain's scout, looks up with fright as he hears that sound again. Looking about, he sees nothing, but his mount is greatly unsettled, twisting, bobbing his head, pawing at the earth, and Tamarak feels a chill pass through him. To turn back he knows is a betrayal of his command, and yet the feeling is growing within him that to remain and to continue on in his scouting is certain death.

He urges his mount slowly onward but the beast twists his

head wildly about, and Tamarak clings fiercely to the reins. The moaning, wailing sound grows. He wants to cover his ears but he cannot release his hold, for he knows he will be thrown and his mount will bolt.

Suddenly, a rush passes throughout his being, and he thinks, *Who are they to take my life from me in the pursuit of people I have never even met ... who have, as far as I know, committed no deeds to warrant their death.*

His mount is spinning this way and that, struggling to break free from the command of its rider. Finally, Tamarak cries out, "You have bested us! I pursue you not. Call off your wrath, you son of the Expectant Ones, you ... Messiah! I see your power. I affirm it. I pursue no longer. Spare me." He reels his mount and thunders off in the direction from whence he came.

Though galloping full out, it is some considerable time before he can make out some of the small fires of the main group that has paused only long enough to nourish their steeds. Glancing over his shoulder, he sees it ... a fierce massive yellowish-brown swirling of dust and wind, and the rumbling ominous voice-like wail calling out from its midst.

Froth foaming from its mouth, the steed thunders past the encampment, as Tamarak calls out, pointing back over his shoulder, "It comes! It comes again!"

Shrieks and cries erupt from the remnants of the original campaign.

The captain angrily jumps up, clasps the back of Noab's garment and pulls him to his feet. "What manner of evil is this? Who are these people we pursue that they can call forth such wrath? You say this is their belief in a *God*, in a *Messiah*? I call it a command of evil forces, and I swear to you, Noab, I will see each of them perish." He throws Noab to the ground, kicking him repeatedly, snarling, "You loathsome cur."

The captain calls to any remaining who might yet be listening, "Mount up. Leave him behind! Let him make his way in the fury of his own people. We will retreat from this, but only for a time! I shall have my revenge."

In a single movement, he mounts his steed, wheeling it about to stand over the cowering Noab, who is looking up, a hand outstretched. "Here is my reward, you betrayer. What good are you to anyone? You certainly are no good to us." He bends to spit upon Noab, reels his mount and bolts off, following Tamarak, who can barely be seen in the distance, galloping full speed away from the encroaching storm.

Noab struggles with the pain from several broken ribs tearing into his side, covering his mouth and shading his eyes against the first winds blasting his face. He crumbles to the ground, holding his side, and begins to weep. "Sweet Lord God, I come to you in humbleness. If I have wronged Thee and my people, I pray that I might be found worthy of Thy forgiveness, for all that I have done has been in the light of what I believe to be truth." Doubling over with the searing pain, he struggles to straighten himself and continues, "If this is my hour, may the grace of your Spirit lift up mine, and may I be taken before the Ancients, that I may know Thy truth, Lord God, and that I might again be returned to Thy path of righteousness."

He glances up, barely able to see. His tears mingle with the desert dust, leaving long, dark, streaking patterns around his eyes and the tops of his cheeks, which are all that is visible above the cloth held over his nose and mouth. As though someone had painted him with a design, one could suppose these are the trails of the past indicating the crossroads and the choices he has met, and which now seem to all be pointing to the central place within him wherein the light of his faith yet endures.

He receives a stabbing pain as a rib pierces one of his organs causing internal bleeding. With a moan, he keels over on his side, the swirling sand now beginning to cover his body.

In a voice softened by the pain, dimmed by the ebbing

forces of life now leaving his body's form, he prays, "Sweet God, I come unto Thee in the humble askance that if I have erred, if I wronged Thy Spirit in some way, see into my heart, and see my spirit in the brightness of my desire only to serve Thee. Unto Thee, now, Lord God ... my spirit comes."

Only a few moments more of pain, and his face softens. His eyes open for one lingering moment, shining with the light of God's peace.

ℰℭℬ

"Are there dwellings here?" questions little Josie of Judy. "Are there places where we can rest and where we might find shelter?"

"Oh yes, I am sure of it," Judy turns to look at Elob for confirmation.

He smiles and nods. "I believe that you shall find great joy in what awaits you. Encourage them to continue on, for I know not the power of the storm being called. It may well impact us too in some ways."

The thumming is stronger now, more powerful, its cadence very rapid.

Elob glances to the sky, evidence of question in his face as he sees the thickening, undulating, eerie coloration and hears the rumbling thunder of another fierce desert storm.

He strides towards the rear of the group followed by Jacob, Joseph, Anna, and Judy, who reach out for a quick embrace of their colleagues passing by, heading inwards, into the great monolithic structures where shelter awaits them. "The spirits of your ancestors resided here, did they not?" Elob asks, turning to look at Jacob.

"Indeed so." Jacob smiles broadly, nodding, his hands thrust into the inside folds of his garment near his chest.

"We have seen them. They have come to us in our councils and gatherings. It is through them and the Great One that we have known to seek you out."

"Oh! Tell us more," begs Judy with childlike excitement. "Please, tell us more."

"There is much more that you will learn and see in the days ahead. But briefly, that One whose light is greater than any we have ever seen came with his companion and spoke to us and we knew that it is He who holds the Promise. So, we sought you out, guided by one of those you call the Ancients, which is how we found you so straight away."

Anna looks at Judy, and the sweetness of their faith is strengthened as their eyes connect again.

"It is written," comments Joseph softly, "that he left those writings for us," glancing down for a moment in sadness, "much of which we had to sequester in the caves. For, as you well know, we could bring little with us. And how wise it was to so do! If we had carried any greater burden, we might not have made the journey." He pauses to look around, to take in the majesty of these rugged outcroppings, which he now knows shall be home for them, for his people and the children, for an indeterminate time ahead. "Look!" He points to the horizon of the distant sky. "It is incredible!" He touches his hand to his heart, "Lord, we honor Thee. We are humbled before the presence of Thy Word."

Having led them to the end of their movement, Elob turns, and they stand watching as the last of the entourage moves into the shelter of the outcroppings. He then turns to look back from whence they came and raises his hands. The Expectant Ones bow their heads, for they know this is to be his prayer and they wish to honor him. Though they sense his way and theirs may differ in some ways, they know clearly that all of them honor the same one God.

Elob stands with his hands outstretched, different from the Essenes, for he holds them with the palms facing one another, arms straight up above. Then he lowers them, palms facing the earth, and brings them back up together again, his palms pressed together straight above his head and down and up. "Om ... mani ... padme ... hum. I summon the spirit within the All. I bring my oneness unto Thee." He continues his mantra-like chanting and prayer, all of this in a tongue unfamiliar to almost all here.

There is a feeling of electrification all about.

Tiny, wisp-like, swirling columns of light come up from the earth and focus upon where Elob's hands are pressed together above his head. "We praise you, Lord God, in the name of these good people, Thy children, and all of us who are Your followers and who seek the presence of Your light. We give thanks unto You for having answered our call, and for granting us the great privilege of serving Your Word."

He stands like this for a time, with a barely audible sing-song humming, then moves his hands apart, that the palms face the horizon and the great storm in the distance. Slowly, very slowly, continuing his hypnotic, humming, singsong mantra, he lowers his arms, palms outstretched.

Anna can barely contain her gasp as she looks into the distance, for it appears that his hands are lowering that great cloud to nothingness.

Finally, his hands are down at his sides, his head is bowed. His mantra continues for a time and then several words are spoken succinctly, clearly, and with power. "I, Elob, son of the Law of One, give thanks and claim this power unto Thy Word."

Silence.

Then, very brightly, he turns, smiling broadly. "So, why do we stand here? Let us join your people. We must welcome them appropriately."

Swiftly, they move to the interior, following the path, twisting, turning, moving upwards, then to the side, then downwards, passing by members of Elob's group, obviously comparable to the guardians of the Expectant Ones, to each of whom he gives a salutation as they pass.

Rounding a corner, they come upon an open area. Judy

notices openings here and there with small lights illuminating the inner chambers.

Elob has stepped forward and gestures with an arm, "We welcome you to your new shelter. You will find sufficient unto your needs within."

Judy turns about and her eyes widen as she sees various individuals here and there, some up on small ledges in front of little openings, others off a bit in the distance where curious structures stand, obviously their dwelling places.

"The children have all been cared for, taken into these chambers," Elob continues, pointing to larger openings at ground level. "You may choose dwellings according to your spirit's call. I might encourage you to look at several of those," indicating some chambers up above, "as I think it appropriate that you be able to look over all of your people. Therefore, I have asked those to be prepared especially for you."

They all express their gratitude and thanks.

Judy suddenly realizes that a heavy bodily fatigue is calling out to her. She glances at Anna, and they move toward the larger chambers to see to the children, coming first to stand before Elob. Holding each other's hands, they bow and gesture to him the Essene gesture of love and respect.

Judy speaks. "You can see into our spirits and our hearts. Of this I am certain. Thus you know without our speaking it, the profound depth of thankfulness that we offer to you. Whatsoever we possess is yours. Say only the word and we shall give it to thee. Speak unto us that which is thy wisdom. Guide us and direct us to those labors that we might do in the joy of service to you, whom we now consider our brethren. May the Lord God continue to bless and guide you, sweet brother." Releasing Anna's hand, Judy steps forward and holds out her own hands.

Elob takes them, and she leans her forehead towards him and pauses.

For a moment, he simply gazes upon her. Then, understanding her intent, he gently touches her head with his own.

When Judy withdraws, Anna replicates this and then states, "With your permission, we shall see to the children now and retire."

"Please do. Rest well. You are safe. You are preserved."

As they move off to choose their sleeping quarters, Anna turns to look at Judy walking beside her, as once again they hold one another's hand. Tears of joy stream down their faces as they pause to glance back at Elob, Joseph, and Jacob.

"It is so wonderful. It is all validated, is it not, Judy?"

"Oh, yes. Yes," Judy returns with a deep sigh. "Only ..."

"What is it, my sister?"

"It is only that ... I grieve for those who know not the truth of the Promise."

In the hearts of the faithful can be found the chapters of all eternity, for the faithful are given the Eternal Record, the Akasha. The Akasha is not the written word of memories found in volumes of an indeterminately huge library which lies beyond. It is, rather, the energies, the fruits of the work ... the faith, the trust, the honor, the love, the compassion, the hope, and so much more, that has been held in the hearts and minds of the Ancients whose words and deeds have woven these deep into the fabric of the Promise.

So unto each of you, we, who were among those, have brought this message to you in the affirmation that what has been sown in the fabric of the past may now be nourished to bloom and flourish and bear forth His fruits of the Promise into your current time.

Chapter Six

The Pursuit Continues

The low flames of a small cookfire illuminate the faces of those seated around it. Elob and the others are speaking softly to prevent the sounds of their voices from awakening the others.

"We have called you here, Jason, you and your brothers called guardians, to ask you to perform a work."

Jason glances at Joseph, then at Jacob, Anna, and Judy. "My brothers and I are ready, Elob, for any work that would serve the Promise."

"Have others been sent?" questions Elob of Joseph.

"They have. We sent them when we first learned of the pursuers. They are seeking all of our people."

"Very good." Focusing again on Jason, "We will be sending several of our own people with you and your brethren to guide you through the wasteland and to take you to a predetermined meeting point. There, we would ask you to find those of your people who have heard the Call and who are willing, and bring them back with you. In addition, the other children must be brought here as swiftly as possible, for some in our group have seen that they are in grave danger."

Jason places a hand over his chest and nods. "With all that we are, we shall fulfill that work you set before us."

Elob studies him carefully for a few moments. A sense of calm comes over his face as he looks into the gentle eyes of this great body in front of him. He can see that within the large frame there is a gentle soul, a sweetness evident in the eyes and countenance, even though if one were to see only the great physical stature, there would be an instant feeling of intimidation. He glances behind Jason to several of Jason's companions, and notes the same essence common in them all ... that all that they are and have would be given without hesitation to the Work.

Without commenting, Elob simply smiles and nods a gentle affirmation to Jason, whose eyes are transfixed upon his, as though he knows precisely what this man of great wisdom and perception has been thinking.

In a single smooth motion Elob rises and extends a hand to Jason, and Jason does the same. Next, Elob raises his other hand and immediately two of his colleagues come from the shadows behind him. "These are my brethren. They will guide you. They have provisions to sustain you, for you have several days journey ahead to the City of Knowledge."

A flicker of emotion crosses Jason's face. Although he has not been to this great place, he has heard much about it. "Is it true that there will be many from the distant lands there?" he questions softly.

"It is true, for it is a place of focus ... of trade, of interaction, and of knowledge. You will find that we have many of our brethren dwelling in and about this location, as well as others along the way, who will support and guide you. My brethren here know of this, for they have traveled this route many times. We shall maintain contact with you throughout your journey."

Jason says no more, but extends to Anna, Judy, Jacob, and Joseph the Essene gesture of love and dedication. He turns, and with the other two, bounds off into the dim light.

80C3

One would be impressed with the swiftness and silence in

which the threesome makes this journey. The two from the School of the Prophets dispatched by Elob move in the darkness of the wilderness as though they are following a trail clearly marked, as though there is a pathway beneath their feet, which they can follow without a thought.

Following them, Jason can feel the coldness of the desert chill as his feet touch the earth. He glances to his left and right, and though there seems to be a luminosity to the south, he knows it is yet some time before the dawn's light will penetrate the darkness around them.

ꝏꝏ

Anna sighs deeply as the last subtle images of their dear guardian and the two counterparts from the School of Prophets fade into the predawn darkness. She muses that it always seems darker just before dawn. A shadow passes through her as she contemplates Elob's comment that some of their brethren are in imminent danger, remembering all too well the events of the recent weeks.

Her thoughts shift to the children. She thinks she hears a murmur of a child's voice off in the distance, perhaps having a vision or a dream, or perhaps stirring because his body has been stressed beyond tolerable limits, muscles aching and spasms causing him to stir and whimper in his sleep. When she finally looks up from deep within her thoughts, she sees Judy gazing at her.

Judy smiles slightly, nods, and places a hand upon her sister's shoulder, her eyes telling Anna that she understands and that she, too, embraces the children with her heart.

Jacob's soft voice stirs the silence. "They will awaken soon. What shall be the procedure from here, Elob?"

"It is going to be a considerable transition for your helpers from what they are accustomed to, and we have anticipated this. We have many who will help. In a moment, I shall call several sisters of light such as you." He nods to Anna and

Judy. "They come to act as emissaries and to assist you however they might. I should like to explain that they are very beautiful souls, as will be self-evident, but also that among our group, they are considered adepts in these works. They bring the knowledge of their traditions and ancient teachings with them from their homelands to this holy place. So, as you encounter that which is unfamiliar to you, I invite you to inquire of them. Explore their abilities, which they will be offering in service to your needs, to the children, and to the Promise. They will also offer these as teachings to the children, and to any of your group who might wish to share in their beautiful talents."

Anna and Judy glance at one another. Swiftly and through unspoken agreement, Judy turns back, her eyes wide, sparkling. "We are always anxious to learn more about truth, knowing very well that it has many facets. It is in the eye of the perceiver and one can learn much through the uniqueness that is manifest in each individual soul. So we welcome, might we call them, your sisters unto our group. We will embrace them as our own."

Smiling and nodding, Elob raises his hand up into the darkness in signal. A beautiful maiden, timeless in appearance, comes forward, as though the shadowy darkness beyond the periphery of the fire's light gave birth to her in some magical way. Several other figures can be seen dimly, coming only to the edge of the shadows and light before seating themselves, but one can see their beauty as though they contain their own light.

The maiden before them now brings her hands together, forefingers touching her chin, and bows.

As she does, Judy notes with interest that in the center of her forehead, the firelight catches the reflection of a solitary gem. It is a focal point of transfixion, for this is foreign to the Expectant Ones.

How and when, Judy muses, *was that placed there?* It seems this tiny gem which appears to have a fire of its own is literally a part of this beautiful body. Her eyes are dark, piercing, dancing with light. The smile is one of sweetness, and yet serenity. Beneath her head covering, Judy can see raven-dark tresses of hair cascading down her garments. The silky fabric, rarely seen in these lands, falls in layers, each one its own unique iridescent color. Within the fabric covering her shoulders and torso are golden threads woven all throughout, reflecting the light.

There is a moment of silence.

She turns to look at Elob who nods, indicating that she seat herself, her graceful fluid movement impressing Judy and Anna as she does. There is a prolonged silence before Elob nods at her.

"I am called Tamma by my people. It is a loving abbreviation of my true name, which is quite lengthy," she says, smiling radiantly at the two sisters. "In my homeland, Tamma is meant to be a part of a prayer, so I am honored to bear this name. I am told of yours, and I greet you. May I call you my sister, Judy?"

Judy beams at the honor that her name has gone before her and nods.

"And you are, of course, Anna. Your deeds, your wisdom, precede you. I, Tamma, welcome you on behalf of our people. You, good sir, must be Jacob?"

He chuckles softly. "I am. And I welcome you, Tamma, into our family."

"And you, sir," smiling serenely, "are Joseph. We know much about you and what lies ahead for you."

Joseph's eyebrows arch in curiosity. "Well, Tamma, I know not what it is that you know about me, but I am at your service. I give thanks to you and to your people for protecting our sweet children and all of us."

Without speaking, she rises, and again Anna and Judy marvel at the incredible grace of her movements. With a subtle gesture of her hand, she bids several others come from the shadows where they have been seated.

They move around to take Judy and Anna by the hand.

"We should like to go prepare for morning. Would you assist my sisters in gathering some items? We believe they will be unto the joy of your children, including some of your familiar foods."

"Really?" questions Anna. "How is it you would know ... Oh, forgive me, of course you would know," realizing that Tamma sees things and that she does know. Familiar foods would of course be known. "Thank you, Tamma."

Anna and Judy move off with them, chattering back and forth excitedly, pondering what foods might now be available to sweeten the children's disposition and nourish their bodies. They are brought to a place where many bundles and urns have been collected.

Judy bends to lift the lid from one of the urns, inhales its aroma, and closes her eyes, "M-m-m, wild honey. Oh, the children will be ecstatic!"

Opening a large bundle, Anna peers within and finds many grains, sumptuous in size, their fragrance filling her with anticipation. Here and there are piles of delectable-looking roots and great containers filled to overflowing with flower petals and herbs which will be used for various meals.

Swiftly, Anna gestures to several of the other maidens who have awakened to participate in the preparation of the morning meal. They begin to mix various herbs and measure the grain to grind.

Judy, having surveyed this wondrous bounty, looks to her new sisters. "May our Lord God bless you all. Such foods we have not seen in many, many days."

One of them responds, "The One God provides, true?"

"It is," and Judy and Anna embrace their new sisters.

Small cookfires are being prepared. Already one can smell the enchanting fragrance of the traditional staple Essene foods. One fire brews a wondrous mixture of teas new to Anna and Judy, as well as to Sarah and several of the others who have now come forward to assist.

"How is this prepared?" asks Sarah of one of the prophet maidens.

"Some of these we have brought from distant lands. Do you like its aroma?"

"Oh, yes. Indeed so!"

"Would you like a small taste?"

"Might I?"

Without another word, the maiden scoops a small cupful from the pot, which is just beginning to simmer. "It is not completely warm yet, but I think the fragrance and body are full enough. Please," holding the small cup between her two outstretched hands, "tell me what you think."

Sarah takes the cup. As she places it beneath her nose, admiring the fragrance, images of fields of flowers, bright skies, and busy insects gathering pollen come to mind. She closes her eyes, taking small sips at first. Then her memory bursts with flavors long forgotten and images of gentle valleys with cascading waters and curiously shaped trees. She opens her eyes and looks at the prophet maiden, "This is magical. Thank you," and offers her back the cup.

"Please," gestures the prophet maiden, "finish it. It will bring life to your body. It is a gift from the One God to my people, and now to yours."

ଐଠଓଌ

"How long before we will have word, Elob?"

"We have been informed that some of your people have agreed. Others have not. Our concern is for those who have not, for they are going to be pursued and there is the possibility of considerable harm befalling them."

Shaking his head, obviously greatly concerned, Joseph inquires further. "Then what are we to do? They are our brethren, our brothers and sisters. Even though we do not share the same visions and they do not hold to the Promise as do we, they are our family."

Elob sighs deeply. "We fear, sweet Joseph, it is already too late for some."

Joseph closes his eyes, bowing his head, and he and Jacob pray a moment in silence.

"Perhaps you might find some solace, however, in that some of our people have seen that not all are lost."

ЄᴐᏫᏵ

The attack has come in the predawn darkness, catching them unawares.

Cries can be heard, calls to God from some as they lie wounded. Several, hiding in the upper reaches of the encampment, whisper to one another. "What happened to our guardians?"

"They must have been overtaken. Come. I saw the children being sent off while the others went to do battle. Let us see if we can find them."

The two comrades crawl their way through the shelter of the outcroppings on the periphery of their camp, past cries of pain from those they love. Here and there off in the distance they can see flashes of metal from the pursuers' weapons, now strewn about.

"Why has this befallen us?" questions one.

"Perhaps the emissaries were only too correct," his colleague responds. "Perhaps we were remiss in our vision, and it is they are who correct. Or it is the will of God. But let us now set our thoughts only on our search for the children."

Around a small outcropping they come upon a fallen sister holding her side where a weapon has pierced her body.

One of them reaches within his garment and, pulling forth a small pouch, removes several herbs with which to make a potion. Taking the outstretched flask from his brother, he moistens the herbs and reaches in gently to cover the wound. "It is not grave, only a glancing wound. This will heal you, as will God."

Tears stream down her face. "Please. Go to the area where we sent the children. Save them. We must do as the emissaries bade us to do. We were wrong, they were right. Please! Save the children. Take them. I will find the others who remain, and if need be, we will distract the pursuers so you can take the children."

"No," responds the tall one. "My brother and I shall do this. You find the others who are able and gather the children. We will lure the attackers in the opposite direction. Speak no more and do as I say. We go now."

The maiden nods, her face brightening as she sees the light in her brother's eyes. "Here." She reaches into her garment and pulls forth a small cloth. "This has been mine since childhood. It was gifted to me by one of the elders. A thousand nights of prayer and the power of God are in it. Take it with you." She turns to look at the other "And with you, my brother. God be with you both."

With only a soft moan, bent over and holding her side, she moves over off into the shadows. Moving slowly, she intuits the location of the children and continues in that direction until she determines that she is close enough. Pausing, she softly imitates the sound of a night bird and waits. Again, she makes the call.

Then comes a feeble response. The trained ear would immediately know this is not a true night bird's call, but someone emulating it. Their prayer is that the coarse attackers would not know this.

She finds the source of the faint responding birdcall. Two children reach up to clutch her with an intensity that chokes the breath from her. Silently, she rubs their backs and touches their heads. As she holds them to her bosom, though their crying is silent, she feels their sobbing little bodies pressed hard against her own. "All is well," she whispers.

"But the others ..." asks one. "Where are they? Why do they pursue us? What is happening, Elba?"

"It is the message of God's will."

"What are we to do?"

"We must look for the others. Come. But, silence."

The sounds of the continued fighting below them are so deafening there is little chance their movement could be detected, so they move off. Soon they find another of the children, and another. Elba sequesters them in a small hollow before continuing her search.

Soon she comes upon a large figure. Since she cannot clearly perceive the identity of this one over the din of the fighting not far away, she makes the night bird sound again.

It responds, and then comes a whisper, "Who is it?"

"Elba."

"Have you found the children?"

"I have found some of them and hidden them away."

Now she can see his face, and recognizes him to be Thomas. Without thinking of what is proper or not amongst her people, she reaches up to grasp this stout form, and they embrace one another for a timeless moment, each feeling the warmth of the other's falling tears.

Thomas gently breaks away. "We must not tarry. You go this way and I will go that, and we will meet back here shortly. Where have you hidden the children?"

"There," she gestures, "in that hollow. I will meet you there." Each moves off without another word.

From the battleground, the sound of the fighting grows more and more horrid, cries and moans echoing all about. These Essene people are noted for their peace, their tranquility, and their love of God, except when there is the threat to that which they hold sacred. The simple-looking staffs, thought to be signets of varying meaning, some ornamented, others merely simple stout lengths of sapling or wood, become fierce weapons in the hands of their skilled intent. They know the physical body well and they know precisely where and how to place a blow or thrust the staff.

Here and there an attacker falls, moaning under an adeptly wielded rod, but the sheer number of the attackers their weapons striking again and again is evidence that these gentle people are only a short distance from being vanquished.

One of the stouter Essenes, having struck his pursuer and seeing him fall, turns and moves swiftly to the far edge of the foray, a trickle of blood flowing down the right side of his face from a gash in his forehead. Glancing up into the darkness, he makes a soft night bird sound.

From the side and from up above, he hears the echoes of his call, two responses. A bit of a smile appears on his face, and he makes the night bird sound twice more. Summoning great strength from within, he turns. For a fleeting moment, he surveys the battleground before him, then shouts a prayer unto God, "God is great! God is one!"

Two of his brothers, obviously other guardians, as evidenced by the signal of their upraised staffs, come rushing in from somewhere in the distance. Joining their brother, they become a furiously whirling trio, standing shoulder to shoulder sometimes, back to back at other times.

Their gleaming staffs strike here and there, filling the air with the moans and cries of the pursuers. Again and again they strike with such force and speed, such precision, that the great wooden rods appear to have a consciousness all their own, and the pursuers are driven back further and further.

"The Spirit of God is with us," the first one calls out in his constant flow of prayer. It sounds to the attackers like a great battle cry, as the guardians continue moving forward, striking under the cover of darkness.

The pursuers redouble their effort, but to no avail. Soon it is apparent that these three are invincible, and the pursuers retreat. A horn sounds, followed by the leader of the pursuers calling his men, those still standing, to retreat, shouting, "Gather unto me. We must regroup." And so they do, some bloodied, others limping.

One, dangling an arm now made useless from where a well-aimed staff has shattered the bones of his shoulder moans, "I thought these people were as sheep following their leader. No one told us to expect this."

"Silence! Fall back and follow me!"

As quickly as they attacked, they leave.

The three guardians come together. Placing their arms upon one another's shoulders and bringing their bruised, bleeding heads forward, they begin a song of praise unto God.

Having seen the completion of the battle, Elba and Thomas emerge from the shadows and cautiously move up to where the guardians are, leading a small group of children. Some of them are weeping and others have covered their heads and faces in the Essene tradition.

Turning with remarkable swiftness and strength, though his body is bleeding profusely, the leader of the guardians speaks sternly to Elba. "You must prepare to depart immediately! Go unto the pathway that leads to the City of Knowledge and do not look back. Go. Now!"

Elba, looking about, hearing moans and soft cries of her fallen brothers and sisters begs, "But we can help them."

"No. The message of God is clear. We cannot best them, but we can cause them a delay. They shall not destroy the children. Go now. Do as I say."

Thomas reaches over to place a hand upon Elba's shoulder. "He is right. We must honor the Promise. Come, Elba. Let us go. I know the way. I have traveled it many times." He turns, walks up to the guardian who has spoken, and embraces him.

The three guardians exchange whispered prayers of love and compassion between Thomas and Elba.

The guardians then move swiftly about the children, touching, embracing, and smiling brightly as though it were just another day. "Children, Elba and Thomas are going to take you to a wonderful place. Gather up what you can now. Quickly. Do not tarry. Remember ... We are eternal children of God. So, fear not. And lament not long over those you leave behind. Look into your hearts and there you shall find all of us, with you always."

The many young eyes and hearts yearn to run back to embrace those they love and others so familiar, but as is their tradition, the children follow without question or hesitation, for they know the wisdom of the guardians is unsurpassed, and they believe.

Scooping up what they can of provisions, they file off into the shadows of the predawn darkness.

The procession moves up and around, led by Thomas and followed at the rear by Elba, who ensures no children wander off and get lost. Here and there they find a few others of their colleagues, so that soon there are six in all guiding the children. Some of the children are barely able to walk because of great pain ... and yet they do.

In the distance the thundering hoofbeats of the pursuers indicate they are attacking again.

Rising above this is the clear cry of the guardians' prayers. It tugs at every heart.

℘)℃℘

"I think we should go to meet them."

"That may indeed be so, Jason," responds one of the prophets, who is serving as a guide. "We have perceived a great battle and we fear there are remnants among your group who are in need of some care. Therefore, we have called several of our brethren from the City of Knowledge who are particularly adept at healing energies. "

"Then let us go now."

Immediately, they head off to the northeast, following another seemingly invisible path, pausing in their journey only so long as is needed to sustain their bodies

The days pass, one by one, until, finally, Jason raises a hand, gesturing to those with him to pause and be silent. In the distance below, he can make out a small group, moving. "It could be the pursuers," he warns, his fingers moving up and down his stout staff, unconsciously readying himself if he needs to use it. Kneeling on one knee, he peers off into the distance.

One of the prophets kneels at his side. After a moment, he reassures Jason. "No concern. I perceive these to be those of your people whom we go to meet."

With some directness, Jason turns to the prophet and questions, "How do you know this?"

The prophet returns Jason's firm, steady gaze with a smile, "Because God has gifted me to know."

There is a prolonged moment of silence as Jason's eyes peer strongly into the eyes of this slight, almost frail form, and then note an inner strength and light there that is unquestionable. "So be it, then," he acknowledges with a smile and a nod of gratitude. Somewhat out of character, he then extends his hand and places it upon the prophet's shoulder.

The prophet responds by reaching up to clasp Jason's wrist. "Go now, we will await you here. We will prepare a camp. Bring them here and we will tend to their needs."

80C03

Now it is Thomas who raises a hand to signal a warning, and all scurry off into the wilderness about them, trying to hide as best they can in what little cover is available in this vast wasteland. Some of the children cover themselves with handfuls of sand, attempting to be unseen.

Jason looks, peering to see who it is before him.

Thomas has a staff in his own hands and has raised it in a

posture ready to strike out if need be. He sees a tall figure striding confidently towards him without concern or caution, and something inside tells him it is a brother. The fatigue, the weariness, the bruises upon his own body suddenly overwhelm him and without conscious thought, he lowers his hands, his great staff falling from his grasp, and slumps to his knees, head bowed.

Elba rushes from behind him, placing an arm about his shoulders and laying a hand gently upon his head. "Oh-h, Thomas. You are ... You are in need, my brother," she whispers with concern.

Thomas struggles to get the words out, "The work is done. Look." With great effort, he manages to raise an arm, pointing towards the horizon. "It is a brother."

Jason is waving and moving at a swift but measured trot. Two of his guardian brothers flank him. Though not knowing exactly what to expect, they hasten their steps, ready with their staffs, which are glistening in the predawn light.

Clutching his side, Thomas falls over and slips to the ground with a low moan.

Seeing this, Jason covers the distance between him and Thomas in mere moments. Pausing only to acknowledge and quickly gesture the Essene greeting to Elba, he bends and scoops up the considerable weight of Thomas as though he were but a light parcel.

Without a word, carrying his own staff and Thomas' in his free hand, he turns, nodding to his brethren on his right and left to continue on. With Thomas over his shoulder, he trots back from whence he has just come, the prophets' encampment, as though his burden were naught.

℘∞CჄ

Jason drops the two staffs to the ground, gently lowers Thomas, and turns to look into the eyes of the prophet who has become as a brother. "Can you save him?" he whispers.

"He is my brother."

The prophet's hands move skillfully over the body, touching, feeling, pausing here and there to make an assessment of some unknown nature. He gestures to others who are about him, and they bring him supplies that have been previously prepared. Small earthen-like mortars are filled with herbs, crushed with a pestle and then warm water is added.

Another of the prophets moves Thomas's garment aside to examine the wound and carefully begins to cleanse and care for it.

"As it is the will of God," states the first prophet, "and as we employ those gifts given us, we will save your brother. Go, now. Leave him and go help the others. All that can be done will be."

Jason places his hand upon Thomas' forehead. "Sweet brother, my spirit I leave with you. Come back to us." Grabbing his staff once again, he turns swiftly and begins his ground-consuming trot with barely an audible sound as his feet strike the earth again and again.

৪৩৫৩

The children have been gathered into a group, thirty-seven in all. Elba and the other four are talking quietly amongst themselves, caring for the children, as Jason's two guardian brethren move about, encircling them as they keep watch, peering off into the darkness.

"Praise be to God," Mariah whispers to Elba.

"Indeed so. We have all the children! It is God's will."

The two guardians on watch react suddenly with their staffs at the ready, then evidence relief as they see their brother Jason running towards them in his measured pace.

His last few footsteps having now been heard by all the others including the children, he calls brightly but quietly, "Come. Come, children. I am Thomas' brother, called Jason. You will like to know that he is being cared for. But quickly now ... Come! We must journey."

Another of the guardians explains to Elba and her colleagues, "We must continue on. Your path will be easily followed if our brothers have not detained the pursuers."

"I thirst," one of the children weakly murmurs.

"And I am so weary," another adds. Their soft moans are repeated by other children.

Jason musters still greater brightness. "All that you could need awaits you just ahead. But you must come now. Please ... now!" he directs kindly, but with an authority that cannot be ignored.

Without another word he turns and trots off into the night towards the encampment where the prophets are. Some distance from the children, he stops, turns, and beckons to them silently with a wave of his hand. Glancing this way and that, he then stabs his staff into the ground and leans upon it, obviously planning to stand as a sentinel.

Soon the children are filing past, led by Elba and the four others, the remaining guardians following at the rear of the column.

"Any sign of the pursuers?" Jason whispers to his companions as they approach.

"No. Our brothers do well. Of this I am certain," one responds quietly.

"Remain here and measure the movement of the dawn," Jason instructs. "Grant us several hours, then follow. But if there is any indication of the pursuers, alert us."

"It is done," the brother whispers, and they come together for a quick embrace, praising God.

Jason turns, moving swiftly to join the group, leaving his two beloved companions behind.

Reaching the encampment, to his joy Jason hears the sound of children chattering and even the sound of their giggles. It would seem that the prophets are adept at bringing forth the light of life from within the children.

Wonderfully aromatic biscuits and hot brews, along with small containers of sumptuous dates and other fruits, are given to each child.

"Look, look!" Andrew calls excitedly to Jason. "Look what they have given us."

"Oh, let me see." As Jason kneels beside the small form of the young lad, his heart is pulled heavily. Over one of Andrew's eyes is a grotesquely discolored lump. Very quickly, Jason recovers from his initial reaction, for surrounding the wound is a pleasant-smelling greenish-white balm, obviously placed there by one of the healer prophets.

"Are these foods not wonderful?" squeals Andrew in delight. "Would you like one?" He holds out his container to share with Jason.

"I would, indeed." Jason reaches his great fingers into the container to select a date, then passes it to and fro beneath his nose. "Mm-m. It smells so good. Tell me, Andrew, is it going to taste as good as it smells?"

Andrew, giggling, and now joined by several of the other children, bobs his head vigorously up and down. "Even better, Jason. Taste it. Go ahead, taste it!"

∞)(∞

Having called them together, Elob takes a very deep breath, measuring his words particularly to soften their effect on Anna and Judy, and begins, "There has been, so we perceive, a very great battle to the northeast."

"Oh-h ..." Judy touches her hand to her heart. "Oh, sweet God. And the children?"

"Safe, we believe. We do not know how many there are, but our seers tell us it is a sizable number."

Anna probes, "Could you gauge for us somewhat the number you believe has survived?"

"Perhaps thirty or so, but we cannot tell definitively. These things are difficult, as there is much that is precluding our sight."

"What would that be?" questions Joseph seriously.

"Hatred."

"From whom?"

"From the opposing forces," Elob responds. "Those forces which are counterpoint to the Light, believing in their limited sight that we mean to destroy them. That is the thought carried in the hearts and minds of the pursuers. This is, of course, the nature of consciousness throughout humankind, as well."

"Why must it be so?" questions Joseph, although, within, he knows the answer, for he knows the teachings. He understands the ways of such things. Perhaps he asks out of a sense of concern for those whom he so dearly loves who have chosen another way.

"They made their choices, and obviously they were not wise ones. If they had at least followed our advice not to remain in their location, many would have been spared."

"Many, Elob?" asks Jacob softly, his heart heavy with this news that the number of those lost is great.

"Yes, many. But be of good cheer. Our people have healed many others of the remnants, so you will see some of your brethren again. And they will be here with us shortly."

Judy and Anna have reached over to take one another's hands and have begun rocking just a bit. So soft that one can barely hear it comes the Essene maidens' sacred prayer, soft, but very powerful.

80CB

In that precise moment Elba feels a stirring within. She straightens up, responding to what she is sensing, looking about as the predawn sprays fingers of light about. "They know," she whispers excitedly to Thomas. "I can feel it."

His eyes flicker open, the incredible skills and power of the prophet healers having worked well. "Oh-h, you think it so? Our brethren know the children are safe?"

Smiling, Elba nods as she touches her heart. "They know. They know much." She glances up to look into the eyes of the small group of prophets that has gathered.

They are smiling serenely, moving their bodies this way and that in silent or barely audible prayer, indicating they too are aware.

The crunch of Jason's footsteps on the rocky terrain draws everyone's attention. "We will rest for a time. Long enough to ready the children, but then we must move on."

For a moment he gestures to each warmly, lovingly. Then, with a serene strength, he moves off into the predawn in a measured trot towards where he left his two brothers.

ℰ⟩⟨ℬ

"Not a sign," one of them tells Jason upon his arrival.

"Very good. We shall have the children ready in several hours, so measure it and then follow. We must move quickly. I know it to be so, for the prophets have said it."

"We will do this," responds one of the guardians.

"Take care, my brother," Jason whispers to this one.

Turning to the other, he places a hand upon his shoulder.

"There is naught we need concern about," the guardian assures Jason. "The Word of God is in this staff," holding it up. "If any care to so do, they can hear the Word of God," and he sweeps his rod, making a swooshing sound.

Jason chuckles softly. "And thou, my dear brother, art the very one to deliver the Word, if so called."

He turns and begins his trip back to the encampment.

ℰ⟩⟨ℬ

This journey is not so arduous as others have been, for the path is known and provisions are supplied. Here and there the children are carried two by two by those who are able. The days pass, and before long the group find themselves approaching the School of the Prophets.

The children can remember only fragments of their recent experience, for the charm of the prophets in their midst lures their minds into what is and what might yet be, placing that which has passed into their being as a foundational rock which may one day be discovered by these beautiful souls. It is not to say that here and there a heart does not long for the familiar warm embrace of a matronly figure, or the kind loving words of a reassuring father's voice. But so light, so mirthful and gay are the discussions and stories from the prophets accompanying them, that the children have become preoccupied with the song of life itself.

ഇറ്റ്

Elob has been discussing with Jacob, Joseph, and many of the sisters what they have to give to the children upon their arrival, as the sentinels come swiftly to the evening fire.

One of the watchers addresses them. "A group approaches."

"From whence?" questions Joseph.

Turning to gesture to the opening of this great School, Elob nods and smiles. "There."

"Oh! They have arrived!" shouts Anna. She and Judy along with the other maidens jump to their feet and scurry this way and that, making ready for something, but in the excitement, not really managing to be about anything productive. One moves a bundle from this place to that, another removes a cover from a cooking vessel and replaces it, still others bump into one another, carrying great armloads of blankets, and on and on it goes.

Jacob tosses his head back, laughs aloud, and claps his hands together, "Well, I, Jacob, am going to greet them. Farewell, friends." He rises to his feet and strides swiftly off into the darkness, raising his voice. "Children! Children it is I, your friend Jacob! I come to sing with you. I come to dance with you! Oh, chi-l-ld-ren ..."

"Who calls to us?" Andrew looks about excitedly.

Jason gazes down upon Andrew's small upturned face. The eye, which had been swollen shut, twinkles with anticipation through the small opening. He smiles. "Andrew, you will love this one. He is called Jacob, and he is a great song-teller."

"A *song-teller?*" Andrew's excitement is growing.

"Oh, yes! He will take a story and weave it into a song. Then he will dance to it and you will want to do the same."

"Me?" Andrew giggles. "I love to dance."

The swift stride of Jacob's sizable form bring him quickly before the group, and Jason turns to greet him.

"What have you here, Jason?" Jacob asks merrily, a bit of laughter in his every word.

Though Jacob's spirit is very bright, his size is so imposing and his demeanor so powerful that Andrew steps back, pushing against the other children who have now caught up.

Throwing his head back, laughing mightily, Jacob bends down and is nose to nose with Andrew. "Hello, young lad."

Andrew's eyebrows are nearly lost into the front of his scalp. "H-h ... he-hello. Are ... are you Jacob? Are you the ... the story-singer, or uh, the singer-of-stories?"

"Me?" Jacob presses his fingertips against his chest in mock surprise. Leaning back, he turns his head this way and that to meet each child's pair of inquisitive eyes. "Well," holding his chin with his hand, "you know, I suppose I am." He swiftly leans down again, putting his nose right up in front of Andrew's. "Would you like me to sing you a story now?"

The impact of Jacob's form and presence having subsided somewhat, Andrew bobs his head up and down, "Yes, I ... I would. W-wouldn't we?" He turns to the other children for some support.

"How are you called?"

"I ... I am called Andrew."

There is a pause as Jacob's eyes connect with Andrew's.

A flood of loving light pours forth from Jacob's great heart, traveling the short distance between their eyes, making Andrew feel warm and good.

Knowing his intent has met its mark, Jacob stands up and moves around throughout the rest of the children.

Elba and Thomas, who are being supported by several of the others, move off to the side, gesturing a greeting to Jacob, who pauses momentarily in his playfulness with Andrew and the others to acknowledge them.

Then, up go Jacob's hands. Clap, clap, and 'round and around he turns, softly singing all the while, *I sing you the story of a boy called Andrew* ... and Andrew begins to giggle ... *mighty is his name. The power of God is in his being* ...

On it goes. The children are charmed as Jacob spins this way and that, scooping up a child here, kissing a forehead there, and their laughter drifts outward on the gentle breeze.

With all its implications, it reaches out to where Anna stands. Suddenly, she cannot contain what she feels.

Her hands come up to cover her face and she falls to her knees, her head bent. No sound is audible from her, but the up and down movement of her shoulders evidences the tears of joy that pour forth from Anna's glad heart.

In the illusion of limitation in the experiences of life there can always be found an opening. It is through that opening that the way can be found unto the Peace of God.

So as you have read in this recounting, you can see that the illusions of finiteness that are clung to with the force of habit by most, are seen by these Expectant Ones in the clarity of what they truly are, that the light of the Promise held within each Essene heart could be brought together as a single force to meet and surpass any force which would oppose.

May the Word of God in the form of the Promise eternal ever be that against which you measure all that you are.

Chapter Seven

The School of the Prophets

As the sound of the children's voices grows, the sisters and all who are to be the caregivers quickly rise and rush off in their direction to meet and embrace these precious gems of God's Promise.

The encounter is met with great jubilation by the children, for among the Expectant Ones, all are looked upon as family. These coming to greet and embrace them, then, are seen by the children as equal to those whom they have so recently lost.

Some jump up into the receiving arms and loving kisses of the sweet maidens, who swing them about, clutching them tenderly, whispering into their ears, brushing hair from a forehead, straightening a garment, and then turning to carry their precious cargo back into the embrace of the School of the Prophets. Some carry two, but all carry at least one of these joyful bundles of hopefulness.

"Are there no others, Jason?" Joseph inquires with some sadness.

"We know of no others. These are the children who came forth. We were not able to move into the area of fighting to search." He lowers his head in sorrow. "We had thought it best to focus our efforts on the preservation of these children, and those ..." turning to gesture to Elba and those with her, "the other four and Thomas."

A heavy sigh comes from Joseph as he contemplates so many he has known, so many he has loved dearly, now lost.

Elob steps forward to speak with Elba. "Did you hear cries or see any sign of others who might have endured?"

Elba shakes her head. "It was hasty, good sir, and so emotional. The darkness that embraced us and hid us from sight also made it difficult to search for additional survivors. Our guardians who went back to help and who then met the second wave of ..." She is barely able to continue. "I am almost certain they could not have survived, for the number of pursuers was surely too great for even them."

Jason, listening carefully, is visibly moved, for among this group called guardians there is a unique bond. Though they may come from tribes far distant from one another, the guardians are as one, dedicated to serving the needs and to preserving the works of all of the Essenes, not merely that group into which they entered at birth.

The conversation continues, when with no apparent cause Elba turns, as if searching the darkness, and suddenly places a hand over her heart, gasping, "Oh-h!"

Judy and Anna move to embrace her warmly, uttering the secret prayers. "We heard it too," Judy murmurs to the sobbing and weeping Elba.

Stepping over to them, Joseph whispers, "What is it? What troubles you?"

"We hear a call, sweet Joseph," explains Anna gently as she and Judy continue to rock Elba. "There are ... There are others. Perhaps wounded, perhaps near death, but life still nourishes their form."

"Please, Joseph," pleads Elba. "Please!"

"No more need be spoken." Joseph turns to see that Elob has left the group. He looks this way and that to search him out, and there, in the distance, he can make out Elob talking with four individuals Joseph has not seen prior to this moment. They are gesturing and pointing about.

Elob is nodding and also motioning, making signs with his hands. Then he embraces each of the four, who turn swiftly, glancing only for a moment over towards Joseph and the group before disappearing into the twists and turns of this craggy, rocky home to the School of the Prophets.

Swiftly Elob comes before Joseph. "It is true, there are others. We must return."

Joseph's concern as he contemplates the arduous and dangerous journey is evidenced by the sound of his sharp inhale and the look upon his face.

Jason, having seen and heard this exchange, steps quickly forward. "Forgive me for intruding, Elob. If you would provide us supplies and if we might rest but a few hours, my brothers and I shall return. We can move more swiftly alone, and without any burdens or distractions, we can make the journey in at least half the time."

"No."

Jason stiffens. "Why so?"

"Two of my brothers will journey with you."

"But we can travel so much faster."

Elob shakes his head, speaks not a word but raises a hand. From the recesses beyond come two figures, striding with a surety and swiftness that clearly indicates these are seasoned travelers. One wears headgear similar to that of Elob's. The other looks quite different, his long hair twisted and fashioned behind with some sort of ceremonial beadwork. Both are tall and lean, and even in the subdued light, the sinewy ripples of muscle indicate that these two are surely worthy of the task ahead.

Surveying them quickly, Jason smiles and nods to Elob, "They will certainly do. Welcome, brothers, welcome to this journey. We would but rest just several hours and then will be at the ready."

The one with the braided hair steps forward, raising a hand in a salute of respect. "Rest you well, good brothers. I and my companion will go on ahead."

"What?"

"It is of no concern. We will meet you at the site."

"But ..." Jason ventures again, turning to look at Elob.

"They have seen your previous journey. They know the way, and they know precisely where the remnants of your people are, as they too have heard the call. Let them go. They are well skilled in the powers of the body and the spirit of the earth. If there are those remaining who are wounded, if any can heal them, these two brothers of mine can."

They gesture to Elob, and not another word is exchanged. They are gone, swiftly melting into the terrain of the desert before them.

Jason, leaning against his staff, now realizes that his fatigue is great. He excuses himself, and he and his two brothers move off to the side. Several of the good workers come to provide them with warm food and drink, which they partake of heartily before falling quickly into a deep sleep.

Another of Elob's colleagues comes forward, gestures an apology for the interruption, and whispers into Elob's ear. Elob nods. This one then goes over to where the three guardians are deep asleep, seats himself cross-legged before them, and closes his eyes. He raises his hands, and begins a curious but beautiful humming chant, rocking to and fro, his arms and his hands outstretched in the direction of the three sleeping guardians.

Joseph whispers to Elob, "Who is that one and what is he doing?"

"To be brief, Joseph, he is empowering them. When they awaken, they will feel as though they have slept for many hours, even though actually they will have slept only for a few. In addition, when they move across the wasteland, the land itself will give them energy and they will find to their own amazement that they will move with a swiftness they have never known before. He is one of ours who knows the power of the native forces and who is a bridge of, might I call it, acceptance between the One God and the One God's expression here on Earth."

"That is remarkable," Joseph comments with obvious admiration.

"Anna, Judy, come over here and sit with me if you will." Elob gestures to either side of him. "And you, Elba, would you join us for a moment? I know you are greatly fatigued, but might I have a moment of your time before you rest? He looks up at one of the good workers, "Here, bring her nourishment." The worker comes swiftly with food and drink.

After Elba has taken a few bites and sips, Judy cradles her lovingly, leaning her head against Elba's.

"I must ask you," Elob inquires softly, "your elders ... Have you knowledge of them?"

Elba stiffens, for the elders are considered sacred, as sacred as the children themselves, and so she wonders at Elob's question.

Elob continues. "There is one amongst your tribe whom we are told must survive. He is called Zamotese. Do you know of him?"

"Oh, yes!" more comfortable with Elob's question, now that he has spoken with concern of this one who is honored by all her people. "All know Zamotese."

"Have you any knowledge as to how he is faring, or where he is? We cannot perceive him through any of the means we employ."

Smiling, Elba nods. "That would be his doing. He is capable of not being seen."

"Ah, yes." Elob smiles. "Of course."

"But, I have no recent knowledge of him."

"Then my brothers will seek him out. Zamotese knows certain works that we value very highly. He knows the pathway to your Ancients." Upon noticing someone's approach, he turns about. "Ah-h, forgive me, Jacob," who is now joining the group. "I did not intend in any way to slight you and your own treasured abilities in this area."

"No offense taken. I know Zamotese well and revere him. He is one of the great ones."

"Indeed so," Elob responds, "indeed so. Elba, go now and rest. Thank you for your patience with me. We here of the brotherhood welcome you."

Elba is helped to her feet by Judy and Anna, who turn to give her over to several of the other sisters and then return to seat themselves in the group once again.

Anna's face is taut with the sorrow and pain of the great loss. "May I inquire, Elob, have you seen any of the others?"

For a moment there is no visible reaction, and then around the edges of his eyes there is a softening, and a twinkling light can be seen. "We have, and there are indeed others. But I must tell you this, in order that there is only truth between us ... Some are gravely wounded, and we do not know if my brothers will reach them in time. However, we will find those who are remaining, care for them, and return them here."

Anna and Judy bow their heads in a moment of silent prayer, offering that which is sacred and which they know is heard all throughout the expressions of God's Spirit.

"What is the status of the children you have recently brought here?" questions Joseph after Anna and Judy have lifted their eyes once again.

"As well as could be expected. Perhaps even better than could be expected, praise God," Anna whispers.

"We have, we think, all of them," adds Judy, "and as remarkable as it might seem, only one of them apparently received any serious injury. That would be Andrew, but he is much better, thanks to your people, Elob."

"It is God who is the power. We are only messengers of His Word, as you know. But you are welcome." Elob's face grows more solemn, "I have seen something else. Approximately a score of this tribe has been captured."

In unison, Anna and Judy both gasp, clutching their hands over their hearts.

Elob strives to reassure them, "All is not lost."

"But," Anna looks up, the tears welling in her eyes, "we know the fate of those who have become captives. The women will be ..." She refrains from completing the thought. "And the men will be chained as beasts for the remainder of their lives, as brief as that will likely now be."

"As I said," Elob continues, "we have other means. Your people would be considered worldly goods, true?"

"Oh yes," Judy looks down, shaking her head, "like beasts of burden or objects of pleasure for those who have wealth."

"Let me tell you a bit more history of this, our sacred land. There were those who came here before us, and though you have seen it not as yet, we shall in time share with you the remnants of their presence, as there are several in our group who are able to retell of those who were here.

"One of the stories passed down tells of old, old teachers, whom you yourselves know by name, who actually found this land and guided many here. It has been this way for many, many generations. Those people built great monuments, very beautiful structures into the mountainsides. And," he pauses, smiling now, "they left us a gift."

"A gift?" questions Anna.

Elob nods. "Means. The means to procure your people."

Judy is stunned. "You mean to ... to purchase them?"

Elob speaks not, but smiles and nods.

"But you said perhaps a score has been captured. It would take a great sum to purchase them."

"God has provided this, and far greater. We have already dispatched several of our people in the garb of wealthy traders, travelers, merchants. They will do all that can be done to procure your people that they do not fall into injury," glancing down to speak these words, "or violation."

A look of hope is exchanged around the group.

"You know where they are?" asks Joseph cautiously.

"We do, indeed."

"Have you any idea ... Do you know when we might know the outcome of this effort?"

"Soon enough." Elob stands. "But for now," looking down at the group, "I must leave you. I have my works before me. Much has been given unto all of us, and it is appropriate that I return to my silence in order that I might offer my prayers of thanksgiving unto God for those things, and to claim the gifts of God yet on the horizon.

"In order that God's gifts can manifest on Earth, we must acknowledge and accept them, that in so doing we become portals through which they can pass and manifest. I shall give thanks unto the Ancients who went before, whose sight was so clear that they would leave for us, the children of their children's children, the means by which these works might be done. Praise be unto Elijah and those who bear his gifts. I encourage you to offer your own prayers as your teachings guide you. Do rest well, dear friends. On the morrow, the sweetness will return. You shall see."

Without another word he turns and disappears into the darkness on the edge of twilight.

There is a hushed silence. One of the good workers comes and kindles the small fire before this little group.

"It is incredible to contemplate," Joseph begins in hushed wonder. "There is the division of our people due solely to interpretation of the prophecy ... we here as one group, and they," looking into the night in the direction of those awaiting rescue. "Yet are we one, two families within the greater."

"How is it we are so blessed," Anna adds, shaking her head in amazement, "to have been taken in by Elob and all those good people with him? They are surely sent of God."

Judy stares unblinking into the fire before them, her face

etched by the flame's light, eyes riveted upon the dancing flames. "It must be so."

One would barely hear them, save for the slight movement of pebbles as they seat themselves, the tall seer and his companion.

All brightly look up, smiling a greeting.

Jacob looks deep into their eyes. "Thank you, dear friends. Your gifts have made all of this possible."

"There is but one gift," the tall seer responds gently, "and that is the Promise. It is the hope that all people would set aside that which is seen as different, that what shall be uncovered instead is that which is alike within all."

There is a pause, and the other seer speaks. "Zamotese is a great one. He shall come, this we have seen."

"Oh!" gasps Anna. "Thank you. Thank you. Elob said it was likely. You are certain?"

The tall one gazes at his companion who is now smiling and nodding, "We are certain."

The group murmurs for several moments at the potentials that lie ahead, and Thomas appears.

"Sit here, sweet brother." Anna motions to an open space between herself and the tall seer. "Why are you awake? Why are you up so soon? How are your wounds?"

Thomas carefully slides himself down to the ground. "Amazingly well, especially considering the journey. It was unbelievable. These people, their healers, are filled with the light of God. I have never seen anything like it, even among our own. Well, none are greater, that is for certain."

"Yes," responds Judy softly. "What mysteries, what wonders must they hold. Look at them! They are as one mind, one spirit, even though there is such diversity. Did you see that one who left with the turbaned one? His hair, his garments, his skin? He is unquestionably from the distant lands."

Joseph smiles. "Yes, I am certain of that. How did they all come together here? How did they know of the existence of this place?" Looking about, "Who would imagine that such as all of this existed in the midst of the desert?"

"How wonderful for us." Judy smiles, as well, a bit more relaxed now. "What a blessing. Is it not always so beautiful to see God's plan unfold? That is, when we do not get in the way of it." For the first time, she leans back to laugh gently, glancing about to make certain her outburst has not disturbed any of the children.

"What do you see that lies ahead," Joseph asks of the seers, "if you will, dear friends?"

The tall one's companion answers, "They have many gifts to give, much knowledge, many teachings that will be treasures to be given to Him who is coming."

"Do you know these?" It is apparent to all that Anna's interest is piqued.

"We do to a degree, for we have spent time with many of them."

"You have?" Anna asks. "What are they like? What unites them all?"

"Well, they are, as you say, very diverse. Many have come from distant lands having heard the inner call, and, most astoundingly, some having traveled for more than one year to reach this place. Some endured great hardships, and others they speak of did not make it ..." His voice trails off. He continues, "They are, as you have discussed, powerfully united. They are on a quest of a sort. Each seems to be seeking something that appears pivotal to them as individuals though contributive to the overall work."

"How would you define it?" questions Anna.

"It is as what we call our truth. They seek to possess it."

"Possess it?"

"Yes, but not in the way you are thinking. They seek to intertwine their being with their truth so completely that they become one with it. That is the means by which, Thomas, their healing was so profound. Those who were your healing practitioners are utterly one with the life-force. As they see the dis-ease or the imbalance, their oneness with the flow of the life-force balances it and promotes healing swiftly."

Thomas nods, smiling, "Very swiftly, indeed."

The tall seer comments, "These are gifts they intend to give unto the children."

"Oh," Judy exclaims, "I knew it! I knew it was a part of the work."

Jacob nods, "I, too, knew. But a little confirmation is certainly welcome." He throws his head back to laugh boisterously, paying not one heed to whether it is heard or not.

Anna and Judy look at one another and giggle, the power of Jacob's laughter invoking that effect.

"Now, Thomas," Jacob springs to his feet, "either you come and rest, or I will gather you up and tuck you in myself. Who knows, I may subject you to a bit of a nighttime song as well." He bends over and helps Thomas rise.

The flickering flame catches the glistening in Thomas's eyes before he swings an arm around the stout shoulders of Jacob. "Thank you all. Thank you all so much. Praise God that we are one."

As they move slowly away, Jacob can be heard. "Now, how about that song, Thomas?" and he begins singing softly.

ဆၠဃ

The dampness of the midnight air amplifies the cold hardness of the stone surrounding Zamotese, yet he breathes in deeply, holds it and exhales. "Unto Thee, Lord God, do I give that which is not perfect in my being."

The sounds of his deep breathing can be heard in the stillness of the night. He moves his hand up into the folds of his garment to the timeworn pouch suspended around his neck. His fingers work their way around it and gently clutch its contents. "Lord God, let Thy Word be spoken here that these, Thy children, are carried according to Thy will on the pathways that are highest and best for them." Again he laboriously breathes in. "This prayer I send out unto existence, now manifested through this, Thy servant, speaking the Word of God."

There is a long exhale, and Zamotese shifts his attention, bringing his other hand up. A crusted rivulet of his blood is streaked across the palm and back of this hand. A moment's flicker of pain crosses his face, then peacefulness, as he covers his solar plexus with his hands, and his breathing shifts to a more gentle, rhythmic pattern. "I feel the pulse of your Spirit on Earth and in all things, my Lord. I submit myself now into oneness with the life of Thy Word and with the presence of Thy Spirit. I, Zamotese, affirm the power of oneness with Thee. I am Thine."

Darkness falls across his consciousness, and all thoughts fade, his heart flickering yet still pulsing.

The darkness is shattered by a burst of white light. Rivulets of color shoot past Zamotese, and he hurtles forward into the light until his journey slows. The light begins to part, revealing a beautiful green knoll with a small waterfall and stream off to one side, and to the other, a cluster of taller greenery. There, stands a shining figure, a hand outstretched in gesture of the signet of the ancient School of the Prophets.

"Good tidings to you, Zamotese."

Now filled with the energy and light and love of the Spirit of God, Zamotese moves easily and swiftly to kneel before the shining figure.

"Arise my brother, I would look upon thee."

Zamotese rises, and in the eyes before him sees a light of hope ... the Spirit of God shining through this servant of God's Word.

"Ancient one, you honor me. What have you to give in guidance to me? What might I bear unto my people ... that is, if I am to continue in this journey?"

"Your journey will continue," the shining one affirms

softly. "Be of stout spirit and heart, for assistance will be upon you soon. With the morning's light, look for them. You will know them by what they shall be wearing upon their heads. One has a cloth wrapped about his head, and the other has hair that shines with the darkness of God's embrace."

"This I shall do," Zamotese avows. "Is there any message of hope? We have endured such a loss."

"Tell them that those of your people who have given all they had to give, the ultimate, are within the embrace of God now. But to know this as well ... Many have survived. They will be gathered soon and you shall see them again."

Zamotese kneels and bows, "Thank you, my Lord! Thank you."

"*I*, Zamotese? I only speak God's Word."

"Of course." Zamotese pauses and then looks up again into the eyes of this shining one. "Is there else that I should carry to our people?"

"Yes. Many teachings, many gifts, have been prepared and are at the ready to be given unto the awakening of the Promise. See that those of the ancient School and those of your people are one, united in heart. As need be, be a bridge of wisdom and light between them. And this remaining message I leave you with, sweet brother Zamotese ... Tell them, *He comes!*"

There are several indeterminate moments wherein the eyes of the shining one, whom Zamotese recognizes as the ancient prophet, and the light from within bedazzle Zamotese. He spins and twirls off into joyful bliss, the ecstasy of the messages given. He knows not for how long, nor to where his falling journey has taken him, but after this timeless experience, his eyes open to the first fingers of light of the new day's dawning, when the stillness of the morning is broken by the sound of muffled footsteps.

He starts at the possibility of impending danger, groaning at the wound in his upper shoulder as he pushes back as far as he can into the recess of the crevasse in which he has lain. He strives to summon his own training and knowledge to send forth the thought of his not-being, but he is too far between the gateway of death and the threshold of life, with portions of him still gone in the lands beyond consciousness. Knowing the futility of his struggle, he simply leans back and resumes his slow deep rhythmic breathing.

Suddenly, a head pops around the edge of the crevasse wall, and after but a single startled moment, Zamotese breaks into a smile. The raven-haired head is just as the prophet had told him, as is the other who has now also come forward, whose head is wrapped in the turban.

Zamotese struggles to speak. "I greet you, my brothers. I was told of your coming."

The smiles are so broad on these two that Zamotese feels better just looking upon them. Carefully, lovingly, they lift his form from the embrace of the crevasse. With seemingly little effort, they begin to move swiftly in a sort of shuffling trot. Each supports Zamotese with an arm here and an arm there, holding him completely off the ground as they consume the distance between the sheltered crevasse and their destination of the City of Knowledge.

After a time they pause, placing him in the shelter of a dune to give him foods and fluids, and tend his wound. Suddenly, the turbaned one rises to move in the direction of a sound, his head now raised above the dune.

Jason, whose steady pace has caught him up to them, is startled at first, as, for a moment, it looks as though a head is moving along on the ridge of sand. He pauses to laugh boldly at the sight.

"We have Zamotese," calls the turbaned one. "All is well. We are preparing shelter and tending to him. Go seek out any others. We shall be here upon your return."

Jason and his brothers smile and nod, glancing down at Zamotese who, though his eyes are closed, raises a hand to gesture a blessing in the custom of their Ancient ones.

ଓ୨୧ଓଓ

Joseph, still seated by the small cookfire, picks up a twig and stirs the coals and ashes about as he contemplates the work before them. *So many children. And what of the other tribes ... What is their state,* he ponders? *How many more shall the emissaries find and return here? How many can this place sustain? How can the Promise manifest in the midst of the wilderness? What of the prophecies?*

Before he can go any further in his thoughts and questions, his spirit stirs, and he begins to pray. "It is I, Lord God, Thy servant Joseph. I know that Thou hast seen my thoughts, and that Thou hearest and knowest the questions that come from my heart. Knowest my faith, as well, and seest these not as doubts or questions but only the concerns of a loving heart for those of Thy children who face such an important and demanding task. I send my love to those who will come. I open my heart and my spirit, as Thou wouldst use me, Lord God, in any wise ... that the Promise be fulfilled."

His head slowly drops forward as his arms and folded legs form a curious sort of support. It is a posture to which he is well accustomed, that he might rest wherever it is that he finds himself.

The days pass and much transpires. What lies ahead is the coming together of the people who hold the expectation of the Promise. Perhaps you will open your hearts and your spirits to be one with that as shall be recounted.

The hearts and spirits of many of you will resonate beyond the ordinary with what is to come. This is our humble prayer. For we have come from on high be-

yond that which thou knowest, according to the Word of God, in order that the Promise might reawaken, and that those of you who hear the Call and know the truth of it within your own being will come forward in the one work.

The light of our Lord God's grace ever awaits you.

Chapter Eight

The Rescue

Reaching across the sky, the first rays of the dawn's light offer wondrous energies for all who are so attuned.

Within the embrace of this energy, a group can be seen moving into the craggy walls of the School of the Prophets. To the forefront of the group are the guardians.

Upon seeing them, one of the children calls out joyfully, "Look! Look, Judy, they come ... our guardians! And they have gathered others!" All the children clamor about, moving into small clusters according to their family ties.

Both groups, those who have already found sanctuary here within the ancient School and those who are their recently rescued brethren, rush towards one another, merging into one large group. There are embraces, cries of joy, tears, and songs. Some grasp hands and dance about in little circles. Others have fallen to their knees to offer prayers. All throughout, the children are touching each other, embracing, calling out a name here or there, weaving in and out. It is, indeed, a joyous sight to behold.

After a time, all have made their way to the central area of the School.

"We rejoice in heart and spirit," Joseph calls out to the large number of his people now before him. "We give thanks unto our Lord God that thou art delivered here into this place of safety, this sanctuary, as we have come to know it. And we give thanks to you," turning to gesture to Elob, "and to all your companions," extending his arms out to the others who are gathered all about, here and there, above, and to his rear.

All gesture in return in their special way, and Elob bows and gives the signet of his people.

"We have much to be thankful for, my people," continues Joseph. "Let us take one another's hands. Look into the eyes of that one to either side of you and see the light, see the Promise shine from deep within them. And join with me now in my spirit as I reach out to Our Lord.

"Lord God, the grace of Thy Spirit is all about. We accept this, and we do so in the joy and honor of bearing forth Thy Word. We give thanks for these, our brethren, and this hallowed ground upon which they have given us shelter. We give thanks this day for the delivery of our brothers and sisters and more of the beautiful children into our fold. We give thanks for the elders who have gone before us and given us the Sacred Covenant, the tenets by which we ever strive to live. Most of all, we give thanks for one another. For in the sharing of our spirit's light do we come to know ourselves and thereby give unto the Promise all that we are and have to give. Bless us, Lord God, with the continued joy and abundance of Thy Spirit's light. So let it be written. Amen." Lifting his head, he turns with a smile at Jacob and a subtle nod.

It is all that Jacob needs. He rises from his seated position and looks into all of the eyes before him. Then, he makes a move with his head to the left as his hands come up in a single clap, and to his right he does the same. Then, clap-clap-clap, and a beautiful song begins to come forth as he sways a bit, turns about this way and that, and then moves down amongst his peoples, calling out, "Come, children. Come, brothers and sisters. Let us celebrate the joy of God's presence, and the joy of one another."

Joyful laughter and song begin. Some have brought forth simple instruments, and the music winds its way over the hollows, between the rocky crags, and up the summits.

For a moment, Joseph's face shows concern, and he glances at Elob who is smiling, nodding at him. "All is well, friend. Fear not. No one from beyond these mountain walls can hear your merriment. Let it flow, and let it course across the sands that surround us. Let every grain hear and know the voice of God's peoples."

Joseph's concern melts into a smile matching Elob's, and he begins to sway back and forth before moving down into the group to intertwine his arm with that of a friend's, and around and around they spin.

Merriment along with the recounting of events that have gone before is shared all throughout the day. Those who are of such talent among the adepts in the School bring forth aromatic teas and unique foods flavored with special herbs and spices, and place them on the great cookfires. Nearby, the children play and roll about, tickling, laughing, giggling.

As the horizon gradually changes to a soft orange-red glow, Jacob, Joseph, Elob, and many, many others gather around a large communal fire. Their evening meal is completed, their prayers have been offered, and even a bit of wine is a part of this evening's ceremony.

Softly, Jacob begins, asking of one of the recent arrivals, "It has been too long since my eyes have looked upon you, Ruth. Are you well?"

"That I am, Jacob. Well, and prepared to be about the work." She glances over at Anna and Judy who are seated close by her.

"I have no doubt that the children would welcome some change. I have always heard too much merriment and idle time can become boring." Jacob throws his head back and laughs a hearty laugh.

Everyone laughs, a wonderful sound after such a prolonged period of challenge leading up to this time wherein their groups have been brought together in this holy place.

When the laughter has subsided, Joseph looks at Ruth, "What of the others? Has anyone heard?"

"We did hear from them not that long ago, though only briefly. They said that they are with us in spirit, and that they will disperse for their own safety, as I presume you know, Elob, and you as well," nodding in honor to the two seers. "And that after a time, perhaps a fortnight or two, they would send an emissary to the place ... Elob, I am told that you know of it ... near the City of Knowledge?"

"I do," he smiles, "and we await them there."

"Oh, that is wonderful! They said to give unto you all their love."

"And what of your group, Elba?" continues Joseph.

She looks down for a brief moment, and then her head comes up as she straightens herself. "I have lost many ... though I am certain they are with us here in spirit. So if all here would, please remember in prayer our beloved guardians who gave their lives that the children, Thomas, myself, and the others," looking to the other four, "could be with you this evening. How is it that God would send us such." She glances across to look into the depth and curious light that emanates from Jason's eyes, and then to two of his colleagues who are seated at his right and left, from whom she receives but a faint smile in acknowledgment.

"Others have been taken captive, but we are told that Elob and the others have dispatched their colleagues with the means to attempt to purchase them, if it is possible. We do not know precisely how many, but we believe a score or perhaps even more have survived. Neither do we know, of this number, how many children remain alive." Her head bows, and all know she is offering prayers for their brethren, and they join her.

Following this, there is a considerable time of sharing

news, not only of their peoples but of the pursuers and their almost frenzied search for these, as their pursuers call them, *heathens*.

Joseph rises and looks about the group. "I think it well that we rest now. On the morrow, we will find a good time to begin planning our works. Let each one in their shelter, light a light of remembrance this evening for those who have gone before, for those of our brethren who have crossed over from the challenges of Earth into the embrace of God, and for those of our brethren who are held in bondage. But let us also remember, as we offer our prayers unto the flame of God, to give thanks for the blessings so bountifully upon us now."

All rise and begin to make their way. Some of the adepts from the School guide the newcomers to their shelters. The others move in various directions off into their time of rest.

ℰↄᏟᏮ

The bidding commences.

"What am I offered? Look, you! This is a stout one, capable of much labor."

Off in the shadows are four men, two of whom have coverings over their heads. Of the other two, one wears a headband. The other simply has very dark, below-the-shoulder hair and wears a plain but bright, beaded necklace. It is he who raises a hand to indicate that he will increase the bid.

The bidding goes back and forth, until finally the auctioneer points to the one with the long dark hair and beaded necklace. "Sold to you, sir!" He gestures for him to come up, pay his coin, and take his new slave.

Again and again it goes, and each time one of the Expectant Ones is brought to auction, one of these four who are now dispersed about the crowd bids the higher bid.

"And now, look you upon this beauty! She is a rare jewel ... pure, beautiful, and young. Look at her. Not a one of you has had better, of this I am certain." He laughs mockingly.

The bidding begins to rise, building to a frenzy ... here, there, up there, then over here.

The dark-haired one moves over to one of his companions. "We must be cautious," he whispers. "Several have noted our bidding." He directs a subtle nod over to the side. Several uniformed guards are looking at them. "And back here, see them?" Two more behind are studying them. One is leaning to whisper, with his hand covering his mouth. "We must remove those we have gathered thus far.

"You two," he whispers to his colleagues, "you take that gate." He cautiously nods in the direction of one of the far gates. "And you ... Take the others and leave by that gate over there. Agreed? We will meet at the appointed place."

A subtle nod, no spoken words, and the two covered ones leave in different directions, taking their purchases with them. One has nine, the other has eight, seventeen in all.

The one with the band around his forehead looks into the eyes of the dark-haired one. "There is great danger here. Do you believe we can bid for her and not be discovered?"

The longhaired one glances about. Apparently the main focus is upon him, for he cannot see that any guards have left to follow the two covered ones. "It is my feeling that the others will do well. Our focus now is on the maiden. Stand over there by those columns near the portico and make the final bid. Make it in gems. Here, take these." He reaches within his tunic to pull forth a handful of strikingly beautiful gems. "That should best anyone's bid, I should think." Smiling, he raises his hand just slightly, allowing their fingertips to touch though their arms remain straight at their sides. Showing no movement, he deftly lets the gems slip deftly into his brother's hand as the men steal a glance into one another's eyes. "I am with you in spirit. Go. Bid for her. She is one of those who are blessed. Do you agree?"

Looking up at the beautiful young maiden being held on the block, "That I do."

One final glance, then, "Go now," the dark-haired one urges. "I will distract them. Take her expeditiously, for no doubt you will be pursued."

"They will not see us. I shall veil our departure."

"Good." His eyes twinkle, for he knows his brother has the power of creating illusion and mirage. "May the Eternal Spirit be your light."

Upon his brother's hasty departure, the dark-haired one moves over to the side and roars out a figure, waving his arms as he does. The guards signal one another and point to him, which is part of his plan. He continues moving towards the opposite side from whence he sent his brother. Again he shouts a number, laughs and slaps one on the back next to him who frowns. "What a fine maiden that is."

"Too rich for your blood, whoever you are, whatever land you are from," and then shouts out a higher figure, then sneers, "It is I who shall have this one."

"Indeed?" mocks the dark-haired one. "Not unless you are willing to pay more than ..." and he shouts another figure. He can see, with a quick glance about from the corner of his eye, that the guards are moving towards him. He smiles knowingly and begins to shout at the man next to him, "You do not deserve a fair flower as she."

Two companions begin to shout at one another, the portly one yelling out another figure.

"Best that, heathen!" shouts a bearded one.

The dark-haired one throws his head back and laughs boisterously, attempting to draw attention.

Others are beginning to gather around this group, as they shout figures one after another.

Finally, no longer able to tolerate the insults from the dark-haired one, the bearded one shouts, and his colleagues pounce upon the dark-haired one. A struggle ensues and the guards move swiftly to the brawl.

To the side of the auction block, the one with the band

on his forehead speaks quietly but firmly, "Auctioneer, look you here. No one can best this." He opens the bag enough to reveal the gems, gleaming even in the bag's shadows.

The auctioneer gasps aloud. "Sold!" he states in a hushed voice, scooping up the leather bag filled with the priceless gems. "Take her! But you had best go quickly. There is not a one here that would not slit your throat to have her."

The maiden is incredibly fearful, tears streaming down her face. But the banded one smiles, and his firm grasp calms her. She looks into his eyes and sees a depth of gentleness that she knows is not out of lust for her body, but love for her spirit.

He leans his head to hers to whisper, "I am come to bring you to your people. Fear not. No harm shall befall you. That is my brother, there, providing us distraction, but we must move swiftly. Come. Are you able?"

"Yes, yes I am able."

They begin to move, leaving the city circuitously through this alley and that passageway until finally they are out into the mid-day sun.

Moving quickly now, glancing this way and that, amid their haste, the banded one removes a large cloth from his shoulders. "Here, cover yourself. You must not be seen."

She swiftly takes the cloth, covering her head and face with it, clutching it tightly to her body. "Thank you. Oh, thank you, good sir. How are you called?"

"I am called Cal, and I am of the brotherhood. We dwell far away. The journey will be long and arduous, but I tell you we shall make it. And you will see your people again."

The maiden begins to weep. "Oh-h ... You have given me my life back, for I would surely have ended it had one of them purchased me."

"I know. I know your spirit. I see your light."

"You ... You have the sight?" she whispers with awe.

"Yes. I have the sight."

The market is now a sea of writhing robes and turbans, a melee of thumps and groans. Everyone is fighting everyone else for no particular reason except that this seems to be the nature of these men. Curses, blows, and orders are shouted from guards as they press into the seething throng.

Standing unobtrusively off to the side, in the shadow of an archway, is the dark-haired one, smiling, speaking under his breath, "You mete out according to that which is in your heart, and now you are receiving that which is within. The Law of the One God is perfect." He turns and moves silently, easily, through the shadows of the passageways.

At a steady trot, with seemingly no effort at all, he follows the footprints of one the group who left by the east gate, a group of nine with one of his brothers.

Soon he can see them, far off in the distance. He stops to look around to see if they are being pursued. Though he hears naught, he senses pursuit is not too distant.

Doubling his movement, within several hours he has caught up with the group. He and his brother adept greet one another in a warm spiritual gesture of kinship, not unlike that of the Expectant Ones themselves.

"Let us pause," the covered one tells the group, "and rest for a time, though only briefly."

The two brothers pass around several skins of water and a bundle with loaves of bread.

As the group takes nourishment, the two move off to the side where they cannot be heard.

"Our brothers?"

" I saw them depart."

"And the maiden?"

"We have her." He smiles and nods.

"Let us affirm our power then, as we give thanks."

The covered one extends his hands out, palms upwards,

and the dark-haired one places his hands atop his brother's. Slowly they grasp one another's wrists and lean forward to place their foreheads against each other's. Even in the day's bright light, a glow can be seen growing around them.

Seeing this, one of the nine Essenes glances over and nudges a companion. "Look, look! Are they praying?"

"I think it must be so."

"But look around them."

"I see naught. What do you mean?"

"The light! The glow. Do you not see it? On the outer is a beautiful shimmering essence, like a pearl, and on the inner ... See? Soft bands of light. Are they men of God?" He turns to look at his companion.

"Of that I am certain. I heard them speak in God's name several times. If they were not of God, they would not so do."

"True. But listen. How strange. Can you hear it?"

"I hear something. It sounds as though they are humming, yet I hear more than two voices."

"I, too. It is as though many voices have joined theirs. Do you think they are magicians?"

"No. I think they are far more than that ... perhaps akin to our elders or some such."

"Well, let us give our prayers, as well. Brethren!" He calls the nine together. They kneel shoulder to shoulder in a small circle and offer their prayer of thanksgiving.

When they have finished, they look up to see the covered one standing quietly beside them. "Have you had sufficient nourishment and water?"

"We have," the Essene to the front of the group responds. "Thank you. May God ever bless you."

"And each of you, as well, dear friends. But come, now. We must not tarry."

The covered one glances at the dark-haired one and momentarily their eyes connect.

Without a word the dark-haired one turns and heads

back in the direction from whence he had come. As he moves away, without looking back he raises a hand to gesture to his brother that he will keep the watch at the rear.

"What is the nature of your people?" one of the Essenes inquires. "Where are you from and how are you called?"

"I am Mellus, and I am to take you to a wonderful place where your people await your arrival."

"Oh-h, sir ..." touched beyond words. "How is it you have come to gain such great wealth to be able to acquire all eight of us? How have you managed this?"

Mellus smiles, nods, and points a single finger upwards. "Your God has provided us the means to acquire your freedom. All thanks should go unto Him."

She strikes her chest. "You ... You know of our God?"

Mellus smiles. "We are not apart from your God, even though you see my brother and me as different from you. In your own teachings, does it not say ... Judge not by that which is seen, rather judge by that which is received in the spirit, in the word, in the deed?"

"You know our teachings, as well?"

"Yes. We know your teachings, and are one with them."

"Know you, then, our elders?" she questions softly as they continue to move along swiftly.

"Some I know here on Earth. Others of them, I know in the beyond."

With a swift movement of her hand, she covers her mouth. In one sense this could be considered blasphemy, for to state such is to imply that one is capable of such oneness with God. Among the Expectant Ones, their holy ones know and revere this oneness, a source of much light to their peoples. But this covered, hooded stranger ... Can he, in truth, know? Can he see, know, and hear those who have gone beyond, those who have left behind the body of flesh?

Mellus turns to look at the maiden with gentle eyes, as though he has heard her every thought. "It is a matter that

---

should concern you not, dear maiden. Rather, think about your people and about the joy that lies ahead, for we have an arduous journey now. But I promise you, you will find a peace and a sanctuary there of such security and comfort and joy that your heart will sing with gladness." A tender laugh comes from him.

She thinks it must be ever so beautiful where he comes from, for in the melodious sound of Mellus' laughter, she hears a resonance reassuring to her spirit.

"And how are *you* called, my lady?"

"I am called Theresa. Thank you for asking."

She glances back to look at the others and is mindful that they have endured much. Several have been wounded in the earlier battle and most all are fatigued nearly to the limit.

Mellus, too, looks back at them and then turns to look into the distance. "Look, there. Do you see that small summit off to the right?"

"I do."

"Well then, Theresa, go back among your brothers and sisters and tell them that there are provisions stored at that summit, and we shall rest there for a time. Go. Tell them. It will lift their spirits. And when we have reached the summit, I shall tend to the wounds of those who are in need."

Her head almost snaps over to the side to look up into his eyes. "Have you herbs and balms?"

"These I have, and greater," he smiles. "Is it not true that if we ask of your God anything in the name of the Promise He will surely give it?"

Her sigh is almost a swoon, for with all else, now this man speaks of the Promise? How could he know? It must be true that he has been among her people. Her heart leaps and she smiles so broadly that her cheeks hurt. "Thank you." She offers the Essene gesture. "Thank you, Mellus."

"Go now ... Tell them," he whispers, smiling to himself.

Having reached the summit, the group is kneeling in the shadow of a tall dune as water flasks and foodstuffs are being circulated about.

As Mellus is studying a deep wound in the upper arm of one of the Essenes, the man turns his head away with a low groan. "Do not concern," Mellus reassures him. "There is no need to mask your pain."

He turns to glance at Theresa who is kneeling next to him, looking at the arm as well, holding the man's hand. "I shall need some water, Theresa."

She rises and rushes over to where the water is kept, is handed a flask, and swiftly returns.

Mellus looks into her dark brown eyes, upturned with hope and expectancy. "Hold the flask here, and when I ask put just a bit on the wound itself."

His hands move swiftly. From some hidden pouch he brings forth a bit of powder, and from another, several leafy-looking objects. He snaps the leaves with the one hand and squeezes a clear fluid from their center into the hand with the powder. Then, with two fingers he stirs the powder and the sap from the leaves in the palm of his hand. "Very well. Now pour the water on the wound."

As she does, he nods and, again with his fingers, moves the water slowly in a circle around the wound.

Theresa hears him speaking very quietly and thinks he is saying, "O Holy One, this water is Thy Spirit, the symbolic and literal fluid of life. I move it in the pattern of Thy eternal Logos, the circle of life, that all within this circle be renewed and cleansed." For a moment, his hand over the wound, he leans his head back, eyes closed, rocking subtly.

Again, she hears a tone or something, words perhaps, barely audible, coming from somewhere deep within him. Not long, only a few moments, but she feels a pulse in her body, pounding through every vein. Her heart ... She can feel it pound. Who is this man? What is his power?

He looks down, and carefully, gently, begins to smooth the paste out over the terrible wound. As he does, he again speaks to the man. "This salve will take the pain from you, sir. This, I promise."

The man looks into Mellus' eyes and immediately feels that this is a man of truth. Suddenly the man speaks aloud, "I can feel it already! My brothers, my sister, look, you! The pain is leaving. What herbs, what potions have you there?"

Mellus is now standing, rubbing his hands together. "We have much knowledge about many things that has been lovingly cared for and passed down through the years as a treasure. Just as all of you know of the Promise, so do we. We are here in various works, for various purposes, as is the will of the One God. You will find, sir, that in several days this wound will be well."

Glancing down, the man can barely see his wound, for it is covered with the reddish powder and the clear thick fluid, which has been placed upon the wound. "If you say it, good sir, I believe it."

"Come now, everyone, rest a time. For soon we must again be moving." Mellus then moves off to the side, as is his nature, to stand apart from these peoples. It is not that he does not wish their company, but that he has works to do, for he has left his three brothers, and their spirits are as one.

Leaning back against the cool shadowed side of the dune, he looks up into the sky with thoughts of his brothers ... the banded one, the dark-haired one, and the covered one. His heart begins to pound slowly, like a drum beating out a rhythm of life. His eyelids flicker and close, and he sees the other nine Expectant Ones now moving with one brother to the forefront. His dark-haired brother is to the rear. Another deep breath, a pause, and now he sees his brother who wears the band about his forehead, along with the beautiful maiden, making his way through the desert.

A smile passes across his face. All is well. He whispers, eyes remaining closed, "Feel the power of my spirit, my brothers." *Thum-thum*, his heart beats, and with the cadence of his own heart's rhythm he sends out a prayer, in part an affirmation and in part a request, made with remarkable calm, strength, and serenity. "We claim you and your power, and we use your power according to your guidance. We claim this and give thanks unto you. Let my brothers know I am one with them."

Thum, thum, thum.

"To whom do you speak?" a voice speaks at his side.

His eyes flicker open and he turns to see one kneeling upon the sand several paces away from him in honor and respect. "Oh, Theresa. Come here."

"I am sorry if I disturbed you. I thought you might thirst, and perhaps be in need of a bit of food, as well."

Sitting up and crossing his legs, he places an elbow upon one knee and outstretches his hand. "How kind of you to think of me. Yes, I might partake of some food and some water. Thank you."

Theresa is obviously very pleased. She moves close to extend these to him. "From what land do you come?"

Mellus, after first drinking deeply, turns to her, "From a land far, far to the east."

"And how did you arrive here?"

"I was a student among several wise old teachers. We were taught many healing ways. That is how I knew of that which I gave to your brother. They also taught us much more. They told us of the Promise. I along with the other students heard this. But when I heard it, something came alive within me. One of my teachers saw it and watched me. This was in my youth. As I grew through the passage of years, this, too, grew within me." He touches the area of his heart as he speaks. "One day, our teachers told us there was naught more they could give unto us, and that it was time for us to go forth and bear the gifts of their teachings to those in need."

"But how did you come to be here?" Theresa gestures with her arms to the desert sands.

"Before I departed, I went to my favorite teacher, for I knew that he could see me, not just this body of flesh but the true me, within. Know you of such things, Theresa?"

"Yes," she nods and smiles. "We know the tenets, the sacred teachings. And I am a part of ..." straightening herself, a glow of pride and joy shining from her as she speaks, "I am a sister. I am a part of a group who shall bring forth the Awakening. We shall help the children discover who they are. Among them, we shall find those who will bear the gifts, the sacred tenets, unto the Promise ... our Lord. And it shall be one of these very children who shall bear Him forth."

Mellus only nods and smiles, "My teacher told me the story of the Promise and of those to the west who were to bear it forth. I knew that was to be my life's work, and my teacher told me this was aright. He gave unto me the means to make the journey. But greater than this did he give, for I spent more time with him. After my brothers had finished their studies as adepts and had gone off, he told me of many things, giving me an understanding of the Promise as he knew it. He gave me this, as well ..." He reaches beneath his garment to pull out a small pouch suspended on a simple thong.

Looking down, Mellus takes the pouch and clasps his fingers gently, tenderly, around it. His gaze warm, compassionate, understanding, he looks up into the soft inquisitive eyes before him. "You ponder what is it? It is a gift that I shall give unto the One who comes."

"Is it gem, or spice, or precious herb, or ointment?"

"No, it is far greater than those, yet only those who have eyes to see would know this."

Looking down and up, she cants her head to the side and asks, "Can you tell me of it?"

Mellus almost begins to laugh, so great is his delight and so amused is he at this young one's curiosity and sweetness. "I will tell you of it," he answers, "when I give it to Him who comes. Fair enough?"

Theresa straightens herself and nods her head with a beautiful, though somewhat serious, gesture of respect to him. "Fair enough. And when you tell me and the others of this gift, we shall tell you of ours."

Now they both laugh softly.

"Come, now." Mellus rises. "I have enjoyed spending time with you, but now we must resume our journey."

"Oh, and I have enjoyed my time with you. I am grateful to you for your gifts to my people and me, and to my brother. Thank you. May God ever bless you."

"He has." Mellus smiles upon her.

When Theresa looks into his eyes, she can see no hint of insult here or forwardness, nothing but reverence along with a wonderfully curious surety.

"Come, my friends," he gestures now to all. "If you would, please follow in single file, and as best as possible step in my footprints. I shall make them of a pace that each of you can manage." He turns for just a brief moment to smile at Theresa, who receives it and looks down shyly.

The coming together of these remnants shall begin a journey of awakening. Not only shall each be given, and give, gifts to one another and to the adepts in the School, but they shall bring about the empowerment of that environment which will support the discovery of the children's light within.

In that which follows next, we shall move across this span of time to provide some reference for that which been given in past. But most of all, we intend to offer you those salient points as might be contributive to your awakening in the present. For know you well that all that you have received here to this point is for the intention of awakening you, of empowering you, that you might see that the path you follow in the present has a parallel in the past.

We encourage you to know yourselves as never before. That whatever the enlightenment in this lifetime, know that what lies ahead can be greater than all of these, and so much more.

Chapter Nine

The Awakening Begins

Some time has passed and all those who were retrieved from the auction and brought to the School of the Prophets have been lovingly received and are by now well settled.

On a summit a goodly number are gathering a bit apart from the main body of the encampment areas so they can speak without concern that any would be disturbed. These of the Expectant Ones are considered teachers, guides, philosophers, seers, prophets, healers. Also gathered here are a number from the School, generally called adepts. Though the Essenes have seen them about here and there, up to this point relatively little exchange has taken place between them and these adepts.

Across from Joseph and Jacob, Elob is seated, and on either side of him are a number of the adepts.

Elob begins, "Have the children adjusted well?"

"I believe," offers Anna, "that they are in the best state of health that I have seen them in for some considerable time, mentally, emotionally, spiritually. In fact, I don't recall ever having seen them quite so at peace. We all thank you, Elob, for this is a gift beyond measure. It is our tradition to return that which is a righteous exchange yet we know not how to repay you for all you have done."

Several of Elob's companions glance at one another,

smiling.

"Well, how interesting," Elob looks about the group, "for this is just the topic we wanted to discuss."

"Repayment?"

Elob laughs softly, and several with him look down, smiling. "Perhaps that is an appropriate word to use in a sense, Anna, but it is not our intent. We should like to share with you some of our insights, if you would like to know of them."

Judy sits up in anticipation, "Indeed, we would."

Close to her are the two seers, both very relaxed, as if they are already aware of what is about to transpire.

Jacob has his knees pulled up, cross-legged. His elbows are perched one upon each knee, his chin supported in the cups of his hands, his head moving ever so slightly left and right, as though hearing some inaudible tune or such. "Yes, we would very much knowing more about you. And, as Anna gave, perhaps we shall find some way to bring about an equal exchange for that which we receive from you."

"First of all, it is very good to hear," Elob glances at Anna, "that the children are ready. Many of them are gathered here now and we understand more are on their way."

A happy murmur moves throughout the group.

Ruth leans forward. "Can you tell us from whence they come?"

"Indeed." He points off to a low summit beyond.

With a flush of quiet excitement all turn to look in the direction indicated by Elob.

"We believe," he continues, as though to quiet them, "that we must make some ... well, I would not call it haste, but we should make plans to move ahead. It is important that the activities begin. We understand that you are to discern twelve from among the children. True?"

Judy looks over at Anna and Ruth, and then back at Elob. "Yes, twelve. It is a truth that the symbol of power for our people is twelve. We follow what we hold true in order that we can maintain the greatest oneness with all that has gone before and with the Ancients, who are our ancestors and prophets of old."

"We concur that twelve is a powerful symbol and much more than a mere number. It will add further potential to those chosen twelve, and though we know you of course have knowledge in this area of sacred numbers we can add to this. Have you guidance as to how they shall be chosen?"

"We do," Joseph answers, "but we welcome any insights that you and your people have."

"Good." Elob now fixes his gaze upon Anna. "Anna, would you tell us about your truths, please?"

Momentarily startled to be called upon to speak on this subject of such majesty for her peoples, Anna, as Judy before her, straightens herself. Without thinking, her hands go quickly to her heart and to her forehead, followed by a barely perceptible glance upward. "What we call truths are the teachings of the ancient ones, recorded and carried forward through the years. We sealed and sequestered these sacred works in the caves where you found us. But not to digress here … For us the truths are as the qualities of the very existence of God. We call them truths because we know that our spiritual and mental intent, enacted in daily life, becomes a bond, a covenant, between that one and God. Is that sufficient?"

"For the moment it is quite so. Know you of our tenets?"

"I have heard you speak of this of on occasion, and I have had the sense that they are similar to our truths."

"They are nearly the same, though we think of them somewhat differently for reasons we hope will become clear to you in the days, weeks, and months ahead."

"That would be wonderful," Ruth comments.

"These tenets, good sir," questions Theresa, "are they similar to what I have heard called sacred teachings?"

"Essentially they are the same, but I should like to allow my very knowledgeable colleagues an opportunity to respond to this. They have offered to help you guide the children, even teach them with you, if, of course, you so choose.

Elob reaches his arm out to the right. "Here is one whom we call Phinehas. Phinehas is not his birth name, but that name is so lengthy that we asked him, when he arrived, to please choose another because it took too long to call him."

There is a moment of silence until the Essenes realize this was intended as humor, and laughter ripples around the rather sizeable group.

"And on my left," Elob gestures to a strikingly handsome, dark-skinned man, "is Zelotese. He is particularly knowledgeable of the sacred symbols, forms, and patterns. Phinehas is knowledgeable of these as well, but also has considerable ... Well, they will speak for themselves and you may question them further if you wish. Please, dear friends, these are as brothers to me. They come to you holding the light of the Promise, I should think quite equal to the love and passion with which each of you holds it within yourself."

A murmur goes all through the Essenes as they glance at one another. Some touch their chests. Others bow their heads, bobbing and muttering soft prayers.

Not Jacob, however, who continues to sit very quietly. Only his eyes move, and ever so subtly his head, as he looks about at each.

"In the quest for discovery," Phinehas begins, "there is the need to inspire. You have among your truths one of these. You call it the ideal, and do correct me if I am misstating this in any way." He smiles broadly. "It is that which you encourage your children and your people, and yourselves, of course, to hold before you as the measure by which you compare all that occurs in your lives. The ideal is also the intent, the destination unto which you intend to travel in the journey called life. Is this a fairly accurate summation, Theresa?"

Shyly she bows her head and glances left and right. "It is, indeed, sir. You honor us with your knowledge."

Phinehas smiles with a slight nod. "What we call tenets, and what we believe you hold as your truths, is that which lies within the heart and mind of the person. It is not that which is known in the outer sense as, let us say, Thomas or Hannah or Mary, or for that matter Judy or Anna or Joseph," smiling broadly at the three of them, "but the very life-force that lies deep within each individual. The purpose of much of what we shall be offering to you and to the Promise will be to help each of the children to discover their truth within ... to call it forth, to know it, to claim it, and then to be guided to live it."

In the silence which follows as the Essenes ponder what has been given, Phinehas leans over.

Zelotese nods. "I greet you from my spirit and my heart of hearts, sweet brothers and sisters, for, indeed, are we not all one?" An excited murmur of confirmation passes all throughout. "Then if we are all one, how is it that in the journey called life there is that which causes some to consider themselves separate from another? If oneness is a truth, and if your truths are rooted in the foundation of eternity and, as your prophets have stated, there is but one God and one people of that one God, how can it come to pass that there is such divergence?

"You look upon my skin and it is colored similar to the others over there. You look into my eyes and they are different than many of yours. And yet, we are one. How is it that the Pattern has come forward to manifest in such differentiation and uniqueness if, indeed, we are all one?

"There are the pursuers who intend to destroy us and the Promise, and to destroy anything that would diminish their dominance. One of their primary weapons is fear. How is it if we are all one that such a thing as fear could indeed exist?" Zelotese leans forward to pass the commentary back to Phinehas.

Phinehas looks about the group. "The nature of reality is that it is held by the perceiver, the one who does the experiencing. If you have not experienced a thing how can you know it? If you have not walked a great journey how can you know the essence of fatigue that is the companion of such a journey? If you have not gone without nourishment to your body and fluids to slake your thirst how can you know the byproduct of hunger and thirst?"

Phinehas does not look, but Zelotese renews his commentary. "If, indeed, we are all one, then when anyone, anywhere, experiences any of these and other things, that experience must at least in some way be known to all. Do you all agree?"

The abruptness of Zelotese' question catches them off-guard.

Jacob, still cupping his chin in his hands, speaks softly. "These are the teachings of our Ancients and we give you the same honor were one of our Ancients speaking to us in your place. We do agree with what you are speaking and are eager to hear more. Your words most certainly ring true within me. What say you, Joseph?" He asks this without looking at him.

Joseph is reflective but his countenance is serene. "I hear in your words, good Zelotese, and yours, Phinehas, truths I have longed to hear again. I concur with my brother, Jacob. We agree and are following what you say. Please, continue."

All are sitting respectfully, reverently, looking at Zelotese with his probing eyes. Each seems to sense that Zelotese with his piercing gaze, would know immediately of any doubt or hesitation merely upon looking at that one.

"Remarkable," responds Judy to Zelotese' silent gaze.

"How so?"

"I can feel, as you look upon me, and I am certain my brothers and sisters can as well, the feeling of being looked upon by one who has what we call *the sight*. It is true, then, that you ... *see?*"

There is no change of expression on Zelotese' face, the penetrating gaze of his beautiful eyes neither wavering nor flickering for a moment. "I see," he responds softly, as another murmur goes through all the Essenes, "as does Phinehas, as does Elob, as do most all here, including," he adds looking around, "all of you."

This is difficult for some of the Essenes to accept, for even in their absolute faith many yet have reservations of their own self-worth, believing that only certain of their elders have the higher sight.

"Is it possible that we know not what we have?"

"It is as we have given, Anna," Zelotese responds softly. "How can we believe on the one hand that we are all one, and on the other disbelieve that we are one? That one would have the gifts of God but not another?"

The sisters are smiling, nodding, and gesturing their dedication to one another with palms outstretched before the group of adepts.

Theresa leans to look at Zelotese and Phinheas. "Please, tell us more."

Phinehas responds, "It is likened unto one who has a great granary. To any who come unto it the owner gives of the granary, again and again and again. One day one comes in tattered clothes, bent, with hands outstretched holding a bowl, and asks of the owner, 'Can you give to me of your grain, good sir? I ask this of you in the name of the true God.'

"Smiling, the owner opens the granary and realizes there is naught within. But he pulls aside the coverings on the small opening at the base, stoops, and goes inside, calling out as he extends a hand through the doorway, 'Give unto me your bowl, sir.'

"Having gathered the very last of the grains from the floor of the granary, the owner emerges, brushing off his garments, and hands the filled bowl to the stranger.

"The man who had asked of him simply glances down at his bowl and then up into the eyes of the owner.

"The owner looks about and at the man and about again.

'I am very sorry, sir. The grain is gone. I have given unto you all that I have to give.'

"Suddenly, the figure before him straightens. The worn garments slowly fall away and in their place is raiment so bright, so beautiful, that the owner can scarcely look upon him. A light comes from the stranger's eyes and now seems to embrace the owner. In a powerful, though gentle voice, the stranger speaks. 'Thou art truly a son of God. I tell you this: Before the dawn's light on the morrow you shall have greater than you can give.'

"The owner falls to his knees and the tall, beautiful stranger bends, extending the bowl containing the last bit of grain from the granary. 'When I am gone from here take this and go back within from whence you have taken the grain. Place it in the center of thy granary and seal it such that naught shall flow out.'

"Reaching his hands up, barely able to look upon the incredible beauty and light of this shining stranger, the owner takes the bowl held out to him.

"The stranger then places a hand upon the head of this yet kneeling man and lifts his face unto the heavens. 'My Father, here is your true son. Give unto him that as will surpass the needs of any who ask of him. And so let it be that all throughout time no measure can equal that which Thou shalt give unto him.'

"Looking back down, the stranger bends and kisses the owner on the forehead. 'I come to you as your brother. In another time I shall come again. When I do, I will call you. I will ask you, *Walk with me.*'

"The owner speaks in a broken voice, tears streaming, 'Say but the word unto me, lord, and I will follow you wheresoever you would guide me. But how shall I know you? What name shall I call you?'

"'I shall give unto you this symbol.' The stranger extends his foot and draws the simple sign of a fish in the sand in front of the kneeling man. 'When you see this symbol and I say unto you, *I am the Son of God, follow me* ... That is how you shall know me.'

"The stranger backs away and the light that comes from within him embraces him and lifts him up, leaving the man kneeling, sobbing with joy."

There is a long pause.

Many eyes are filled with tears. Some in the group are bobbing and striking their chests, speaking the Holy Words.

"Is it not so," Phinheas continues, "just as in this recounting, which is one of many we shall share with the children, that this is what God has given unto us? If you believe you can see then the sight is yours. If you believe that you can hear then all the beautiful utterances of the Earth and beyond are yours. Any such as is before you, so as you look within it, you will know that place wherein the Oneness still dwells. Not the greatest mantle of all darkness or illusion or fear can extinguish the Oneness within. That Oneness is the truth of which we have spoken and is similar to your sacred truths. We shall honor you as we ask you to honor us, and together this will form a powerful force." Phinehas falls silent.

Zelotese allows a moment for those assembled to receive what Phinheas has given, and then speaks again. "There is no number greater than the number One for there is no thing that does not contain that number. Whether we devise beautiful symbols, ancient teachings manifested in patterns and designs, taught through weaving, found in the chanting of mantras, heard in the drumming of the external as well as the drumming of life within, when one states *All are one*, it is possible to infer *All are one with God*. This statement is an invocation, and in that invocation there is power.

"We shall not offer you that which we have to give with the intent of creating a quest for power for power's sake or knowledge for knowledge's sake, but shall offer these as our gifts to the Promise ... which comes.

"For the Promise is the Son of God. He will manifest to light the Way to make it passable and to invoke the memory of oneness, not only in those who will hear His words, feel the touch of His hand and the warmth of His smile and the joy of His laughter, but in all those throughout time who hear and know the truth of His words as those words endure.

"We have seen that the recounting by Phinehas has touched you ... even you, Jacob." Jacob only blinks and smiles. "Then we ask of you, touch your self in just that same way. For you," he raises his arm and points a finger directly at Judy, "are a Daughter of God." Her face flushes as the light clearly embraces her. He raises his other hand, "And you there, Thomas, are a Son of God. Say it."

Thomas, startled at being singled out, looks this way and that, then glances straight across at Joseph who simply nods. "I am a son of God," Thomas responds.

Zelotese shakes his head. "No. Heard you not the words and the power as recounted by my brother? *I AM A SON OF GOD*. Not, *I-am-a-son-of-God*."

"But how can I say this?" Thomas is flushed. "I do not feel worthy to say this."

"Now you have demonstrated where our work must begin," Phinehas interjects. "So we have done as we intended to do for this gathering. And we thank you all. Zelotese and I now have other works to attend to. We have brothers who are journeying afar. Others of our group will come to their assistance but we wish to join them in spirit and give to them of our power, for their course is perilous as they journey on behalf of the Promise." He turns to Thomas. "Bless you, Thomas, for in that which you deny is the presence of the potential for your own power. It is often so."

Zelotese and Phinehas now rise. Each gestures, palms upstretched towards the group, and as though they are locked in unison in some strange invisible way, they rotate around together, looking for a moment into the eyes of each one in the circle. Then, coming around to face one another they smile, fold their hands, bow, turn, and walk away up the slope behind a craggy outcropping. And they are gone.

There is silence for a moment. Elob then gestures to his left and to his right, and two others move closer to him. Their faces and heads are covered with garments, such that one can only barely see a nose poking through an opening. "I should like you to now welcome Madra." He extends his hand to place it on the shoulder of the one to his right.

Her head yet covered, Madra turns towards Elob and he nods. She then reaches up to remove the hood of the garment and there are gasps as her abundant hair spills down across her body. Even in the subdued light the reddish cast is apparent. As her emerald green eyes sweep across the group like a great gentle ocean wave each one feels as though she has embraced them. "I am sent here to this gathering that you would know, particularly those of you who will bring forth the young maidens, that the power of God has polarity, depicted in the expression of nature itself. In our lands and our teachings we have many methods of discernment, and these I will share with you. But most important is the quest for one's own joy. For when all else fades away or is taken by any who strive to thwart the Promise this inner joy will ever be present to sustain." Madra then leans, looking past Elob to the figure on his other side.

Elob turns and extends his left hand.

Again, there is a moment of silence.

Anticipation grows but not a word is spoken, as the second figure turns to Elob. Nods are exchanged before delicate hands come up to remove the covering upon her head. Again, sumptuous hair cascades down, this time raven-dark.

"Never dwell in the illusion of limitation," she begins. "Seeing the power and potential of being unlimited is seeing and being the power of God. Your truths empower you to do just so. I am called Louisa. It is not my true name but I shall be known as Louisa until I have accomplished what you call the ideal, which is when my true name will come forth.

"When you look upon a rivulet of water such as we are blessed with here in this beautiful haven perhaps you ponder from whence this rivulet comes. Perhaps on occasion you walk along beside it as it journeys downward noting it has grown larger. Continuing on, you may even reflect for a moment at how narrow it was in comparison to the mighty brook passing alongside you at this point. Again you may journey on, until the stream's song can be heard as it rushes past the rocks and impediments that would seek to limit it, yet onward it goes. Much in this can and will be shared with the children, such as, if one's faith is like this rivulet of water journeying through one's life, acknowledging that rivulet is the first act of empowerment.

"There are, in essence, twelve acts of empowerment. As Zelotese affirmed for you these are points of power. They are what you call your truths and what we call tenets. Each of the twelve Maidens who is to be chosen must carry one of these to her utmost ability. It is our joy to have the opportunity to guide each of them, as the rivulet of water, unto the truth she shall carry and know as the song that is within, as the song of the mighty stream continuing on its journey towards oneness with the Source, which is God. We have seen into these children and we believe we already know some of those who will be among those twelve who shall be chosen." She smiles, leaning to look at Madra.

"But it is no matter that we know them," Madra resumes. "It is that, together, dear brothers and sisters, we shall guide them to know *themselves*. Again, there is much that we will share and much that we will learn from you as *you* share. For true oneness to manifest all must give unto it that which they have to give. In that giving none is greater or lesser by that measure which is eternal, which is the Spirit of God. Now, we too must leave you but we shall return on the morrow."

Madra and Louisa rise, gesturing as did Zelotese and Phinehas, with the palms of their hands extended to each one in the group as they turn slowly around in the center of the circle. Ending with a smile and then almost laughing with each other, each extends a hand to clasp the other's and off they go, along the pathway their two brothers just followed.

Again there is a long hush before some of the Essenes, as though they had been in some sort of dream state, begin to rub their faces, their eyes, and then to speak, softly at first and then the conversation and excitement grow.

Jacob finally takes his chin from his cupped hands, sits up straight brushing off his garments, and looks this way and that. "I believe this calls for a bit of song and even a bit of dance." He lifts his sizeable form and stands easily, to the smiles and chuckles of the others, for not one is without complete love, compassion, and far more for Jacob.

Hands upright and clapping, swaying his head this way and that, shuffling and turning about, he begins to sing, gesturing to his sisters and brothers to join him.

Soon all are dancing.

In a few short steps, his circular dance has brought him face-to-face with Elob. He stops, hands in the air in mid-clap.

"May I join you, brother Jacob?"

Jacob's brings his arms down to give Elob a mighty embrace, which he reciprocates. They stand, hands upon one another's shoulders, gazing lovingly at each other, their eyes speaking volumes, their mouths saying nothing.

It is Elob who exaggeratedly moves his head to the right, emulating Jacob, and brings it back to the center, then to the left, and back again.

Jacob throws his head back and laughs. "Ah, you have the sacred power of dance, I see."

Around and about they go, their voices intertwining in song, as joy permeates the entire atmosphere.

A few of the sleeping children stir, for while the sound cannot actually be heard the power of Jacob's love is a bond, connecting them even in slumber. Some turn over, smiling. Yet in slumber their heads move just a bit as they imagine dancing with their beloved Jacob.

Over to the sid, a sleeping child softly calls out. One of the attending maidens glances over to see if all is aright and then smiles as she realizes this child is simply singing in his sleep.

In yet another sleep area we find a child also in dream, a tear forming in the corner of the eye. We pause to look in upon her vision ...

She sees the Promise.

Chapter Ten

Dreams and Visions

The prayers, the cleansing, and the morning's duties have been completed, and there is an inordinate amount of laughter at the morning meal. The children, enjoying this time of oneness with the entire group, can be heard laughing as many recount having had the same dream, the same vision, proudly identifying themselves as having danced with Jacob during their evening slumber. Some giggle, some emulate his dance. Others simply sit munching their breakfast, rocking to and fro as they have so oft seen him do.

Off to the side a small group is seated quite close to one another, their smiles indicating that they, too, are a part of the celebration of the event that occurred during the dream state.

One turns to whisper to another, "How did it look to you, Mary? What was it that you saw?"

As she lifts her eyes skyward, her face glows. "Such light and beauty! The angels of God were all around and there were songs so beautiful I have not heard such ... here, at least." She glances at her companions with a smile.

"How curious," her sister adds, "that while the others danced and sang, our vision was so different."

"Tell us of yours, Editha," Mary coaxes.

"Well, I was walking through a beautiful meadow and a bright figure came upon me and asked me to speak my name, and so I did. Then he bent and knelt before me, and held out his hands. They were aglow! I did not know in my heart of hearts if I should place mine in his, for the light of them was so bright there was a stirring thought within me that if I were to touch his hands I would not return."

"Oh-h," sighs Mary, "that is wondrous!"

Hannah leans in excitedly. "What happened next?"

"I did it ... I put my hands in his. And I felt the glow of his light pass all through me. Then I awakened."

Hannah giggles. "Does it not always seem that just when the dream gets fun, it ends?"

All three laugh rather boisterously, for they each see the truth of this, remembering the previous evening's vision.

Editha smiles at Hannah. "And yours, Hannah, how did you see him?"

"Not clearly, for the green growth was so thick and so beautiful I could barely make him out. Yet I knew he was there. And over to the left, in an alcove in the lush green, as though it had been prepared by someone, was a shining white bench just large enough for him and me."

"Do you know his name?" probes Mary gently.

"I know it, but I cannot remember it."

They giggle again.

"How shall we speak of this?" Mary glances up and gestures to the others. "Look at them."

Many have gathered into small groups here and there, and are dancing or playing together in their circles.

Hannah watches them playing. "What will they think of what we have seen?"

"I know not," Editha responds, "but we must tell our elder sisters. They will want to know of these dreams, especially Mary's."

"Why mine?"

"Because yours had angels in it."

There is a moment of silence, followed by laughter.

Mary, having placed her bowl of food in her lap, reaches up and pushes each of them playfully on their shoulder. "Well, yours had angels, too. What else would you call that?"

Several of the elder sisters are keeping a continual watch over these three, for it is believed that they are candidates. As such, great protective care is taken with them. Not they alone, for all the children are revered, but these three they believe shall be among the twelve chosen.

It is Anna who has noted with particular interest the separate activity of the three and has slowly, inconspicuously, woven her way through the groups of the many other children to a position just a few paces away from the little group. Gathering her garments, she kneels upon the ground, places her hands in her lap, and sits looking upon the three.

She shifts her awareness, her vision, just a bit and begins to see the glow coming from each of them. While the essences of each are of differing hues and intensities, and the patterns are swirling, there can be no mistake ... the energy she and the others have been watchful for is here!

At the sudden soft pressure upon her shoulder Anna is startled out of her thoughts and turns to look up into the eyes of Ruth, who has also noted this energy.

At Anna's gesture Ruth sits beside her and whispers, "Let us call our sisters over. I believe it has begun."

They look to catch the eyes of their elders sisters and in a short time they have been joined by a number of them.

They gather not only these three but a score more children off to the side here, while other groups of children varying from twenty to thirty in number have been taken here or there for specialized works or merely for the joy of play.

Here in this little group, Judy begins, "Did anyone have an interesting dream or vision last night, other than dancing with Jacob?" She laughs heartily, which casts an air of ease throughout the children gathered.

The children each look from one to the other, some smiling, others looking down shyly.

A small hand comes up. Judy smiles and nods at her.

"I had a dream that puzzles me, dear sister."

"Tell of it, Elizabeth."

"There were two great giants standing on either side of me. They seemed so great and yet I could not find cause to fear them, only to look upon them with awe. One was brightly attired and seemed to be smiling very warmly. The other wore dreary garments, dingy and tattered, and the face was not joyful. In both did I see something that seemed the same, yet outwardly they were so different. What does this mean? Is it God telling me to watch out for giants?"

The laughter of the children is contagious and all the elder sisters look at each other and burst into laughter.

Judy is still laughing, "Perhaps so, for one needs to be mindful that giants may not notice those who are smaller," and the giggles come again. She leans in to emphasize her point. "I am only joking, of course, sweet Elizabeth. What the vision tells you, as I see it in my heart, is that there are two great forces in the world, and throughout your lifetime you will walk between these ... the one brightly bedecked and warm and smiling, and the other lesser so. Yet, if you look from your heart you will see that they are in many ways the same. Can anyone offer why that might be so?"

As is traditional a number of the older children are in the outer circle, for the Expectant Ones are taught early on that the older, stronger, always preserve and encircle, symbolically and literally, those who are younger and weaker.

A hand comes up in this circle of older children and a tall, slender young lad rises respectfully. "My teacher, is it possible that this is to show us how there will be temptations in differing ways and how, if we look at these temptations, we will see the presence of God within them? Then if we know that which is our power perhaps we can call forth goodness in place of the temptations. Could it be something like this?"

All the elder sisters are smiling and nodding.

"It could, indeed," Judy affirms. "That is wonderful sight on your part, Benjamin. You are to be commended."

The elder sisters offer a bit of applause.

"Now, then, who else had a vision, a dream they would like to share?" Judy's eyes pass over the group. Some of the children lean their heads this way or that to think, not clearly recalling what the night's sleep offered them. She comes to Editha, whose gaze is warmly, though strongly, fixed upon Judy, as though asking, *Please! Ask me!*

Judy stifles a small chuckle. "Little sister, Editha, had you a vision?"

"Oh yes, my teacher, I had a wonderful vision. So did Hannah, and Mary. Mary's is the greatest, is it not, Mary?"

Mary flushes with embarrassment and looks down. "I do not see it so. I think each dream, each vision, is a very special gift. I do not see mine as greater or lesser than my sisters'. Both of them had beautiful visions as well. You tell yours first, Hannah."

Hannah begins to giggle and relates her vision.

"What do you think, little sister Hannah, all of that greenery means in your dream?"

Her hand comes to her cheek and she rubs it vigorously, then rubs her forehead as though trying to stimulate some thought, some answer. "Since green things are alive, could it mean lots of life, Anna?"

"That is a very good answer. Is there anything else you can think of?"

"Well, it was guiding me. Like great walls of living things, guiding me to meet this wonderful person who was at the end of the garden."

"And how did he look to you?"

"I cannot remember enough to tell you the color of his eyes or his hair. I do remember that it was all so sweet and that it left me ... hopeful, very hopeful."

"In what way?" probes Anna.

"That I will see him again!"

The children giggle as the elder sisters glance about, smiling yet indicating clearly that this is purposeful work and therefore serious. Immediately the children quiet themselves, some looking down, others now intrigued at this exploration.

"Editha, recount yours if you will, since Mary has chosen so wisely to have both of you recount yours first."

The three giggle and touch each other playfully.

Editha recounts her vision, and eyebrows arch.

"Have you seen this Shining One before?" asks Ruth.

"Oh yes. I have seen him. But you know when the sun is bright on the horizon and you try to see something that is in between you and the sun? You cannot, no matter how hard you try." She rubs her eyes as she remembers. "It hurts your eyes to do that and so I do not. Well, it was like that, sort of. I saw his light. And when I got over my shyness," she looks down, "I put my hands in his."

The sisters quickly look at one another, their faces having become very serious.

Ruth encourages Editha to go on. "How did that feel?"

"It felt good for a short time. But then it woke me up."

The children giggle again, and even the elder sisters chuckle.

"Well, Mary, your sisters have told their visions and have shared all their thoughts. Now will you share yours?"

Sitting up on her knees and straightening her garment, folding her hands in her lap, she tilts her head upward and her face becomes bright. "I went up into heaven, and ... I heard them singing."

"Who did you hear singing, child?" questions Judy.

"At first I could not tell. Then they came from the beautiful colored clouds. Some from here," she gestures with her hands, "and some came from there. Soon there were many and they all sang beautiful songs together."

"Do you know these songs?" Anna asks.

"Some I know, others I know not. But they were so very beautiful."

There is a silence.

Mary then gathers herself, again straightening her garments tilting her head up, as is her mannerism. "Then, I, too, saw the great light. At first it was way up there," she points into the sky as though the entire group can see as she recalls her vision, "and then the light came down and came over to me, and soon it was all around me." She becomes very still and looks down.

"What happened then?" questions Judy softly.

"The light went inside me."

Again, the elder sisters glance quickly at one another.

After a brief pause to collect herself, Anna continues, "That is a beautiful vision, Mary. And you, Editha, and Hannah, all three of you the visions are very beautiful. Please do share with us any others of this sort." Then, glancing quickly at her sisters, "But before we go about our day's activities, could you tell us, sweet sister Mary, what happened when the light went into you?"

Mary looks up again, her face very soft now. "I began to spin. And then, just like Editha, it woke me up."

The children giggle again, and then a strong *thum-thum-thum* sound startles the entire group out of their sharing.

The elder sisters rise to their feet and move quickly through the group.

Striding swiftly towards them is Elob and with him are Jacob, Joseph, and a number of others. He directs his comments to Judy and Anna. "May we speak with you?"

Judy and Anna quickly give instructions to their sisters as to the day's activity for the children. Aware that the children most certainly have picked up a sense of urgency from Elob and their elder sisters, they turn, smiling and gleeful, saying so that all can hear, "Tell the children to have a wonderful day.

Today's outing will be to gather herbs." Then they say directly to the children, "Everyone pay attention, for there are to be valuable lessons."

The children, more at ease now, follow their elder sisters.

Several of the guardians, who have appeared from nowhere, move alongside them at the outer periphery, glancing for a moment back over their shoulders towards Elob, Joseph, and Jacob.

"What is it?" Anna asks Elob, once the children have moved away from earshot.

"There have been visions. The group coming, the ones from near the great sea, are being pursued. We are dispatching a number of our brothers. We have made several additional mounts ready and have come to ask if you would send some of your guardians with our brothers. We fear it is urgent. They are almost set upon."

Judy clasps her garment, looking down.

Anna's gaze is steely. "How many do you require?"

"Might we have four?"

"It is done." She turns and gestures to one of the other maidens off some distance, who comes quickly forward. "Call the guardians."

The maiden runs off, and within moments the guardians appear, again as though from nowhere. The situation is quickly explained and soon the thunder of hoofbeats can be heard.

"I never saw them, never heard them ..." Judy remarks incredulously. "I never knew there were horses kept here."

"There is much more to this sacred place than you have perceived as yet," responds Elob. "In time, as the situation permits, we will show you more of it."

They move to a high position to watch the group of mounts carrying the guardians and some of the brotherhood, galloping at great speed towards the sea.

They are stumbling, some of them breathless, their bodies wracked with the weariness of carrying the children and whatever belongings have been considered too sacred to be left behind.

The handful of guardians with this group has fallen back to meet the pursuers, prepared to give their lives that the Promise will survive.

Several of the elder male members have positioned themselves between the sisters and the children in the event that the guardians cannot withstand the onslaught of the attackers, now visible as a great cloud of dust not far behind them.

"You can do it," a sister encourages one of the older children. "You can do it."

"But my legs ... They will not move well anymore." No tears are present as he responds, only his concern that he might fail.

"Think of the Promise of our Lord God and it will help you to have the strength. Come. Come now!"

On they struggle, until the hoofbeats of the pursuers can be heard very near.

The guardians take positions just alongside the wadi where their position gives them the advantage of a higher bit of ground. Long woven ropes are strung across the opening between the wadi walls with the intent of unhorsing at least some of the pursuers.

One of the guardians makes a stout loop and secures his end of the rope around a large rock outcropping, sending the loose end across to another guardian on the opposite side. He ties it around another outcropping, leaving the middle loose, lying on the ground. A third guardian quickly covers it with dust. Two others are at the edges of the openings, their stout staffs at the ready.

The first attacker to enter the wadi, the leader, is knocked from his horse. He is not the captain but a trusted aide. The vengeance of the captain has swept through his ranks and the pursuit of these evil ones, as he calls them, is now relentless. Down the lieutenant goes and two with him, followed by a fourth. The rope is then lowered to admit two of the guardians and then the others who were tending the ropes, all with staffs swinging.

The sound intensifies as one attacker upon another strives to best the guardians. One of the guardians is down, for three attackers swept upon him. Another guardian comes with a stout stroke and an attacker falls to the ground, lifeless. Swinging around, the other end of his staff catches another attacker under the chin, flipping him as though he were made of rag. He falls moaning to the ground. The third assailant swings his sword, catching the guardian beneath the right arm. Gasping, he falls to one knee but swings his staff around catching his attacker across the shoulder, to the sound of shattering bones.

So it goes, the sickening sounds of battle, until two guardians are all that remain. Standing back to back, fighting off at least a dozen, yet do they stand their ground.

Finally, the pursuers take positions above, loosing arrows upon them.

The one guardian falls. Silently, his eyes close.

Not a sound, the other then falls to his knees, dropping his staff.

The pursuers stand in the open now, knowing that the battle is complete, watching as though mesmerized by the courage, the valor, of these who are called by many, warrior priests.

The one guardian reaches his hand up and grasps the shaft of the arrow where it penetrates his chest. So silent is this wadi where just previously there had been battle that the snapping of the shaft as he breaks it off is amplified.

The warrior priest holds it for a moment in his hand,

looking at it, and then slowly, with no spite, no anger, no hatred, his fingers uncurl around it. It falls to the ground, and he slumps forward.

Then, from this weary one comes the soft sound of humming. Or is it ... Could it be that he is singing?

His hands come up to his sides, trembling from the brutal stress his body has endured in this battle. The attackers near him can hear, "Sweet Lord ... Receive my brothers in the embrace of my love. As it is Thy will, should it come to pass, receive me as well. Forgive me my actions against these others whom I know are likewise my brothers, though they know it not, even as I, in this moment of my death, forgive them."

He falls limply to the ground.

There are moments of silence as the exhausted pursuers that remain stare at the lifeless body, pondering what manner of "evil" is it that asks for forgiveness for defending the lives of his people.

One off to the side throws his lance to the ground and with surprising forcefulness shouts, "I shall pursue these peoples no longer. Do what you shall to me, Lieutenant, but this is not my battle, my war. How can these people be called evil who ask their God for forgiveness for defending their very lives?" He stares with steely defiance at the lieutenant, who stands speechless. The soldier turns briskly, catches a loose steed, and in a single motion, mounts it and gallops off back from whence he came.

Moments later, another follows suit, and another.

Finally, the lieutenant, as though gathering himself from a dream, shouts, "Stop! Remain where you are! You know the orders. Those traitors, those deserters, will be dealt with. You know that. The captain will see to it. I assure you, if you leave, when you are caught your death will not be as easy as that big lout's over there." He points to the guardian's body.

"Take time to bandage the injured, grab a bit of nourishment, and tend to the mounts. Then gather them and your weapons. We will pursue the deserters."

୫୦

The sound of the battle in the distance has brought chills to the sisters and the children, some of whom are burying their heads in the shoulders of those who are carrying them, as they struggle to run across the rugged terrain.

A cry comes from one of the sisters at the forefront, as thundering hoofbeats sound once again. "They are coming again! Quickly, hide the children!"

All scurry off into the crags and dunes, doing what they can to hide. Some cover the children with their own garments, brushing sand and whatever is available across them, hoping they will not be noticed.

The horses come to an abrupt stop.

In a swift motion, one of the guardians comes quickly to the forefront. "Is it you, Jason?" He peers into the dust kicked up by the galloping horses. "It is you!"

The Essenes standing near this one fall to their knees with tearful utterances of joy and thanksgiving.

"Where are my brothers?" Jason questions directly but tenderly.

One steps forward and points in the direction from whence they came. "I fear it is over. I-I fear ... they are lost," she whispers, and her head begins to bob up and down with muffled sobbing.

Jason reaches his mighty hand over, placing it upon Stella's shoulder. As she looks up into his eyes he extends his arms to her and then embraces her. "All is well. We have a goodly number here. That one there is called Zelotese. He is one of our patrons and we are quite certain he is sent of God. He will guide you. Do as he says, for he knows the Promise."

"Oh, praise God."

"I must leave you now, but do not fear. We will stop them."

He turns and gestures, and all with him wheel their mounts, offering words of encouragement and tossing down small parcels of food and water as they gallop off.

One of the guardians removes his cloak and as he races by, handing it down to a bright-faced child. "Here, my son," he calls over his shoulder, "for the chilly evening."

The small round face looks with awe and wonder after this one whose life is dedicated to the Promise of God, as though he were an angel in physical form.

Soon the sound of the hoofbeats can no longer be heard.

In the silence, the adults move about, tucking in garments, wrapping bruised bleeding feet, one telling a story.

After a bit, Zelotese gestures, "Come, my friends. Let us resume our journey. All is well, but we must continue on just for a time, and then, soon, you will be within the embrace of the safety of your God's love."

The children murmur at the hope of this, and the entourage continues its movement.

ℰↃ◯ℬ

The onslaught of the guardians alongside the brotherhood astride their mounts catches the lieutenant and his soldiers off guard.

The mere sight of this thundering cadre bellowing great songs of praise unto God, whirling rods and staffs about that glisten in the sun's light as so many shafts of light, throws the resting soldiers off balance. They run this way and that, some stumbling, one being dragged by a horse galloping off in its own fear.

It is all very swift. Then it is over.

The lieutenant, several ribs obviously broken by a blow to his chest, hisses, his voice raspy from the dust of battle, "Well, finish me, evil one."

The guardian merely leans upon his staff. He is bruised in several places and has a large welt over his forehead but this does not dim the light in his eyes nor the curious smile upon his face. "No, I shall not do you in, Lieutenant. I believe that another shall, however. For we have collected your mount and are sending you back to your captain. If you will notice," the guardian gestures about, "you are alone."

Rising up on one elbow and clutching his chest, the lieutenant demands, "Finish it! You are the victor this time. Finish it. If you let me go, I swear ... I will find you."

"It would be well if you did not," the guardian responds, dropping the reins of the lieutenant's mount across his face. "While you can, you had best depart. Some of the others may not be as forgiving as I. For we have lost many dear brothers here this day. So, by the time we have tended to them you had best be gone." He wheels about and strides off.

Pulling himself up, the lieutenant struggles to mount his steed, and finally, awkwardly, unable to sit erect, he urges his mount to return to the encampment.

℘○℃℞

"Some of them are injured. We must help! We must go to meet them." Theresa's face is filled with concern.

"No. That would be unwise," Elob smiles reassuringly.

"But I have lived through what they are experiencing," Elba cries, in support of Theresa's request.

"And you lived through it because you followed the guidance of those who believed what was aright, true?"

Recognizing that she had spoken from emotion rather than from her own guidance or inner wisdom, Elba looks down. "Of course, you are right. Forgive us. It is just that our hearts are calling."

"They will be here soon enough," Elob responds softly. "The better choice would be to make ready. They will have thirst and hunger, and will be in need of shelter and rest, for they are greatly fatigued. Some are wounded. I have called several of my brothers to help you when they arrive. For now, the better course of action for you is to make the preparations." Without another word he turns and strides off up the craggy pass through which all of the brotherhood seem to come and go.

Off to the side stand Jacob and Joseph.

"What shall we tell the other children?"

Jacob smiles, "It will be difficult to mask the truth."

"Ah, that is so, but we have brought them to such a wonderfully open and receptive place."

At this point Anna and Judy walk up and join them.

Joseph continues, "It would not be well to cast a shadow of fear based on what our brothers and sisters have just experienced."

"I agree and I cannot overcome that with a bit of song or dance, for the arriving children will surely recount their experiences."

Judy interrupts, "They are strong enough. They know what lies beyond this place, and they know through their own experiences what it is like."

"Yes, but what Joseph is actually referring to is whether the pursuers will now know the pathway or have a general idea of where we are, and that the children are sure to contemplate this. Having said this, I now offer this as an answer to my own question ..." He throws his head back and laughs, but not vigorously enough to call attention to them. "We *use* this. We use this as a tool to teach them. For as Phinehas and Zelotese pointed out worthiness is perhaps one of the first things to learn, to understand. What are the underpinnings of worthiness, what limits its flow to a child of God, if not fear? And we certainly have a fearful event here."

"Wonderful idea," Judy responds, and Anna nods.

"Well then, that is how we shall proceed. Call in the groups and let us gather to welcome our people and tend to them."

Off to the side is the sweet voice of Madra as she rocks this way and that. She is kneeling and several small candles are burning between her and Louisa.

After a time, they look up to gaze steadily, unblinking, into one another's eyes.

"Tell me, Louisa, what do you see?"

Louisa, who has been softly humming, weaving a little this way and that, straightens, still holding Madra's eyes in her gaze. "I see that we are triumphant and that they will soon arrive."

"That is wonderful."

"And what do you see?"

Madra is now smiling. "I see more children, one in particular whose light is in their midst. Look you into my eyes and see what I see."

Nodding, Louisa does. Her eyes move in and out of focus and the vision is there: a small child, perhaps four or five years of age, clutching a garment that a small boy gave to her, a gift to him from a guardian.

"Yes," Louisa, too, is now smiling, "I believe you are right. I believe she is one of them."

"Do you hear her name?" Madra questions coyly.

For a moment Louisa's face shifts. Wrinkles appear around her eyes as she squints, and then her eyes relax and a smile comes over her face.

"Andra."

A Message from the Guardians

Whatsoe'er there is that finds its way into your lives, know that there are those guardians sent by God who stand at the ready. Whatsoe'er the path may bring unto you, know that the blessing lies beyond it. As the guardians and those with them were willing to give all, know as well that there are those forces of God willing to give all for you.

We are permitted to tell you that those who were called the guardians are we. So as we fell in the service of our Lord God and His Word and Promise, so are we yet willing to give all, that the Promise might be reborn.

We shall go where there is conflict; where one is in need, there shall we be. Should it be the course of that journey for that soul to cross beyond the veil of finiteness into these and greater realms, we shall stand at the ready to embrace them and escort them into God's Light. If you would send your prayers unto those who are in need, we shall be the bearers of thy prayers, adding ours as well, as gifts to those who are willing to receive same. We claim our oneness with God and with you.

Glory be unto God's Word. Blessed are those who claim His Promise.

Chapter Eleven

Humming Giants

Several months have elapsed. Many more stragglers of the Essenes have been found and guided to the School, and the number now is a goodly one.

It is a beautiful day, and the children's laughter can be heard all about.

A distance from the encampment where the children are, a large group of the Essenes has gathered. Among them are many of the revered elders and seers who have been found, much to the joy of those who look to them for their light and guidance. Included in this gathering are many from the School of the Prophets.

Elob is speaking. "It is important that we commence now with the preparation for the works which lie ahead. Let us begin with a prayer of gratitude and affirmation unto the One God for the gift of so many of you having found your way here to this, our place of study and reverence."

One of the elders is called upon to offer the prayer and does so eloquently, after which Elob resumes. "In offering ourselves in service to all of you, we should like to offer some of our insights that we have found helpful to members of our group. We have discussed some of these with your elders and seers and know these are pertinent, if not immediately relevant, for you to consider." Elob turns to his left, nodding to Zelotese to continue.

"As the unfolding of the Promise progresses," Zelotese begins quietly, "we know that some things will need preparation well in advance. Our two groups appear to agree that He who will come shall be guided through many experiences of this realm called Earth. Accordingly, many gifts will be prepared, awaiting Him, and thereafter will carefully be given. We have seen that there will come a time wherein this One, whom we shall call the Christed One, or the Christ, will honor our people by journeying to the lands represented here by our brothers and sisters." He gestures to his left and right, above, and behind him. "This will serve in numerous ways.

"First, there will be the reinforcement of those teachings which we humbly offer to you and which we believe will benefit the Christed One.

"Second, we have been foretold of His journey to many of our lands, wherein He will teach those of our people who are open and aware, just as, upon His return here, He will teach the people in these lands. Is there confirmation from you of this?"

There are murmurs and short discussions.

Among the Council of elders, which represents all of the Essene tribes, one stands. A hush falls over all, for this one is very respected and revered.

"We have seen that of which you speak, Zelotese. So we do concur, and we honor you and your brothers and sisters. I speak now on behalf of all of my colleagues and all of our people. There will be challenges which will come, similar to that which we have already met and endured and, thanks to the grace of God, surpassed. Some of these will affect certain of our people moreso than others. We shall look into these challenges to the Promise for the gifts they contain. For if we anticipate them and prepare ourselves, strengthening our faith and our love of the All, naught will withstand our inner strength."

Many heads bob up and down, and many silent prayers

are offered at these words.

"Wisdom tells us that, as we anticipate the many paths that lie ahead, we can gain much by recognizing what choices and what directions would best support the work. We concur with our brothers and sisters, who are so gifted and so filled with love," gesturing to the adepts from the School, "that it is important that some order be developed now.

"Therefore I, Benjamin, and my colleagues, ask you to look into your hearts and spirits. Look for that place wherein the Call resonates within you. Then, we ask you to answer that Call. Come forward to assume the tasks, the responsibilities, and, yes, the blessings of the many different works that shall be needed. At the forefront of these is the need to prepare those who will serve as emissaries, envoys who shall go forth into the near and distant lands to make a way ready and passable for the Promise to traverse and enter into those lands, as has been spoken of by Elob and Zelotese.

"These will be arduous works, for these servants will be separate from our community. But our love and our faith will be with you, and Elob and his brethren will support you in spirit in their unique ways. Further, from the adepts, there will be one to journey with each group, to serve as guide unto the distant lands. Many of these, as some of us we know first hand, are diversely skilled in languages and customs that you will encounter if you should choose to be one of these peoples.

"We tell you now, in order that you can consider it as you decide, that while we shall make every effort to provide for you all that is unto your needs, there will be many challenges. Your dedication unto the Promise must therefore be sufficient to endure in the midst of those challenges, to accomplish that work should it fall on your shoulders alone."

A murmur passes throughout this large group, as they contemplate the hardships, the dangers, and the possibility that it could be a journey from which they might not return.

Some hearts are visibly heavy with these considerations.

Heads bow in silence as some search within for clear answers and decisions. Others look up into the beautiful cloudless sky.

Benjamin continues, "There will be the need, also, for those of us to dwell among the peoples and the activity in the near lands. While this second group of servants to the Promise will not be so far removed from the greater groups, they will face no less challenges than the first who will travel afar. Already as many of you know, we have some who have become accepted into various communities and social structures in the near lands. You will be guided to these people, and they will help as best they can, knowing full well that their positions cannot be revealed, but must be kept inviolate. For certain of these will play important roles in the journey that lies before the Christ.

"Others of you who are skilled in various trades, crafts, abilities, will be asked to work with the adepts, and they with you, of course, that we can develop that which will be most contributive to the Promise ... that which is held within the spirits and hearts of our blessed children."

Benjamin continues in such manner, covering all the logistical needs that lie ahead. Here and there, some stand or indicate by raising a hand, knowing almost immediately in their hearts and minds that this is the work unto which they are called. As each does so, the group celebrates them, calling their name aloud, rejoicing at the gift they are offering to the Promise.

So it goes for a goodly time. Several of the other elders speak as well. The two seers from the distant land, who have been with the Essene primary group for quite some time, also offer their insights, and on it continues.

At one point Anna and Judy are called to the forefront, along with Madra and Louisa from the school of the adepts.

"We have agreed," speaks Benjamin again, "that these four shall, in essence, head the planning and direction for the children. With them shall be a group of our brothers who will support and offer the counterbalance to the feminine energy. While recognizing that the feminine force, whether one considers it native to the Earth or eternal of God, is the primary one, we have called upon Joseph and Jacob, along with Phinehas and Zelotese of the adepts, to be the balancing energy to these four. This group of eight will comprise a council of sorts. To this council we shall contribute four of our own to guide and to provide insight and blessing. The total then makes up our sacred number." He pauses to gesture in reverence. "We ask you who receive guidance in dream or vision to bring that to this council.

"We have called upon all of the seers, those of the School and those of our own peoples, and in vision we have seen many things as guidance, for which we thank our Lord God. Some of that which we have perceived is unclear. Thus we know there are pathways to be met and works to be about before that can be discerned.

"Now we shall begin. We have called upon all the seers of the School and of our own peoples, and in vision we have seen many things as guidance, for which we thank our Lord God. Some of that which we have perceived is unclear, and thus we know there are pathways to be met and works to be about before that can be discerned. Regarding the Maidens, we shall fashion a means whereby, until the clarity of identity comes forth, none of the children will know which are the candidates. Additionally, we believe that the sacred trinity ... spirit, mind, and body ... must be summoned forth from every candidate so that each Maiden chosen shall thereby represent the trinity to the Christ."

A long silence ensues, as they consider the children and all that has been given.

"Occasionally, we will send groups of the candidates apart from the others. The purpose for this is that an opportunity for the Promise to manifest always be preserved, and for each sacred Truth, or Tenet, as called by the School of the

Prophets, to be preserved as well. In other words, should there be a mishap which befalls one, there will be three others who can be reviewed to take her place."

The possibility of this raises a murmur of emotion among this large group. "Though we know there are challenges which await us, and we know not the nature of some, fear not, my brothers and sisters, for we have not foreseen such an event or mishap."

One of the Essenes, a slender young man, raises his hand, and Benjamin nods at him. "If I am understanding correctly, we will have in total four groups of these maidens?"

Benjamin merely nods.

"How will this discernment be conducted? Is there a plan for such?"

Benjamin glances at Elob, who nods and answers, "Not all of this, Thomas, is known as yet. Much of it will be framed as the needs arise. Essentially, though, we shall begin with what we know, which is to take smaller groups here and there to study various things, giving us all the opportunity to observe them each more completely, and to ascertain. And, as Benjamin has stated, our intent in separating these groups somewhat is not only to aid in the discernment, but also for the preservation and insurance as indicated ... that no matter what hardship might befall us or them, there will always be those remaining to carry the truth forward."

Thomas works to smile in the face of the mere thought of such an event and, finally, unable to, looks down.

"Hold your head up, Thomas," Benjamin counsels softly. "This is a time to rejoice. Do not build the future out of today's fear. I know your heart and your strength are true. Then, call upon those, my son.

Thomas looks up, his eyes brightened, his face visibly indicating that he has done just so.

So the conversation continues as others offer insights and suggestions. By the approach of twilight, much has transpired, which the scribes have recorded. Many of the people are chosen, and their works are now being discussed with them.

Within the next several days, with their diligence and dedication, these people move into the effective manifestation of their plans and schedules.

℘℃

The sounds of the children's delighted laughter can be heard bouncing off the craggy walls as Jacob leads them, twisting and turning, pretending to be a creature following a path that cannot be seen by those who are in physical body.

Mingling with Jacob and this little group of twenty-four children, are Madra, Anna, and a number of the other of the sisters along with several of the brotherhood.

In the midst of winding along Jacob's makeshift path, Madra asks light-heartedly, "Who knows how to see?" She has already become well loved by the children for her cheer and something within her which resonates with them.

Some of them glance about, looking to their beloved Anna. All the while, Jacob, pretending to hear not, continues bobbing and weaving, moving slowly along.

One of the children in the center raises her hand timidly. "I know how to see."

Madra, smiles brightly. "Jacob, may we pause?"

Jacob stops and turns abruptly. Two of the children walk right into him, giggling, and are tousled by him as they do. In a swift movement, he seats himself, resting the two who collided with him one upon each knee, who are joyful to be so honored.

The teachers move among the children, who are all now seated.

"Sweet Josie," Madra encourages, "since you know how to see, tell us how you do it and what it is you see."

Sitting cross-legged, her hands in her lap folded one upon the other, she looks this way and that, and sees twenty-three pairs of tiny eyes looking at her with anticipation. She glances down, embarrassed at the attention, and then looks up. "I have learned to see, of course, with my eyes. But I also see in here." Her thumb pokes her own chest.

"Would you explain that for us?" Madra asks.

"Yes, I will."

One of the other children giggles and Madra looks at her. "You have something to offer, Abigale?"

"She sees with her heart. I have seen her do it many times. Is that not true, Josie?"

"Yes, I do. When I feel things, I know to look not only with mine eyes, but with my heart. It feels like a buzzing." The children giggle. "Then, after the buzzing, there comes a thing, like a tingling, that goes all through my body." She points from her toes to the top of her head. "I can tell if it is a good tingle or a bad tingle. If it tingles good, I know that what is before me is good. If it tingles bad, I know to watch out."

There is a long silence.

Madra, glancing to and fro, catches another pair of eyes staring at her steadfastly. "Ah ha," nodding to her, "is it possible that you are seeing now as well, sweet child?"

"Yes. I see *you*."

"How are you called?" asks Madra.

"I am called Eloise."

"What do you see, when you see me?"

"I see that you have a light glowing from within you."

"Can you see into me to see this light?"

"Oh, no," Eloise giggles, leaning and twisting this way and that. "It is so bright, it shines outside you. See there?" She points to the area around Madra's head. "See the pretty blue, and over here the pretty pink?"

The children are leaning and turning. Several of them stand to get a better look.

"I see it!" shouts one.

"I, too. I see it!" another calls out.

Madra smiles and claps her hands. "Well done. Well done, children. Now, let me offer you a contest."

The children all murmur with joy, for they know that such events have at their ending a reward of some sweet treat.

"When Jacob leads us onward again, whichever of you can see something that has that same light as you say you see around me, raise your hand, and we will stop. If anyone else can see the light, then you shall have won the contest."

There are happy giggles and clapping, but several of the children shake their heads to and fro. It is apparent that they cannot see the light around Madra, so they presume that they shall not see and win the contest.

"And for those of you who don't *know* that you can see," Madra continues, smiling at several of those whose faces are now much brighter, "if you can find a flower, you shall also win a contest."

These children now clap their hands together, for many feel quite adept at this second challenge.

"Now for those of you who might not see *or* find a flower, if you can hear the call of a creature and can tell us what it is, then you too shall win a contest."

So it goes, as Madra essentially presents all of the children with something to excel at, and off they go again, following Jacob, who occasionally raises his hands up, murmuring a little song, leaning this way and that.

The children, of course, are emulating him. Here and there, some are concentrating so hard at seeing or finding a flower or listening for something, that they stumble into one another before bursting forth in spontaneous laughter.

ରୁଠଓ

"When shall they be dispatched, Elob?" asks Joseph.

"I would think at the change of the season. Several months should be adequate for preparation."

Joseph looks down, "I shall miss them."

"Indeed, and they will miss you and your people as well. So we will unite after each day's evening meal and prayer at an agreed upon time wherein we might all join one another spiritually, even though we are apart physically."

Joseph, looks up, his face brightened. "Your people know how to do this in a remarkable way, do they not?"

Elob smiles and nods, "And we will share that with you, Joseph, and any of your colleagues who are so inclined to participate."

Several of the Essenes who are also present raise their hands, asking to be included.

Elob nods, "Come with me, then. I should like to share something with you."

As they move up between the rocky outcropping, soon they are upon a small group, beautifully, softly chanting, who pause only for a brief moment in their work to smile and nod before returning to their chants.

Elob moves those who are with him off to the side a respectful distance from those chanting, that they can speak without interfering. "There is considerable power in what they are doing," he begins quietly. "Yet in your sacred prayers, in your chants, in your song and dance, you are in essence doing the same thing, with the potential for similar power."

Joseph studies them carefully. "I know you have purpose in explaining this. Has it to do with our just previous discussion?"

"It does," Elob nods. "Soon they will reach a point, the four of them, when they have attuned themselves, so to say, to sight beyond the finite. Because they are accustomed to the essences of the brothers and sisters with whom they are striving to connect, it is like following a pathway well worn into the earth. These two of my brothers and sisters," for there are two of each, "feel the same energies, the essences, of those with whom they are connecting ... But wait. They are ready."

One of the brothers straightens himself and leans his head back. Without seeing him, for their eyes are closed, the other three pause, their voices becoming silent. Next comes the sound of a name being called. It sounds like *Eson*. Again and again ... *Ee--so-o-on.*

One of the maidens makes a soft tone, and then we hear her speak. "We are with you, my brother."

There is silence, and then one of the others comments, "He is well, though weary. We must send him that of ourselves to nourish and infill him."

Immediately, they place their hands upon one another's shoulders, and begin a gentle, almost imperceptible swaying.

From a distance not too far, another group has picked up the energy, and from them comes the low rhythmic sound of *thum-thum, thum-thum.*

"You see," Elob explains, "the sound is the same as the heartbeat of Eson. So, when he hears and feels the pulse of his own life, he will know to reach out to touch these four in response to their greeting."

"What is the purpose of such action?" asks Judy

Smiling, Elob pauses a moment. "Consider your question, Judy."

She does so, and then responds, "I see principles. I see concepts. But what is the intended manifestation of this?"

"It is very straightforward. Where there is fatigue, there will be this energy and the recipient will know it. When he awakens from his own prayerful meditation, it will be as though he has slept a goodly time."

"Truly?" questions Judy, with some amazement.

"Truly."

"What other works? Tell me, please."

Elob is stimulated by the excitement and genuine interest from this one who is as a priestess to the Expectant Ones. "Were there to be an injury, or were a disease to befall one of our brethren, it would be tended to."

She gestures with her hand. "From here? How so? I know the power of many of these works, but if your brethren are at a goodly distance, how is it that they can receive this aid? Who is there to tend their wound, or heal their body?"

Elob, smiling, gestures upward. "Our God, yours and mine, is one and the same. My brethren know this. They *live* it. So within the Spirit of God, which is in life itself, these four can raise their consciousness, so to say, and become one with their spirit form. Spirit is not limited. That which governs the Earth and finiteness cannot fetter the power of one's spirit. This, of course, I am aware that you know."

"That I do," responds Judy, "but what I am striving to understand here is how this functions."

"It functions because all of them, all of *us,* know it, affirm it, and believe it with all of our being. Thus, it is a small thing to shift from this, the finite," he gestures about, "to the infinite. From that shifted position, carrying our consciousness from here to our spirit, which is there," gesturing beyond, "has become a matter of considerable ease. Because, to anticipate your question, dear Judy, we have lived it, we have therefore become it."

Beginning to realize the nature of the gifts being offered, Judy smiles excitedly. "I have seen this. I have experienced it, as have we all." She gestures to Joseph and the others. "But to see you and your brothers and sisters *doing* it, is truly a gift of God. I am inspired. Will you show me the way?"

"That I shall. It is not unlike that which you performed with your two brothers there." He points to the tall seer and his companion, who smile and nod at the recognition. "The storm," Elob adds softly.

Judy reflects for a moment. "Yes, I remember only too well the calling of the Word of God. I remember. I was ... forgive me, my friends ... most apprehensive, particularly," and she looks down and then up and laughs softly, "when they each placed a hand upon my knee."

Elob smiles and simply nods, glancing at the tall seer and his companion, who merely smile in return, no inference, just an acknowledgment. "This was done to unite the energies. Because time was of the essence, they could not expend the time to explain to you. If it was awkward for you, as surely we can understand, perhaps you would understand that it was of some difficulty for them as well."

Judy's face brightens, for she had not considered this. She glances back at the two seers, who smile now with a bit more emotion showing. "Oh, forgive me," she apologizes softly. "It is a valuable lesson, is it not, Elob," turning back to look at him, "that we tend to see things from our own perspective, and to react based upon that with which we are familiar and know to be true and right for us."

"Yes, it is indeed a valuable lesson. What is also important here is that you did not let this inhibit you. You went beyond the potential limitation to claim the power of your spirit and what was at hand, which they could see you were capable of, which is why they called upon you."

Judy is obviously pleased. This knowledge has freed some aspect of her, apparent to those here who have the sight.

Suddenly the *thum-thumming* stops, and all cast their attention upon the four seated across the way.

Their hands still placed upon one another's shoulders, they lean forward until their heads are touching. Judy notes that they, too, have been seated knee to knee, and that their group is very connected, literally as well as spiritually.

They lean back and begin to laugh, as they know their task to be complete.

The laughter is contagious.

80C03

"Look at all these wonderful flowers," Jacob gathers them up and placing them into the woven basket before him. "It looks to me like everyone here has won the flower-gathering contest. But Madra, Anna, who has won the other contests?"

"Oh," exclaims Anna joyfully, "we have a goodly number. This one heard the call of an owl."

"Goodness," he responds "in the mid-day? That must be a very spiritual owl," and all the children giggle mightily.

Anna goes on to explain that many others heard different creatures, and then there is a pause. "And this one," she continues softly, "heard a voice speak to her."

"Indeed so?" questions Jacob. "Who was it, Rebekah?" The child begins to giggle. "Please, stand and share this with us all."

Obviously quite pleased, she stands, straightens her garments, and shifts her weight from one foot to the other, moving her fingers between one another, first in front of her, then behind her. "It said, *Good day, my child. I know who you are.*"

The children giggle again.

Shaking her finger at all of her little friends, Rebekah continues, "I looked all about to see if one of you was playing a trick on me."

Many of them shake their heads to indicate, *No, they would not do this.*

"But it was not any of you, nor was it anyone I could see. Yet, did it speak."

"What else did the voice say to you?" questions Joseph now, the seriousness of his question shining through his outer appearance of mirth.

Madra has been slowly moving closer to Rebekah, weaving in and about the children who are seated cross-legged.

Rebekah continues, "The voice said to me, *One day I shall give you a shining gift.* And I said, 'How will I know you? I cannot see you. What shall your gift be, and why is it that it will shine? Is it a gem?' And the voice laughed and said, *Yes, sweet Rebekah, it is an eternal gem. Be watchful, I will speak with you again.* I called it again and again. I said, 'But who are you? I know not your name. Please!'" and she begins to look down obviously saddened, "But it did not answer me."

There is a pause, a moment's hush, and then a gentle hand upon her shoulder. Rebekah looks up into Madra's eyes, which are filled with love. "The voice will speak to you again. That was the Promise. And the gift, I am sure, awaits you. But of importance now is this: You, sweet daughter, have won this contest." She swoops down and lifts her up, parading around among the children with her, as they clap and laugh chanting, "Rebekah has won the contest for hearing."

Anna, looking over to the side, sees a pair of small eyes wistfully staring. "What is it, my child?" directing the attention of the group.

"My teacher, I saw naught. I heard naught. There was naught for me to win a contest."

"Oh, my child. Come to me here."

The child rises and walks awkwardly through the group of children to stand before beloved Anna.

Anna pulls her to her side, embracing her, "Is there anything about our journey that you would like to share?"

"Well, I did see some curious things, but they were ... you know ... *real!*"

Laughter comes from the sisters, teachers, and guides.

"Well, what caused you to notice them? Was there something of distinction?"

"Yes, to me. But no one else seemed to see them."

"Perhaps you have a certain gift."

"Well, I do not know. It was strange. I went to this great rock, and when I put my hand upon it ... because I felt something from it ... I could feel a strange energy ... you know ... like you feel when the thunder talks."

The children giggle again.

"What kind of thunder?" questions Jacob lovingly, but with a hint of seriousness.

"It was not scary, but it was strange." The silence all about encourages her to go on. "It was the same as I feel when I close my eyes to offer my prayers before sleep. Sometimes when I do that, I hear a voice, too."

This time, only a few of the children giggle.

"What does that voice say to you as you enter into your spirit rest?" questions Jacob further, the seriousness still evident in his tone.

"It calls my name, first of all. *Ze-phor-ah*, *Ze-phor-ah*, over and over again. And then my mind does a little dance. It moves all around. I bump into lights and colors, and they make me feel good. And then, I feel that same thing as I felt from the rock. It is like a giant humming. It is like ... you know, like Editha's giants were going to sing."

Everyone laughs at this.

Jacob is smiling, but glancing from Madra to Anna and several of the others. "When you touched the rock, where did you feel this thunderous giant's voice?" Jacob mimics, bringing laughter again.

"Always the same, Jacob ... right here," she stands up and pokes her thumb into her solar plexus.

"Ah, ha!" Jacob exclaims, his interest and great love evident. "Then this must be a part of your life's being, for is it not written that this part of the body knows such things."

"This I have heard," Zephorah agrees, excited that an authority is giving approval. She smiles, tipping her head up just a bit as she glances at all her peers, as though to say, *See?*

"Well, then, Zephorah," Jacob announces, "you have won a very special contest."

"I have?" she asks eagerly.

"Yes!" Placing the children who have been sitting upon his lap on the ground, Jacob rises. "You have won Jacob's tummy contest," he announces, and reaches down and tickles her tummy, at which everyone giggles and laughs, especially Zephorah. "But what you have also won is the same thing the others have won." He turns, gesturing to all the others. "For all of you children shall have delicious treats upon the conclusion of our journey! And, Zephorah, I would be honored if you would ride upon my shoulders and tell me more of the humming giants."

All laugh and applaud and cheer for Zephorah, who raises her hands up to Jacob.

Jacob bends and sweeps her up, perching her upon his shoulders. Off they go, Jacob bounding this way and that, his hands wrapped around her dangling legs, as she giggles and waves to all her friends.

ᎻᏣᎾᎿ

Zelotese stirs the embers of the fire, as those who are gathered begin to share the experiences of the children, telling of the giant and of the calls and the sights.

"I am certain of these five," pointing to the marks of five on the parchment which the scribes had made at his direction that indicate the children.

The parchment is passed about the group, and as each recognizes Zelotese' choices, smiles flash here and there.

Anna is the last to receive it. "Some never spoke," she speaks softly. "I think the number is too great. Some are shy."

"This I have seen, as well," Zelotese agrees.

"I, too," Judy adds. "We must make the number smaller. Let us use the sacred number, and take these five as the core group and continue to add the others to it. They will show us who they are. Of this, I am certain."

"I was particularly troubled," continues Anna, "by Mary. As you know, she is within herself very much of the time."

"This is true ... very introspective," acknowledges Phinehas softly. "That is a powerful sign as I see it."

"You think it so?" Ruth questions.

Phinehas looks at her and gently nods.

Madra looks about the group and smiles, "And Rebekah ... There is a child filled with the fire of life! It needs to be channeled to find its pathway."

"As is true for them all," Elob responds. "Then it is done. We shall separate them into groups of twelve and compare our observations of their actions to discern who might be the other seven."

Louisa leans forward, "There may be an easier way."

"We are open," Ruth smiles.

"I think it would be well for there to be more discussion of their visions, their dreams. To that end, there would need to be, in my humble opinion, more preparation prior to slumber, that they shall have their spirit, mind, and heart opened to remember and to know."

"To the best of our knowledge, these things we do in our evening prayer and ceremonies," responds Joseph. "Have you other methods?"

"We do," she responds gently. "It is time, I believe, for them to learn more about the seven temples that lie within the body physical."

"Ah, you are speaking of the energy centers."

"Yes. But many of us we believe that these are not only centers of energy, but powerful steps. We can bring several of our brethren to assist, perhaps one or two in each of the groups of children. We will show you the techniques and methods that we will offer, that you might tell us if you believe them acceptable to the level of receptivity of the children."

Anna responds quickly, "Wonderful. When can we begin this?"

Louisa laughs, "Now?"

"Now is a good time," Anna and laughs with her as murmurs ripple about the circles.

"Then come with me. If those of you who have no particular interest in this will excuse us, we shall tend to this."

Joseph raises a hand, "There is no need to excuse yourselves. We are all interested. Please, stay and share with us."

"Very well. We shall do so as succinctly as possible. Then you can reflect upon it, and if you wish, on the morrow we can answer any questions you would have."

"Agreed." Joseph is smiling broadly, for he is always one willing to receive new knowledge.

"Much of this you will know. Some will be new. But if we might begin by seating ourselves cross-legged in this manner," she gestures, " and quite erect."

All follow her lead.

"The earth is the base of the energy of life. We believe that the life force of God is resident within the earth itself in many different forms, such as in plants as they are rooted into it. So, much of our needs are found within or upon the earth itself. As one affirms this, it is a step-stone. Many means can be utilized to activate this center, and this is a part of what I am suggesting that we share with the children prior to sleep."

Louisa pauses. Her hands are together in her lap. Next, she utters a single tone, which she repeats again and again.

All note that her eyes are closed, and they believe they can see a bit of shining emanating around her.

"If you will now, replicate this." All do. Her hands still together, she raises them to the next chakra, or energy center, and repeats the process, and then again with each successive chakra.

Now her fingertips are pressed against her forehead. "This is a place of sacred sight, as I presume most of you know." Nods of affirmation come from all. "What is important that we wish to bring to prominence in the children is that they recognize that they control this."

Some of the Essenes are obviously moving into new areas of thinking, for their faces are bright with interest and with anticipation of what Louisa will give next.

"Applying pressure with the fingertips is not a casual thing," she extends her hands, "since these are the instruments of our minds and our hearts. The hands and the fingers do the work of the mind and the heart's intent. The hands and fingers are instruments of power, literally and spiritually.

"The energy centers we have activated here, using our hands as tools, combine to form one great orb of energy that envelopes our bodies in differing forms and differing ways." She glances about to see that everyone is understanding.

Many are smiling, for they know of this.

"We can direct where our hands are and what works they do." She reaches her arms out. "My hands are now at this moment beyond my unique energy, my life force, and have become an instrument of my uniqueness. So in my prayer work, I reach out to affirm my oneness with the God of All, and I bring that back, touching my forehead, thereby making a connection between my sacred sight and the All.

"For now, I would not go beyond these six chakras with the children, for the seventh center is of its own import and work. Therefore, I believe," glancing around the group, "it should be held aside, to be explored when all twelve candidates are known."

Judy looks at Louisa with gentleness, "I am not sure I agree with that, if you will forgive me. I think it is important for all the children to be equally prepared."

"I agree with you and in due course all will receive equal in kind. But what I am intending is, first things first. Because time is of the essence, the work with the seventh center should not detract from ascertaining the twelve and from the importance of their discovering their sacred tenet."

"And by this, you are also referring to what we call our truths?" Judy smiles warmly.

"One and the same, with a variation of how we see these and how we utilize them."

"This I am eager to learn from you."

"And I from you," responds Louisa, "for I know that the power of your truths is equal to our tenets. How say you all, then, to my proposition? Shall we give these teachings to the children? Do *you* feel any different, having followed this exercise to the center of the sacred sight?"

All are smiling and nodding.

"Indeed." Anna gestures, "It is like a fountain of light being raised up into my body. Tell me, do you perceive this coming from the earth, or from above, or both?"

"There is, in truth, no separateness, but for sake of description, and for the children's understanding, we will teach them to draw it from within, from the base of the spine or the foundational energy center, and draw it upward. In this way, should there ever be a need in the body, or the heart, or the mind, they will have this as a resource which is more literal and understandable. For they can always put their hands down and touch the earth, can they not?"

Everyone chuckles at this intended light-heartedness.

"Then, I suggest that we show them how the energy also comes down from above, and, as Zephorah discovered, comes together in the center of our being. That is a magical child, that one. Believing that she had not the abilities, the gifts, the talents of the others, and quietly waiting to be called upon is a special blessing, a gift ... a truth that is unexcelled."

Among these very learned teachers who are calling forth the little Maidens, there is the understanding that a concept, which they considered a living thing, becomes empowered with a great force called Joyful Expectancy. It is the Principle upon which the opening of the children shall be strongly based, for being guided to anticipate is as being guided to create.

A concept is as a blueprint, a pattern. As more and more behold it and take it within themselves, it moves inalterably to become a reality. It is the expectancy of the concept's manifestation that is a key, not only to empowering and awakening the children, but a key good for all.

We have given this information from the eternal references of the Maidens themselves. It is our prayer, humbly, that we have presented this in a manner which has stirred something within you ... the expectant child.

Chapter Twelve

Spilling Down All Over Me

As all are milling about, one of the children runs up to the teachers to ask excitedly, "Is this a good root, Isadore?"

"Oh, let me see that one. Yes, it is a very good one. But, see here? Whenever you see this particular color, you know that it is like the sun ... very hot."

Theresa giggles and runs to join the other children.

"Oh, Judy, see how bright the children are! They are bright in spirit, but in heart and mind as well. How quickly they learn, and how wonderful their sense of the fullness of God's gifts to all who are willing to seek them."

"Undoubtedly, that is your doing, Isadore." Judy laughs softly. "I have never known one whose knowledge of plants and herbs is so complete. To the rest of us, it is as though you and the plants are somehow united."

"Actually, I always think of it in just that way, and that is the key I am trying to impart to the children."

They are interrupted by the laughter and excitement of Andrew as he runs up to them and without a moment's pause jumps up to perch himself on Isadore's lap.

She quickly embraces him, swinging him to and fro. "Well, Andrew, what have you found?"

"See here, Isadore? This plant has tiny flowers! And if you look inside, it is like the plant is looking back at you!"

"Oh-h, let me see that! Yes, it is looking back. And listen carefully. I think I hear it speaking ... *Hel-lo, An-drew.*"

Andrew giggles. "What does this plant do for us?"

"Well, if you take these petals and spread them out to dry in the sun, once dry, you can keep them for very long periods of time. Then, if someone's body is too warm, you know, here," and she places a hand upon his forehead, causing him to giggle again, "or here," placing a hand on his tummy, and he giggles all the more, "you can take this and mix it with hyssop, and it will make the person feel better. But you only want a few of these tiny buds. It is a very strong plant and will heal them very quickly."

"Can I tell the others that I found it?"

"Yes, please do!"

Andrew scurries off, and the children excitedly gather around him as he begins to share his discovery.

"I believe he is blessed."

"We think so, too, Isadore," Judy responds pensively. "What have you seen in any of the other children?"

"Many carry the light. That one over there ... see her?"

Judy looks to see that Isadore is pointing to Zephorah. "Yes, we know her well."

"She has a uniqueness in her heart and mind that sees things differently than most people would. She sees with the heart of one who feels a connection. It is something that, in my opinion, we all would do well to nurture."

"We agree in that regard about Zephorah."

They continue their conversation for a bit longer before rising to go forth and wander among the children, speaking to a number of them here and there. It is a very bright day, though not as warm as usual, and thus it invigorates the plants and all living beings. Finally, it is time for nourishment. All gather in the shade of a large outcropping, and other Essene women come, bringing food and teas. After the blessings, they lean back or stretch out to have a bit of a rest.

Some of the children are lying on their backs looking up into the sky through the shade that embraces them.

"Anna ... How will we know when He comes?"

"Oh, Timothy, our holy ones will tell us."

"Why do those people love us so much?" asks Rachel.

"And which people might these be?"

Rachel giggles and answers, "Those people." She points beyond the outcropping to the summit, where they so oft go to visit with the adepts. "The people of the great School."

"That is a very beautiful story. Would you like to hear it, children?" Anna teases sweetly.

That is all it takes. The children all scamper about, snuggling up to various Essene maidens, who are quick and joyful to receive them.

"A very long time ago ..." Anna begins.

"How long?" Andrew interrupts.

"Sh-h," she responds, laughing.

Andrew looks down smiling, glancing up this way and that. "Well, those things are important, are they not?"

Sighing and looking up into the sky, Anna speaks in a muted voice, but loudly enough for all to hear. "Lord God, thank you for the brightness of Thy son, Andrew. But could you ask him to be silent long enough," glancing down at Andrew with a great smile, "that I might tell this story?"

Andrew, looking up into her loving eyes, smiles and falls silent, waiting expectantly for the story.

"Long ago, there were great challenges upon the Earth, and many people did not like one another. They formed into groups, and sought to gain power and dominion over one another."

"Excuse me," questions Hannah, "what is dominion?"

"Dominion means rule." Anna smiles.

"Thank you."

"The more one group would gain strength, the more the others would strive to match it, until the lands were divided.

The people were no longer one. Some lost sight of God. Some lost their remembrance of what is holy and true. They began to use what they called gods, which were actually statues, to dominate the people, ordering them to worship these idols and monuments that were of strange things."

Young Jason raises asks, "What do you mean, strange?"

"Well, some of the statues were part human and part animal, and others were wholly animal. And these people were ordered to worship them."

"Why would they think an animal would be God?" asks Rachel.

"It was a way that they could control the people."

Rachel's eyebrows arch. "They believed that animals control people?"

The Essene women all giggle.

"It was rather like that. They worshipped the idols, believing that the power of certain creatures could be used to help them gain things that they wanted."

"I know some of the creatures they used," Timothy adds excitedly, "lions and elephants!"

"Yes," responds Anna. "Now, children, may I finish the story?"

"Yes, yes!" They clamber closer to one another.

One child has snuggled close to Anna. "We will be silent so you can finish, but may we ask questions *after*?"

"Yes, Hannah, you may. So, a wind came into the Earth, and upon the wind was the Word of God. In a distant field, a simple farmer felt the wind. He was one who had not forgotten that there is but one God. Stopping his labor, he turned to face the wind, and he knelt and offered a prayer, for this good farmer saw that all was of God. As he knelt and prayed, he heard the Word of God. So in awe was he of what he heard, that his spirit awakened even more."

One of the children begins to speak and quickly covers her mouth.

Anna nods approvingly and continues. "Afterwards, he went to his family and told them what had happened. They called their friends together and offered a prayer, and their strength grew, for others began to hear and see and came to join their number.

"Then, upon a time later, a child was born into this family. One of the elders looked upon him and saw a light, a very beautiful light. So his father ... Remember, he was the simple farmer," and all the children nod at one another, "the father said unto his friends and family, 'I shall call him Elijah, for I know God speaks to him. I hear the same wind and the Word whenever I am with him.'

"Well, the community grew and grew as still others came unto it. It was a peaceful place, distant enough that none of the quarrelsome tribes paid them much heed. As Elijah grew, people would come to him to ask him for a blessing. The more they asked of him, the more he listened and the more he heard. And when they came to him, each offered a gift."

Another child, with a word halfway out of his mouth, stifles it and begins to giggle, looking down.

"But it was not a gift as you would think of it, of the material world. It was a gift of their knowledge or of their memory, for portions of the ancient teachings had been handed down to each of them from their ancestors. So they were like living records. Can you imagine? They gave the gift of that record to Elijah! So he grew stronger and brighter.

"There came that time of his life whereupon he went forth. As he wandered through the lands, he sought that which would bring him even greater oneness with the God whom by now he had come to love so deeply.

"Long before this, it had been written that the hand of God would be placed upon a prophet who would foretell of those times ahead for our peoples. Elijah knew about this. But he did not know that while he wandered, seeking, it was he who had been chosen! He spent many of his youthful years journeying, looking, asking, listening to seers and prophets and to those called magi. Yet each time God would speak to him, and Elijah would know it was not they who had been chosen. So he journeyed on, long and far.

"Finally, one day as he trod up a mountainside, he came to a beautiful spring where the water cascaded down some beautiful rocks and passed beneath the shade of some wonderful old trees."

"Oh-h," Zephorah sighs, unable to contain herself, "that sounds so-o beautiful."

"It was. And is, for this is a very real place, and this is a true story. May I continue?" Anna rebukes good-naturedly.

"Oh, yes, please. Forgive me!" giggles Zephorah shyly.

Anna turns to smile at her sisters before continuing. "Well, while he rested beneath the shade of one of those trees, leaning back against a beautiful rock, he took from the stream to quench his thirst, and then he fell into sleep. As he rested, God came to him.

"*E-li-jah* ... He called. *E-li-jah.*

"Finally, Elijah awakened. He looked about and said, 'Who speaketh to me? Where art thou? Show yourself!'

"And a great Light came before him, and he was taken into God's Spirit. At first, he feared, for he thought perhaps he had wronged God somehow. And the voice spoke unto him, *Be of good cheer, Elijah, thou son of God. I bring unto you joy. I shall guide you unto those who are righteous. You will speak unto them that they shall triumph over those who worship falsely and who lead their peoples into limitation and darkness.*

"'I, Lord?'

"There was silence ... And Elijah knew that the Light had spoken truth. So it was, then, that he went forth, listening and hearing the Word of God, guiding great rulers unto triumphant victories over those who worshiped falsely.

"It came to pass that the rulers recognized Elijah as a prophet of God, and some of these rulers sought him out, seeking to vanquish him. An evil king sent two hundred of his prophets and soldiers to do battle to vanquish him. But Elijah spoke to God, and God smote them, and a fear went forth throughout all the lands: Here, truly, is a prophet of God.

"Many came unto him bearing their children and bringing others whom they felt were to serve God, and it came to pass that Elijah grew great in his strength and compassion. While it is true that many continued to come against him, each time, the Hand of God or one to whom Elijah had given a blessing of God, would come to his aid ... and he always triumphed.

Anna bends down, her eyes passing over the gathering of children, "And do you know where that beautiful spring and that very special tree and rock are?"

The children look at one another in silence.

"Has any of you seen such a place?"

All of the women are watching these children, more than forty of whom are gathered here.

A tiny hand comes up over to the right and back a bit.

"Come. Come up here, child."

Shyly, a small girl makes her way to stand before Anna.

Anna reaches out to pull the little one onto her lap. "Tell us what you have seen."

"We come from the place called Carmel, and there is such a tree and such a rock, and a beautiful stream. It has given our people life and nourishment. Our elders say that it is a holy place. Is that Mr. Elijah's place that you speak of?"

"That is it." Anna confirms, reverence in her voice.

Another hand comes up now. "I know this place."

And another. "I, too, know it, dear Anna. Are we blessed because we know it?"

"I am certain you are blessed. But come here, you two, and join your sister."

They come running up and surround her. Anna embraces them as she continues speaking, looking about the gathering. "Where we are now, called the School, and the holy place that you know and which has blessed you, were both created and blessed by Elijah. But it is the holy place that you have come from, the sacred mountain of our homeland, that we shall return to in a time. When we do, we shall call upon the beautiful spirit of Elijah and other Ancients to guide us."

"Can we not call upon Mr. Elijah now?" questions Zephorah, and the little maidens all giggle.

"Do you think we can, sweet Zephorah?"

She shrugs her shoulders, tilts her head left and right, looks around at the other little children, and wrinkles up her face. "Why not? Is he bound to a place? Is he like the roots we have been gathering?" She stands, "Or is he like them?" She points to two large winged creatures circling in the sky above.

"How do you come to think such things, Zephorah!" Judy smiles, and then steals a glance at Isadore.

"I do not *think* it. It just rises into my mouth from somewhere inside me, and I just speak it." She giggles.

"Do other things rise up into your mouth?" asks Judy, striving very hard to keep from laughing.

"Oh, yes! It happens a lot. Sometimes I have to cover my mouth or it spills out." The children giggle all the more.

"What are these other kinds of things that want to spill out of your mouth?"

"Well," she looks down, moving her foot back and forth in the soil, "uh-h ..."

"Just give us a little example." Judy is still smiling and encouraging Zephorah, but also intent upon discovering more about this from her.

"Well, earlier, I told Mathias," pointing to Mathias, who is leaned back against the rock outcropping, and who brightens at being singled out, "*You had better not walk there. There is a bad insect there,* and he listened to me when the words spilled out. And we went and looked, and there it was ... one of those stingy things."

The children giggle yet again.

"And, what else?"

"Well ... I knew that plant that Sarah has in her lap was smiling at her and the words just spilled out when I told her."

Judy calls Sarah up and asks to see the plant. Passing it to Isadore, Isadore nods. "Well, Zephorah, the words that spilled out of you were quite correct. Isadore states that this is a very powerful healing plant. And our healers say that God smiles on us through this plant. Have you ever heard that?"

"Oh, no." She shakes her head, looking down and then up. "Those healers do not speak to me very much," and the children giggle all the more, causing her to as well.

"Well, thank you for sharing with us, Zephorah." Judy glances at several of the other maidens, who are all nodding. "So then, children, it has been suggested that Elijah is ..." and she sweeps her arms all around, "everywhere."

Oo-os and *ah-hs* come from the children.

"In this rock?" questions Timothy.

"Yes."

"Up there?" Hannah asks.

"Yes, up there. Perhaps that very winged creature."

"What about down here in the earth?" Andrew stomps his foot.

"Well, it is the teaching of our people that the Spirit of God is, indeed, in the earth, and that if one is attuned, if one listens and looks, he can know and be one with the Spirit of God by being one with the earth."

Isadore nods. "And is it not from the earth that we gather our food, and the herbs and plants that make us well?"

The conversation continues in this manner, until finally the sisters gather the children into a circle.

Seated in the center is Judy. "Now, children, do like this." She brings her hands up, placing them together, the tips of her fingers just beneath her chin. "Move your hands out and in, up and down, and then bring them back here," placing them against her chest. Now spread them wide and speak these words: *I ... state your name ... call upon you, Lord God, to guide me.* Bring your hands slowly together, this way, that they are outreached in front of you."

Some of the sisters move about, showing the children, adjusting hands here and there.

"Now, bring your hands back and place them flat against your heart."

Judy watches the children carefully. "Now, bring them up and place them over your eyes. Close your eyes, and look. Let your body be free. Let it move with that within you."

The children peek, and look, and see Judy swaying just ever so slightly, as is in the tradition of the Essene elders and maidens. "When you feel the Presence, you will know it. You will feel the difference. But you must close your thoughts, close your sight, close your hearing. Then, reopen all of these, but do so beyond your body."

"How do I do that?" questions Thomas. "Every time I try, my eyes pop open and all I see are my hands."

Some of the children giggle, but some are seemingly beyond the voice of Thomas. One of the sisters scurries over to him and whispers in his ear, explaining to him, showing him. The rest of the children are striving. They have heard this many times, and some have become quite adept at it.

Judy begins to look around, shifting her sight to the fullness of her being so that she can see the children in their completeness. Anna and many of the others are walking about. Some of the children turn, hearing one of their elder sisters approach. But some do not; they instead are swaying, and the sisters are noting this very carefully, to know which of the children have moved beyond their finite being.

80〜03

The evening meal has come and gone, and the children

have been prepared for slumber. As has now become the custom, several of the adepts from the great School come to join them at this juncture prior to sleep. The children have been divided into their smaller groups and are seated.

Here, in one little group, an adept is teaching. "Do you feel the energy, the movement up and down your back?"

Some of the children, seated admirably straight, smile brightly and nod. Their hands are together and they are sparkly clean, inside and out.

Looking about the group, the adept next asks, "What do you feel, and where do you feel it?"

Abigale answers, "I think it is stuck."

The others giggle.

The adept, smiling broadly, encourages her. "Can you tell me where it is stuck?"

"Right here," Abigale points to her throat. "It feels stuck here." She glances around and sees the elder sisters watching her. To one side, sit Anna, Ruth, Isadore, and Judy, and slightly beyond is the elder Theresa and many others.

"Does it get stuck there often?"

"Yes, it does. It gets stuck there a lot!"

The adept gestures to Judy, and Judy motions to Theresa the elder, who goes over to talk to Abigale. She then places her hands upon the child's shoulders.

Soon Abigale is smiling and her eyes close. "It is not stuck anymore, thank you."

The children giggle again.

"Does anyone else have stuck energy somewhere?"

They look to one another, and a hand comes up.

"Yes, you are Mary. Is that true?"

"Yes, I am," she answers sweetly.

"Is your energy stuck?"

"No, it is not stuck, but it *is* spilling all over me," to which the children burst out laughing.

"Tell me, how is it spilling all over you, sweet Mary?"

"It is spilling out of the top of me and running down."

"How can you tell that?" the adept questions further.

"Well, it feels all warm, and ... like someone is hugging me, and it makes me feel tingly and sparkly."

"Do you like how it feels?"

"Yes, it feels very good. But is it supposed to do that? Spill all over me?"

The adept quickly glances at the elder sisters, receiving in return bright smiles of affirmation that, unquestionably, this is one of the twelve candidates.

The adept returns her attention to Mary. "It does not *need* to do that, but it is a very good thing when it does. Tell me, Mary, does this happen often?"

"Oh, yes," she sighs, "almost every time. It spills right down all over me." She looks down and now she, too, begins to giggle. "Sometimes, like now, it tickles a little too."

The children all giggle yet again.

"I want mine to spill over me too," Kelleth announces.

The others quickly join in that they, too, would like this to happen to them.

"Well, then, perhaps our sweet sister Mary can tell us how she does it. Could you, Mary?"

"Well ..." She wiggles her body just a bit, brings her hands up, and closes her eyes. "I do all the things you told me to do, just like you told me. See?" She opens her eyes to gain approval. Receiving it, she continues, "Then, I think about the Spirit of God in the earth, like our sister, Isadore, taught us. And I speak to it."

There is silence as all of the sisters can see clearly that the other children are striving to do just that.

"Is there anything in particular that you say to the Spirit in the earth, Mary?" questions the adept.

"Yes. I tell the Spirit of God in the earth that I love Him. And when I tell Him that, He sends the light and the ... you know, the tingly things, right up my body. Oh-h, it makes me feel happy, and it makes me feel good. And the more God's Spirit makes me feel good, the more I love God. So, I tell Him that, and He gives me more light and more tinglies, until pretty soon, it comes right out the top of my head and spills over me. I guess it must go back down into the earth again." Her eyes pop open. "Do you think so?"

"I am certain of it, for all that is of God is never apart from God, and that which is God that goes forth, always returns to its home ... which is God."

One of the other maidens raises her hand.

The adept looks at her and nods, continuing to keep an eye on Mary. The other sisters are moving about silently, to observe the energies around the other children as they strive to emulate Mary's guidance

"Yes," nods the adept, "speak child."

"What you said, that what goes forth from God always returns to God. Is that what happens when we set aside our bodies?" Her eyes begin to glisten with tears, "Like our sweet guardians? Did they ... return to God?"

The children are looking at the adept and Anna, who has come to seat herself beside the adept.

"It is very true." The adept nods to Anna to carry on.

"It is good to remember always that you are here on Earth in your current physical body for a pathway which has importance for you. That pathway has a particular purpose in service to God and to our brethren. When that purpose has been fulfilled, then the journey is complete. It is very much like laying aside your clothing when you no longer need it. When that time comes and we lay aside our physical body, the angels of God, and our elders and Ancients who have gone before, await us. They await each of you, and they hold beautiful new garments for you to place upon your being, your spirit. And then, you will be reborn into all that you are and all that you can be."

It is now little Kelleth who speaks. "Why can I not be all

that I can be now?"

"Perhaps you can," answers Anna, "if you believe it so, and if you follow the teachings which are intended to guide you, and if you listen to the voice of God within you."

"I do not hear it very often," Kelleth responds, and several of the children chuckle. "Sometimes I do, but it seems to me when I need it the most, it is ... well, it seems gone somewhere else for a time, because it does not seem to hear me."

Some of the children giggle again.

"Tell us of such a time, Kelleth. And, we will come back to you in just a moment, sweet Theresa. Is that acceptable?"

"Oh, yes. My mind is thinking anyway. Go ahead and talk to Kelleth because I have to listen to my mind." She looks down and closes her eyes.

It is very difficult for Anna to keep from laughing aloud. The sweetness of these young maidens, and their innocence and honesty, brings such joy that laughter is sometimes almost uncontainable, the laughter which comes of love.

"So why does the voice of God not hear me all the time?" Kelleth asks again.

"God hears *every* word, sees *every* action, knows *every* thing."

"Well, I do not understand that at all. If God hears it all, why does He choose not to answer me sometimes?"

The other young maidens are very intent upon this, for all have experienced it.

"Can anyone answer Kelleth's question?"

They all turn about and look at one another, some shrugging shoulders, others with a hand upon their cheek, turning their head this way and that.

A hand comes up. "Yes, Mary, how would you answer your sister Kelleth?"

"Sometimes I think that God wants us to work at it a little bit, and if we cannot get it after that, then He will tell us. You know, dear Anna, like you and the other sisters do with us. You make us try. If we cannot find it or understand it, then you tell us. Is that what God does, too?"

Again, the sisters brighten and smile at the wisdom.

"Yes, Mary. There are times when God wishes us to try just a little harder to learn, to see, to know, and to answer the questions ourselves or meet the challenges that are before us."

"Did the guardians have to meet something?" questions Theresa again. "Is that why they were ..." and she looks down, "taken from us?"

Many note that Theresa is heavily focused upon the loss of the beloved guardians who gave their lives to protect them.

"It was perhaps, sweet Theresa, that they have works elsewhere. Their journey, their pathway here, was completed. Our people whom we call warrior priests are so at one with God that God gives them the power of Elijah. They serve you, Theresa, because they see the God within you. They fear not death, for they know the teachings of those who have gone before, the very teachings of Elijah for example, that death is but a doorway, and that beyond it are those we love waiting to, as I said, give us beautiful new garments of light."

"Could we get wings, too," questions Rachel, "like the angels have?"

"Perhaps so," smiles Anna "I suppose that is between you and God."

"Are the guardians still with us then?" questions Theresa.

By now, two of the sisters have positioned themselves near Theresa. One slides forward to put a hand about her. Her left hand is upon Theresa's front shoulder, and her right hand comes along behind, moving gently across Theresa's back, the light evident as her hands move again and again.

A sweetness flows into Theresa's face. The visibly tense sadness that has been there begins to soften. "I know the answer to that, do I not?"

"You do," Anna responds.

"My heart is telling me that they are here right now. Can

I close myself and see them?"

"Yes," responds the adept, "and if you lift up the energy of God in your body and perhaps even let it spill down over you, you may hear and see them. For their love for you, sweet Theresa, is equal to the love you hold for them."

"Oh-h, that is a lot of love because I love them so very much."

The sisters again look at one another with a nod of understanding.

ℰᏅᏟᏋ

The children have been prepared for sleep, and the sisters move about, placing a blessing upon the foreheads of the little ones, making the sign of the Expected One. Some of the children are moving their hands up and down as they have been taught, clearing away what could be called the debris of thought and energy from the day that is now concluding.

Judy begins to hum a sweet single tone, and off to the side a bit, Theresa the elder, and next, Sophie the elder do likewise, and the evening prayers begin. It is a soft chant, asking that God would guide and God would care, sending forth blessings of their spirits' light to those they love and to those who are in need.

Sleep comes swiftly to the children, for the day's activities have been many. The teachings have been great, and revelations have been found in varying forms and degrees, even though for the most part the children do not see these as teachings, but rather only as grand adventures.

Here, one in dream begins to spin and roll into the dark, warm embrace of God. In the distance she hears the sound of her own laughter, and she answers it. She hears, too, a voice call out to her again and again, *Sophie ... Sophie.* "Art Thou God, calling me?" she questions in her dream. *Yes. I am your God.* And Little Sophie spins off into the light, laughing, and speaking with God.

Another child has moved as though sliding down a shaft of light, multicolored in great, beautiful, billowy swirls. As she moves downward, downward, she feels the essence of each color touch and caress her. And below, she sees the familiar beautiful orb of light awaiting her. She bursts forth into it, and finds herself walking upon a path. Involuntarily, she reaches down and grasps her garment, and she spins about this way and that, her body and her head swaying as she sings a small song of sunshine and light. She follows the pathway, which is embraced by beautiful blooming bushes on either side. Passing beneath an arbor covered with sumptuous, bright yellow roses, she comes up the path, and there He is ... the Shining One, standing by the bench. She begins to giggle and laugh as He extends His hands out to her, and she rushes to Him. He sweeps her up, and they spin around, and all becomes color and light, and they laugh together as the Shining One tells Hannah of her beauty and God's love for her.

Another finds herself, after walking through a beautiful mist, standing on a small pathway, which weaves in and out of great boulders. She sighs very deeply, and with a sparkle in her voice, "I guess I will have to walk through here again." She begins to move gaily through the boulders, when suddenly she sees them... the two giants. They look down upon her with light around their heads, smile, and call her name.

She speaks to them. "Why are you always so great? Why do you not meet me in a smaller form? You give my neck an ache." The giants begin to laugh and hum. As they do, their size diminishes, until ... there! She can look into their eyes, *Hello, Zephorah. Will you play with us?* "Yes, I will." She takes one of each of their hands, and off they go, bouncing down the path, now covered with flowers, not a boulder in sight.

8)(3

The children are excited to share their dreams, and as each of these is retold, the sisters note the symbols.

One who has the knowledge to record such things does so, creating the symbols of the dreams on a great scroll, with Anna taking the names of the children.

Later, she and Judy discuss the dreams with Elob and some of the others.

"What do you think of these visions?" Anna asks Elob.

"They are moving ... awakening."

Zelotese nods, "I believe it is approaching the time for other teachings and works to be given. The knowledge of your Ancients is very powerful, and while we know of it to a large extent, the greater teaching in this area will come from your people because your spirits are one with it."

"You think that is a significant point?" questions Judy.

"I do, indeed. In fact, you are probably the one I would choose to oversee the next levels."

"And what levels would these be?" She smiles.

"The ones you already know." He smiles back, recognizing that this was something they both knew.

"It is time, then, to focus upon their purposes, their reasons for being? Is it time that they begin to seek their truth?"

"Why is it, sweet Judy, that you ask me these things when you know the answers before you ask?"

"Perhaps it is because I so honor you, and all your brothers and sisters, that I value, if not treasure, your affirmation."

"You honor us, and you honor me. But you, of all you here," nodding to the others, "know that the true authority and guidance is God."

Judy nods, smiling, "I also know that God speaks through you, and so my honor is not only to you ... which, indeed, is mighty ... but it is to honor the God within you."

Zelotese straightens himself and looks down, bringing his hands up to gesture a salute of reverence to her. "Can there be any question or doubt why you are called great among your people, when all that comes forth from you bears the wisdom of God."

Judy does not look away, nor down, but only smiles.

"It is self-evident that you believe yourself to be a Daughter of God. *This* is where I would begin. Help them understand this about themselves."

Judy's eyes, softly fixed upon him, are highlighted by the flickering flames that have cooked their evening meal, now dancing before them as the embers begin to appear. "So shall it be then. I thank you, Zelotese, and all of you." She gestures to the others.

"I would like to place some petitions before the group," Ruth begins now. "Will you hear them?"

"Of course." Elob smiles and nods.

"We seek to awaken ... not in the sense as though some are greater or lesser, but according to the Promise and the Prophecy ... We seek to awaken certain gifts and qualities in the twelve, and we ask that you hold these in your prayers as we shall do."

"Name them, then," declares Elob, "for as you know, the power is in the speaking of the name."

Ruth begins. "Mary. Zephorah. Andra. Abigale. Kelleth. Hannah. Theresa. And we should like to embrace in the loving intention we have just affirmed together those whom we know are yet to be made known to us, those in our group who are yet to become awakened ... and perhaps even some as yet to join our group."

"So be it then," Elob states. "We shall hold these in our hearts and prayers."

Chapter Thirteen

Journey to Truth

Several years have passed. It is a beautiful day and many of the Essene women have gone on an outing with the children.

They are in the process of searching not only for certain plants and herbs, but for the signs of those things that can inspire the children and evoke the strength and character that is uniquely theirs as individuals.

As the group comes to rest in a particularly beautiful spot, they gather to sup. Having nourished their spirits, hearts, and minds in prayer and song, as is the custom, the elder maidens receive questions and ask them in turn, still searching for the remainder of those twelve, who they know will epitomize the twelve levels, the twelve truths, the gifts to be borne to Him who comes.

"Anna," questions Theresa, "when shall we return to our homeland?"

"Is there a longing in your heart?"

"Yes. I dream of this often."

"Tell us of your dreams, Theresa."

"I see us all," turning to smile at all of her companions, who by now are near and dear to one another, forming one inseparable, joyful bond of light, "walking along the seashore. I remember it only vaguely as I retell this, but in my dreams it is very clear."

"At what age do you walk by the seashore?" asks Judy.

Theresa smiles, "I am older. We are all older."

"Can you estimate how much older?"

"Well ..." Theresa turns her head this way and that, glancing up and then back to the group. "Mary, your hair is longer." Mary looks down and giggles. "And Andra, you are considerably taller." Andra smiles, flushing. So it continues, as Theresa turns to one and then another.

"Then, what would you estimate your age to be?" probes Judy further.

"Perhaps a year older or a bit more. It is difficult to tell, for everyone seems the same, just mostly bigger."

The children and teachers alike all laugh.

Judy glances at Anna, and then over at the other elder maidens and some of the adepts who are usually with them on the outings. "Then could you suppose, Theresa, that that is your answer?"

Theresa's face becomes more serious as she reflects on this briefly. "I suppose it could be. That seems like a long time. But then we have been here for a very long time, have we not?"

"Yes," smiles Anna.

Another enters the discussion, "Why is it that some days seem longer than others? Like today. It seems very long."

"Why would you think that is so, Hannah? What is different today as compared to yesterday, or the day before?"

"Well, yesterday we did chores. We worked on making fabrics, then we worked on making utensils. Then we wove, and then we did scribing. It was busier than today. Today we are out here in the beauty of creation. Perhaps it is the vastness of the day compared with sitting in one place and doing all those ..." She looks down, giggling, for she knows all things, even chores, should be looked upon as gifts and blessings, "... wonderful little tasks." As is typical of her, she looks up to see if Anna has perceived her inner thought and flushes.

"It is not that I do not find joy and purpose in doing those things. But out here," she sweeps her hand about, "I remember the vastness of God. I remember the beauty of creation." Then she looks down, recognizing it is likely that some follow-up comments will come from her beloved teachers.

It is Judy who begins the teaching, "When you were weaving the beautiful fabric, for which you have such skill," causing Hannah to blush, "were you not putting your thoughts, your heart, your very spirit into the cloth?"

Hannah quickly looks up. "Oh, yes! I love doing it, and I love thinking about who might wear it and of myself hugging them as the cloth is wrapped around them. I think about the beautiful colors and how, if they come to look at them in a time of need, the colors might invoke joy. So, yes. Even in the making of the utensils," and the children all giggle, "which everyone knows I am not very adept at, I was thinking about what the utensils would hold, who might drink from this bowl, who might place food in this container. It gave me joy, and I put that joy back into what I was working on. But out here ... Well, my spirit is free, and the day is vast and filled with wonder." Hannah looks around to see most all nodding.

"What does that have to do with time?" asks Editha.

"Well, when I am in our village, sometimes in my joy of the things we are all about there, I forget what I feel when I am out here. Out here, I am constantly aware of the presence of God, and this makes the day vast."

"Then would you say," offers Judy, "that time is relevant to how you feel, to what you see, and to what you think?"

Andra responds now, "I certainly would."

"Would you share that with us, then."

"I always look for my truth. In whatever I am about, I try to see it through the eyes of my truth."

Mary nods, "I do that, too."

"And I, too," Abigale adds.

All the children respond accordingly. Andra sits for a

moment, not knowing what to say next.

Judy smiles at her, "Tell them how you see, Andra."

She takes a long breath, something she is known for before sharing something important to her, "I look for the excitement and power of my truth."

"And what is your truth, Andra?"

"Wisdom. Wisdom is my truth."

"How is it that you see through the eyes of wisdom?" questions Anna now.

"Well, I remember everything that I have been taught, and I remember that I must think before I give birth to my words. Like you taught me, Ruth," she looks over at her beloved teacher who smiles and nods, "because I know that my very words are creating. I think about all that I have been given, all I have learned, and about the experiences that Jacob taught us. Remember?" She looks around at the other children. "He taught us to mix knowledge with experience in the golden bowl within, and season it a bit here and there with a dash of love, a bit of compassion, a ... what does he call it? A smattering of understanding, and patience, and all the other virtues, which are your truths, my sisters.

"Then I think ... *I can make this little bit of time larger than it seems to be because I choose to.* And as I choose to make the time larger, it gives me lots of room to walk around in my mind and in my heart. Then I can speak the words that my truth gives me. Others think only a moment or two have passed, but I have had large portions of time.

"So, then, when I hear words back, I look at them through the eyes of this wisdom, and I can see in their words their many experiences, their knowledge, their understanding, and Jacob's smattering of this or that." Everyone smiles. "So that is how I see through my truth, very clearly."

"Oh-h," sighs Zephorah, "truth is so beautiful."

"How so?" questions Ruth, still smiling.

"Because, as we have journeyed to find our truth, we

have found ourselves, have we not?"

The elder sisters look at one another smiling.

"Yes, I believe one could say that," Anna acknowledges softly, "when you find your truth, you have found yourself."

"I like living in my truth."

"How does it make you feel," questions Judy, "to live in your truth? Is your life different than before you knew of your truth?"

Zephorah shakes her head and, as is her custom, rolls her eyes, which makes the other children giggle. "I cannot even remember not knowing my truth, to tell you the truth. But I do remember feeling lots of things, like I was carrying around big stones."

"Big stones?" Ruth's eyebrows arch in loving support, for she clearly knows Zephorah's thought.

"Yes, big stones. I could not see them. I did not really know what they were, but I knew I had them. Some days while the other children were laughing and having a good time, I had to try very hard to join in because the stones were so heavy. I could not even take a deep breath to let laughter come forth because they just got in the way."

Some of the children chuckle, so she glances at them with youthful sternness to tell them this is serious.

A bit embarrassed, they encourage her. "Tell us more about these stones. What was it like? How did you come to know them?"

"That is quite a long story."

"We have plenty of time," encourages Judy.

"Oh, good. I like to tell this. It makes me feel good all over." The young maidens laugh and clap their hands. "First, when you, Louisa, told us about the column of light within ... the ascension, you called it, of the Spirit of God through all of our being, and the movement back and forth to embrace all that is ... I found a stone. Remember, Mary, when you used to get the energy stuck?"

Mary laughs, "Yes. It has not been stuck for a long time. Thank you very much." She looks up, gesturing to God.

After the laughter subsides, Zephorah continues, "Well, I found one of the stones in the way of the light."

"What did it look like?" questions Anna.

"It looked like sadness. It looked like memories. It even looked a little like fear. So, when Louisa told us that all energies are what we make of them, Hannah and I worked together. Remember, Hannah?"

Hannah smiles, bobbing her head up and down.

"We let our spirits embrace ... like you taught us, Ruth. When her spirit touched mine, she gave to me of her truth of joy, and that gift helped me transform the sorrow into joy. Some of those memories, I actually came to see as gifts! We looked at them, together, just as if they were real gifts all wrapped up. We even took some leaves and rolled things up to symbolize those memories, and we wove a basket ... That was a pretty one, didn't you think, Hannah?"

Hannah nods, smiling, "You still have it, do you not?"

"Yes, I do. Well, when we looked at them all wrapped up like that, we could always find, like you said, Ruth ... if a thing looks unpleasant the way it is, turn it over in your mind and heart, and see what is on the other side of it. We did that.

"At first, the things we wrapped in the leaves looked pretty much the same, but then we named them. We named one side what seemed to be, and the other side what we believed God was gifting to us. Then we rolled them up in the leaves again and put them back in the basket.

"And remember, Hannah? I carried them around in there. Each time we unwrapped them, the stones seemed to get smaller and smaller. After awhile, it was almost like looking at little grains of sand, like down there that the ants are piling up." Everyone glances down to see the ants busily at work. "As we kept doing that, I began to learn, and Hannah learned from what I learned. Right, Hannah?"

Hannah nods again, supporting her sister.

"One day, Hannah said to me, 'How many stones do you have left inside you, Zephorah?' I looked about and closed my eyes. Then I placed my hands on my heart, and I could feel the warmth. That is when I knew that my heart had nothing stuck. So then, I placed my hands to the bottom of my back, then to the front, and then here to my spiritual entry and exit point in my tummy, and then back to my heart, and I looked at Hannah and laughed. Nothing was stuck anywhere. No more stones. Remember, Hannah? We took the basket full of the rocks, still wrapped in the leaves, to your holy place that you found. We blessed them and put them back into the spirit of the earth."

Judy is focused very intently on Zephorah. "How did you bless them?"

"We looked into the future."

"You did that mostly, Zephorah," comments Hannah, "for that is your truth, not mine."

Zephorah smiles and again nods a loving gesture to her dear sister. "Well, we looked into the future together. You did it, too."

"Yes, I did it, too," Hannah smiles in return.

"And I saw the energy! I saw the life going into the earth, being taken by the Spirit of God. So I said unto God, 'Thank you for giving me these experiences, and thank you for helping me to see that I have choices. I can choose how I shall carry them from now on. Now Father, Hannah, my good friend, and I come to You in her holy place, and we wish to give them to You, that You can pass them on to another who may have need of the gifts they will offer to *them*, as they have to us.' So we made the special symbol, you know, Louisa?"

Louisa smiles and nods.

"We made the design and we put them there in the earth and said our prayer of blessing. Then we held hands and danced around them and sang. Now I have no more stones."

"Have you no more sadness?" questions Judy.

"Oh, I can see the sadness if I choose to, but most of the time, I only look at it for a short while. Like Hannah says, 'Always choose that which brings you joy. Why would you choose otherwise?'"

Now everyone giggles again.

"So, then, tell us how you see through your truth."

"My truth is the eyes of God."

Anna's eyebrows arch. "Really?"

"Yes," nods Zephorah. "Well, I have called it by different names. I suppose I might find other names to call it in times ahead. But it is truly that I look through the eyes of God."

"How do you do this?" Ruth asks lovingly.

"I do it like this." And even though they are sitting a bit apart from one another, as Zephorah straightens herself, Hannah straightens herself too, as they have done together so often in past. Both of them close their eyes, but it is Zephorah who speaks. "I put my hand on top of my head and I say, 'Here is the center of my spirit.' I put it here so that my spirit and my thoughts shall know one another and be able to help one another. Then I touch my forehead with all of my finger-tips, like you said, Louisa. And I say, 'Let my spirit-mind open my true sight.' Then I put my hands to my throat and I say, 'Let my words communicate what I perceive, what I know.'

"Then I bring my hands to rest upon my heart, and I feel the joy of the gift of life God gives me, and I let that move out from me. As it does, my sight goes with it. It takes me to things and I can see them. I can see with the movement of time, as we just talked about it. And like you, Andra, I take time and command it. And like you taught, Judy, pausing for a moment, then I say to time, 'I am Zephorah, Daughter of God. I am one with you. Carry me in your embrace forward, as I embrace you with my spirit-mind and my heart.'

"Then I feel myself being lifted up. I feel movement, and I hear and see sounds and colors, and I can detect fragrances.

Then my sight opens, and I can see what lies ahead. That is how I do it." She giggles as she opens her eyes and rocks to and fro.

Hannah begins to clap, as do the other sisters.

"My goodness, children, you have done so well. Would anyone like to tell us what truth is?"

"I would!" Abigale exclaims excitedly, and she stands up, straightening her garment, without a nod from any of the elder sisters, who simply smile and look at one another.

"Truth is that which is inside of everyone.

"Truth is that thing which is always there to pick you up if you fall down, to help your tummy when you have a bad thought, to bring a healing when you have an injury.

"Truth is that which helps you see others as you would have them see you. Truth is that which tells you, *Honor all things, and all things will honor you.*

"Truth is the light of Oneness that comes to us when we are in our ceremonies and prayers.

"Truth is the light that comes in darkness to guide us should we have lost our way.

"Truth is the power of God that we can call upon when another is against us.

"Truth is the spirit of looking forward. Expectancy. You know, Hannah ... looking forward to what might lie ahead, and truth helps us to build it.

"Truth is like the flowers that bloom so profusely when the rains come," she glances casually to the side, "which is not all that often here," and everyone chuckles a bit.

"So, truth is the Spirit of God seeking to speak and act through me and everyone." Abigale grasps the hem of her garment and bows here and there to the group.

All the children yell out praise and clap their hands, as she seats herself erectly, straightening her garments.

"That was wonderful, Abigale," Judy smiles. "So, how would you see through *your* truth?" adding quickly, "And there is no need to stand up again," which Abigale is usually quick to do.

"Oh, well, I see through my truth as understanding and compassion. When you have understanding and compassion, you know that all things are brought to you to experience. Like you do, Andra, with your bowl inside you, and putting in all the seasoning and experience like Jacob said. The only time I had fear and sadness," turning to glance at Zephorah, smiling, "was when I did not understand. When one of the adepts," glancing up at Louisa, "spoke to me in one of their languages or tongues, I got a funny feeling inside me."

"Why?" questions Louisa.

"Because I did not understand."

"Did you ask them to help you?"

"Yes, of course I asked," Abigale replies, causing the children to laugh again at her matter of fact nature.

Louisa smiles very broadly, "And did they tell you?"

"Yes, they told me," Abigale states, quite adult-like, "and that is what I mean. When they told me, I understood. If I had left those funny swirling feelings I had inside me alone, they could have become fear, you know."

"We know," smiles Judy.

"Well, they left because I asked. I said, 'Can you help me understand your beautiful words? They are like a song to me, but I know not their meaning,' and they would smile and tell me. I can speak some of their words if you would like."

The elder sisters cannot contain themselves. They burst into laughter, followed by the children.

Abigale looks about, and then down.

"No, no," Judy offers softly, "we are laughing at the humor in what you have given us, not at you, Abigale."

"Oh, I know." She turns her head this way and that. "I always have a way of making people laugh, especially when I try very hard to explain something."

Anna smiles at her. "Well, I suppose that is because you

have such wonderful understanding."

Abigale brightens immediately and straightens herself, sitting very tall and erect. "Oh, thank you, my sister. I suppose that could be so," and the other children affirm this.

"Well, as I was saying, when I truly understand a thing, I can see, just like Hannah and Zephorah did, that it has more than one side. That what you see or hear is not always all there is. So I ask. Sometimes I do not ask aloud. I ask of God, and then I do this," and she puts her hands over her forehead, then her ears, then her mouth, and then over her heart.

"Why do you do this?" asks Ruth.

"I do it because when I put my hands on my forehead, I say, 'Let my thoughts be still and open, that new thoughts can come and build understanding.' I put my hands over my ears and say, 'Lord God, bless me with the guidance that will help me to understand and have compassion.' And then I put my hands over my mouth so that I can say, 'Bless the words that I speak, Lord God, that they will carry understanding and compassion to all who hear them.'

"Then I put my hands over my heart, as you have all taught us to do because then I can feel my life-force, and as I feel this, I know I am also feeling the life-force of God. When I do this, sometimes I rock, and sometimes I hum the sacred sounds. Then, I become still and very quiet. I mean still inside, and quiet in my movement and everything.

"And then I listen. And I hear God say, *Hello, Abigale. What you seek is this ...* And I see that what might have been sad or dark has a purpose. God shows me the purpose. Like that this one will slow down and pray more, and that is why they have injured their leg. And like, the purpose for this unpleasant food," glancing around and giggling softly, "is so your body can tell the difference between what is good for you and what is not so good." The children giggle and clap at this. "These are some of the things I do. I can go on, dear Ruth."

"I think those are enough good examples."

"Well then, once God has told me these things ... Well, He does not always tell me. Sometimes He shows me. I see pictures of them in my head. Then I feel them in my body, and it changes and the swirly stuff inside becomes calm, like a beautiful breeze passing through my body, and then I have understanding and compassion. You know, maybe those are two different truths, though they always seem to go together. What do you think Anna? Are they different?"

Anna glances at the other sisters, for she knows one day these sweet children will come to know there is truly but one truth, that what they are each exploring and discovering and claiming at this point is but one of the twelve sacred points on the symbol of life itself, one of the twelve facets of the jewel to be presented to Him who comes.

She turns and speaks gently to Abigale and all of them. "It is good for one to remember that a gift is only a gift when given and received freely. Look you."

She reaches within her garment and pulls out a small, beautifully carved amulet. Rising, she walks over to Abigale, bends, lifts Abigale's hand, and places the beautiful amulet in her palm.

Abigale and the other children gasp at its beauty.

"Now then, that is a gift to you."

"For me?"

"Yes, it is yours. I gift it to you."

"Oh-h," Abigale sighs, clutching it to her heart. Closing her eyes, she tilts her head up. "Thank You, sweet Lord God, for this gift given to me through my sister Anna. I have not ever possessed a thing of such great beauty."

There is silence for a moment.

Abigale's eyes open and her hand opens, outstretched before her. "Oh. You are teaching me, are you not?"

"All of life offers us teaching, is it not so, dear Abigale?"

Her eyes flutter closed, and then open again. "I understand your meaning, according to that which you just spoke to me. You have given it to me freely. But you also said I must receive it freely. What does that mean?"

"Look with your truth, and see it."

"Will understanding help me to see this?"

"Well, if it does not, I am certain that compassion shall."

Abigale goes through her routine as she has just demonstrated. There is absolute silence as the children revere the holy place into which they know she goes.

Only a brief time passes, and tiny little tears begin to run down her cheeks. "I understand," she whispers.

Without speaking, she rises and walks over to Mary, who is kneeling upon the ground. Opening her hand to reveal the beautiful amulet, she looks at Mary. "My Truth tells me that if I receive this gift from my sister in the spirit in which she has given it to me, that I would in turn give it to all those for whom I hold love. I love you, Mary." She bends and places the beautiful amulet into Mary's hand.

Mary's head bows. When next she looks up, Abigale is smiling brightly. Mary stands and they gaze at one another, and then embrace, leaning to touch their foreheads and upraised hands as they have learned to do to symbolize and complete their oneness.

Abigale turns without another word, goes back to her place, and sits down, her face serene, a light from within evident about her, which the elder sisters duly note.

There is silence as Mary remains standing, her fingers caressing the amulet, looking into its color and beauty. Glancing up, she looks about, and walks over, extending her hand to Little Sophie, also called Sophia. "I add love into this beautiful gift which our sister has shared with me, and which our sweet teacher," glancing up at Anna, "has gifted to us. In the spirit of the truth of love, I gift it now to you."

Sophia shyly accepts. As her fingers touch the smooth surface and explore its intricate carvings, she begins to weep.

"Why dost thou weep?" questions Ruth.

"Because Mary's love is so bright, it makes my heart sing and I weep at the beauty."

Mary, who has knelt before her, their knees touching, places her hands upon Sophia's shoulders.

"The sweetness of Mary shines in this amulet, as does Abigale's and yours, dear teacher. Is it true," she lifts her tear-filled eyes turn to look at Ruth, "that when a thing has been in the possession of others, that it is not the thing itself, but the thoughts of those who have held it and the intentions of the giver to you that give it its true beauty and its meaning?"

"What you say is true. Many on Earth do not pause. They have not the willingness to open and to see in the manner as you have described. Yes, whether it is a beautiful amulet such as you now hold, or a prayer asking for peace or healing or understanding, or the intention of those who wish to build something, the intentions of each person who has been a part of that thing are within it and passed along."

"So, my sisters and our teacher have built something into this object?" Little Sophie asks, turning the amulet over, looking at it curiously.

"If everything is of God, which we know to be a truth, then is it not so that the intention of those who would intend a thing is that which gives it its essence, its power?"

"I think it so, but how do I know?"

"You look through your truth, sweet Sophie," explains Judy.

Little Sophie's eyes seem a bit distant for a moment and her head tilts this way and that, as her eyes flicker closed. Then they pop open.

"Have you seen it now through your truth?"

"I have, and it is true what you say. I can see the love around it, the brilliance of you, Mary. And the depth of understanding and compassion of you, Abigale." Looking around the group, she comments, "While others of you have not yet touched it, I can feel your intentions because we are one, so if any one of us touches this, we have all touched it."

"What a beautiful message," observes Judy. "Children, let us do this. Close your eyes, but first, Sophia, hold up the amulet that all can see it."

As the light bounces off it, the luminescence of the gem's multi-colored facets creates an opalescent tranquility dazzling to the eye. "Now, close your eyes and go to your inner place of sacredness."

The children move about, their hands touching their bodies in the manner described.

"Now, with your hands upon your hearts, go to your life's being, the center of oneness within you, and from within that center of being, come and be one with sweet Sophie."

Sophie wiggles a bit in anticipation. Then she begins to smile and her eyes flicker as she feels her beautiful sisters and affirms them one by one. She comments softly, indicating to each that she knows of their oneness with her.

"Now, open your eyes. Who among you that has not physically touched the amulet can tell us of it?"

There is a moment of silence, and then off to one side comes, "I can tell of it."

"Very good, Kelleth. Speak it."

"It has carvings in it, and the symbol of the moon ... the one that is like a bowl on the side. And there is the symbol of the sacred tenet of ... I think it is of the adepts. Is that true?"

Anna smiles widely and nods. "It is true."

"And there is carving on the back that is our symbol."

"What is that symbol, Kelleth?" questions Anna just to verify that Kelleth knows this.

"The outline of the fish."

"Yes, that is true."

"I can feel how smooth it is. I even, in my spirit, held it up to the light and saw the colors."

"I saw them, too," adds Hannah. "They are so beautiful. They lifted me up and carried me like rainbows of color, like the reflection on our beautiful seashore ..." Her voice drifts off as she briefly recalls times at the sea.

"How very, very good, children. How well you do. Unquestionably the Spirit of God is upon you all."

The children look at each other smiling, touching one another. Mary is hugging Sophie and they are rocking.

Sophie pauses. "May I give this to someone now?"

Receiving nods from her teachers, she does so, and 'round and 'round they go, gifting it until the last one has received of it. It is Kelleth. She pauses a moment, then stands and strides up to Anna. "I have gone into my oneness. You taught us ..." she turns and smiles at her sisters, "that a gift, if truly, freely given, and truly, freely received, must always return to the giver."

The children all clap and cheer, laughing, some of them rolling about upon the ground in their joy.

"So now, I speak for my sisters and myself ... You are the temple of our holiness and love. It is appropriate that such a symbol as this, of beauty and power, be kept by you."

Kelleth reaches out and, to the glee of her sisters, ceremoniously places the amulet back into the hand of their dear teacher Anna. "But ... might we sometimes hold it?"

And all of the elder sisters laugh heartily.

ℛ⳼⳦

"Micaiah is returned," announces Joseph. "Let us call to council."

The evening meal, prayers, songs and such have been completed around the dwindling campfires, and here and there the twinkling of the stars, incredibly bright on this night, illuminates the new moon.

Micaiah stands. "Enos, brothers and sisters, I am come to you from the outer world with news. The king is dead. His son is taking reign. God's blessing is upon us, and the scourge to destroy our children appears to be passed. Though we have not certainty of this passing, those of us who are in the outer lands recommend to you, our council and our dear brothers and sisters," glancing at the adepts and Elob, "that we begin to disperse our families slowly back into society. It is also our recommendation that we send emissaries to re-establish the encampment at the Holy Mountains, that we can reawaken the Temple of the Prophets and the holy ones. We believe that it is time, and we have come to you to ask whether or not you see it so, as well. I ask of you, revered seers ... Ask of Our Lord God and then speak it, that we shall know how to proceed." He ends gesturing a blessing.

Enos stands and turns to Benjamin who rises, offers a prayer, and chants the sacred names of God. Some of the adepts with Elob rock and sway. Others form into geometric patterns, as is their custom. Then, silence.

When sufficient time has passed and it is apparent if most if not all the seers have, each in their own way, asked of God and received their answer, Benjamin begins to move throughout the circles and groups, going to each of the seers, the prophets, while Elob does the same in the opposite direction.

Now they stand together again.

Benjamin takes a few moments to look into the eyes of many of those present. "Our dear brethren, brothers and sisters, you have provided for us these past years. You came in answer to our prayers and saved so many of our people. I and my colleagues honor all of you. As a symbol of our love, our honor, our reverence for you and your knowledge and your belief, and, most of all, to acknowledge our oneness as brothers and sisters unto the Promise, we wish now to ask Elob to speak for us." With great gestures and bows of reverence, Benjamin turns, stepping backwards away from Elob, who stands smiling.

"We all agree that the vision is clear to which God has guided us, and that you are correct, Micaiah. It is time to proceed. Many of our people must now make their way back into the outer worlds. We must establish ourselves in the various communities and societies, so that when the Promise comes, we can give shelter and aid, guide, provide that unto the needs, and support and call forth those who are to walk with Him, so as He speaks it to us.

"It is our combined perception that this should commence immediately, for time draws short. But a few years remain before the Maidens are ready and the Chosen One will be made known. We must make the Way passable.

"Micaiah, our prayers have been with you and those who have served with you these past years as you faced untold danger and hardship. God blesses you. We shall inscribe your name in the holy records."

Micaiah nods and bows.

"These, now, are our recommendations." He turns to Enos and Mathias, and to all the others of noteworthy stature. "The parents of the children should be sent to diverse locations. Those of you who have come from relatively nearby villages and towns and provinces, we encourage to return there to rekindle friendships and associations. Those of you who are to offer services to others, trades if you will, we ask to resume those and become a part of those environs. It will be a time before the remainder of us, in small numbers here and there, can slowly begin to join you. Therefore, there will be a space wherein the children will not have your familiar love and embrace, but we believe the bonds are strong and that they are as one great spirit awakening under the guidance of beloved teachers, prophets, and seers," gesturing to Judy, Anna, Ruth, and the elder Theresa, "and so many others."

"Yet we must prepare, for there will be the testing for the young Maidens. And the work ... the calling forth of their truths, and the discovery of their oneness and their purpose ... cannot be allowed to falter." Turning to look at Joseph and Jacob, Elob avers, "The two of you will be sorely missed."

Joseph stiffens a bit, but Jacob only smiles.

"It is important for you, Joseph, and you," glancing over to Zechariah, "to become established in your villages, for reasons which we cannot fully reveal here. You must depart soon, perhaps on the morrow, and journey with Micaiah. We shall send our guides and council and several of the adepts to watch over you, but at a distance. We will also call upon the guardians, that these can be dispatched as well, for you are to be preserved at any cost!"

Standing over to the side, the guardians nod and hands come up immediately to volunteer for this dangerous task, until every guardian has raised his hand. They grasp one another's shoulders, smiling and gazing into each other's eyes.

"So, you can see that will be provided for." Elob turns back to those he has named.

Jacob stands, straightening his garment. "Might I speak?"

"Please."

"I think we would do well to close with a joyful song and dance. But before we do, let us ever remember and affirm, each of us, our purpose. We are each living extensions of the expressions of God, as all of you know, some far better than I, God's humble servant. But what I do know is that a glad heart can endure whatsoever comes before it. The offering of a bit of song and a little dance, even if one is alone, as I have so oft been myself, can invoke the presence of the All. When you do so," glancing to his brothers, Zechariah, Joseph, and a number of the others, "you will see us standing here at our future council fires, and you will feel us, just as you shall this evening as we lock our arms, in celebration that He comes.

"Praise God. Come. Let us sing. Let us dance. Let us all rejoice."

Chapter Fourteen

In Command of God's Spirit

The shadows are long, and in their embrace, one can find comfort from the heat and intensity of the day just past. So do we find the sisters, the candidate maidens, many from the School of the Prophets, and others of the Essenes all gathered here.

Approximately one year has passed. The young maidens now have a great degree of understanding of their nature and that which is called their gift, their truth. On this particular day, having had an active day of searching, discovery, and application, we find their demeanor is casual as they await the call to the evening prayer, meal, and celebration.

"How is it that you are able to bring about the elimination of an injury? We have seen you do this more than once," Abigale asks one of the adepts.

"Ah, this is a very good question, and a subject in which you have some considerable knowledge, Abigale."

"I do? Hmm ... I do not seem to know about that."

The other children look about, as they reflect upon the meaning here.

"It is a part of all that you have learned, for healing is not an action. It is not something that you *do*, like digging a hole, or weaving a cloth, or cooking a meal."

"Well, it *looks* like you are doing something," comments Zephorah.

"Yes, it does. It looks very much like you are doing something," agrees Kelleth.

"Perhaps so," the adept responds, "and perhaps there are times when doing things is certainly appropriate. For example, opening your spirit might be appropriate."

"What do you mean, opening your spirit?" Zephorah questions further.

"You do this often. It is the exercise my sisters have shown you, which you do easily now prior to your slumber."

"Are you saying that when that energy goes up through the top of my head and spills down over me, that is opening my spirit?" questions Mary.

"Indeed so."

"Oh-h. I thought that was the joy of God coming up from the earth and passing through me because I told God I love Him."

The children giggle a bit, for Mary's happy sweetness is evident in her demeanor and in her words.

"You have learned much about herbs and roots, and the many things that God provides in nature that can be used for teas, for herbal potions, for balms, and ointments, and all that sort. You know those that are capable of cleansing your body inside and out, and you know how to combine them, at least to some degree." The adept glances over at Isadore. "You know how to use them to heighten your ability to, how shall I call it, be *well*, in the total sense."

The children continue to reflect on these comments.

"Well, what is the difference between when you *do* something and when your spirit opens?" questions Andra.

"The opening of spirit is according to that which you feel guided to do. Your elder sisters may feel a bit differently," she adds, glancing up to look at Ruth, Judy, Anna, the elder Eloise, and so many of the sisters gathered here. A general consensus is given subtly and so the adept continues. "You build an attitude of knowing. That is like some of your truths, so I am told." She smiles at the children. "Knowing is a state of placing yourself in the flow of God's Spirit, which is the life force. When you encounter an individual who is in need, you know immediately, do you not, that something is amiss."

"Oh yes," exclaims Hannah, "they would not be ill if there was not something amiss." She smiles, looking around with pride at her knowledge.

"Well stated," the adept responds. "Knowing that then, when you place yourself in the flow of the life force, you become as an elder ... one who can command that force."

"Command it?" questions Kelleth. "Are you stating we command the Spirit of God?"

"Does that trouble you?"

The children look about at one another and their beloved teachers and sisters.

"Oh, children," Judy encourages, with a smile, "you are about to be given a great gift."

"But would the Spirit of God not get angry if I try to command it?" questions Rachel.

"Have you not commanded it often?" the adept asks.

Rachel reflects with deep seriousness, obviously sorting through her life's events and the teachings given to her. "Well, we command ourselves. We have learned how to take command of our own beings and to travel the beautiful path to the sacred place within, where we meet the Spirit of God and say, *This is our need ... We pray Thee, if it is appropriate, would you fulfill it?* But we do not say *Do this* or *Do that.*" She glances about, obviously deeply into the emotion of this topic.

"Listen carefully," the adept resumes. "You command the *Spirit* of God, not God. The Spirit of God is God's gift to you and to all the creatures upon the Earth, those which fly above, and all the creatures of the seas. God's Spirit is life itself. The power ... think about what I am sharing here ... is through the Spirit of God. Do you understand?"

They glance at one another and at Anna and Ruth.

"It is fine, go ahead and speak up," states the adept.

"Well," offers Zephorah, "I think we understand some of what you are saying, but we could use a little more help. Thank you very much."

The children giggle.

"Let us step back from the question. Look within yourselves, and find your sight and your hearing. Take a moment and do so now, please."

The children wiggle and straighten themselves, doing whatever works best for them to help them remove their thoughts. All become very still.

"Now, open your eyes again and perceive my words from within and without you. Quickly, all eyes look directly at the adept. "The greatest gift of all is constantly offered to everyone and everything. It is the Spirit of God, which is life. It is offered to you every moment of every day. It is with you no matter where you are, no matter what you do. Regardless of any circumstance, that gift is ever offered."

Some of the children close their eyes, and open them, and close them, and open them, obviously striving to see from their spirit self as well as their consciousness from Earth.

"I am accepting the gift of life with every breath that I take, am I not?" questions Mary.

"You are, indeed. But when you know it, affirm it, and use it as an act of self-empowerment, then the gift is truly received. Some pass through life and see this not, ever ... the importance to affirm the gift from God of life itself."

"Well, how does that relate to my question of healing?" questions Andra.

"Perhaps it is that the affirming, the claiming, and commanding of the Spirit of God must go before all else. But do you not wonder why they are dis-eased in the first place?"

A tiny hand comes up, and it is Eloise. "I think they are dis-eased when their heart does not have gladness."

"That is a very good answer. Does anyone have any

other thoughts on this?"

Almost every hand comes up.

"Wonderful." She points to Theresa.

"Perhaps they have a sadness. Perhaps they have lost someone. Like when we lost the guardians."

The adept merely smiles at this and nods.

Another hand comes up. "It could be that they have taken something into their body as a food, and it has created an angry tummy, and perhaps that is their dis-ease."

"This could well be, Rebekah," responds the adept.

"Perhaps one of the stingy things stung them."

"Yes, Zephorah, that could be, too."

"Or maybe, they were not looking where they were going, and they fell and hurt some part of their body," suggests Editha, smiling, looking about.

"This too is very possible. Is there anything else?"

Turning this way and that and sort of wriggling in her position, Mary slowly raises her hand. "Perhaps," she begins, "their spirit does not know their body. Perhaps they have lost sight of their spirit and that has saddened them, separated their heart and mind from the beauty and guidance and the loving replenishment that comes from God."

"Excellent, Mary. Now consider this, children: If one is in dis-ease, whether something has befallen them, or something has grown as an imbalance within their body, mind, or spirit, is it not so that the power of God in the Spirit of God ... always around us, remember ... has not been accepted, has not been seen? Often, the Spirit of God is asked for only when the body begins to fail."

"I understand what you are saying," offers Zephorah again, "It is the gladness that comes from being one with God that keeps us well and in a state of joyful ease. Is that true?"

"It is true. Even so, it is possible for events and circumstances to occur and to affect one. Nonetheless, should that occur we should remember the connection between the state of ease and oneness with God, the embrace of God, and claim the gift of God's Spirit ... which, again, is always present."

The children begin to smile.

"But what is it you *do* when you *do not do* a thing? questions Andra, pressing her point. "Like when you take from those herbal pouches you carry, when you do not do that, but you need to offer them healing, what do you do?"

"This is what I do ..." The adept brings herself quite erect. Her legs crossed, folded beneath her, she places her hands upon her knees and her eyes close. "If you wish to be complete with the Spirit of God, begin by being complete unto yourself. See how I now bring my hands to my feet?" and she bends, holding her feet, and touches them with her forehead.

"Oh-h," observes one of the children. "That looks a little difficult."

The adept comes back up. "Not for me. But mind you, this is the preparation for making *me* complete. It is not the only way. It is simply my way. If it suits you, use it. If it does not call to you, then do not let it be a limitation for you."

"Well, if it works for you, why would it not work for us?" questions another.

"I am not saying that. What I am saying is, if you do not find this joyful, then use that which helps *you* feel complete. Like you, Mary, with the energy that spills down over you. You do not do as I do to make that happen, do you?"

"No. I simply get quiet, build my consciousness into recognizing God, and then tell Him how much I love Him."

"It is like Ruth teaches us all the time." Kelleth smiles at her and receives a smile in return. "When we begin to do a thing, we first think about it, then we take it into our heart, then we take it along the golden path to the temple within. Having done these, if we find it to be good, we proceed, putting that goodness before what we do."

"Yes, and you expect goodness to come," the adept responds. "Like sowing a seed. You expect a plant to come forth from that seed. You and the seed are one through the Spirit of God. It is that oneness, the same as between you and the seed, that also exists between you and one who asks of you to be healed. The seed of that person's potential is always present, is it not? So, you give your spirit over to oneness with the Spirit of God. Just as with your breathing, if they ask it of you, you are, in a manner of speaking, breathing the Spirit of God on them."

The adept looks about to see how the children are doing with all of this. Abigale is nodding, but slowly.

"Would I do that like this?" Abigale purses her mouth and blows very hard.

"You could do so, but you might look a bit odd."

The children all chuckle.

"It is not the physical thing that you do, so much as it is your intention and your holiness that goes with it."

"My holiness?" questions Abigale.

"Yes, your holiness."

"You mean I am holy?"

"Yes, of course."

She shakes her head to and fro. "Well, that part is not very clear at all. I see the holy men and women of our people, and they have great lights around them." She turns to check with the other children, who nod vigorously. "I do not see any light around me," looking at her hands and feet in the depth of the day's growing shadows.

"How does one go about seeing one's self?" questions the adept.

"Well, I can hold my hand out," and she does.

"Keep holding it out there, Abigale, against the dark shadow of that outcropping," the adept directs, and rises to walk around behind Abigale, who is still holding her hand up. "Do you see the light around your hand?"

"I see a little, but not like the holy ones. They glow like

the sun sometimes."

The children all agree.

"Well then, we shall have to make you glow so that your hand can be like the hand of God, that the Spirit of God can flow through you to answer the need of another."

"I would like that a lot!" She bobs her head up and down vigorously.

By now all of the children are holding their hands out and have positioned themselves close to Abigale, hoping as they do, that whatever she receives will spill over onto them.

"Now, do this ... Close your eyes, and with your other hand, balance yourself as you have been taught so well."

Abigale brings the palm of her other hand up to her solar plexus, then to her heart, to her throat, to her mouth, to her forehead, and then places it flat upon her head, and states, "I am Abigale. I am your daughter, Lord God. I come to you in joy and expectation." She brings her hand slowly down over her forehead and over her face, perceiving areas that might need cleansing or releasing, and when she reaches the point just below her throat, she makes a little swirling motion, pauses, and her hand continues downward, finally coming to rest, turned upward, in her lap.

"Now, open your eyes and look at your hand."

"Oh-h! It is much brighter!"

"Now, close your eyes again." Abigale's eyes close, as do those of all the others. "Breathe in the Spirit of God, which is ever about you." Audibly, all the children breathe in very deeply. "Hold it a moment. Now open your eyes and breathe the Spirit of God out towards your hand."

Abigale's eyes pop open, and she breathes slowly, deliberately, towards her hand. As she does, she exclaims so sharply that she begins to choke on her own breath, and coughs and sputters. "I saw it! My hand was golden like the holy ones!" She turns to look at the adept. "It was golden like your hands are when you work for someone who is not well."

"You see? If you do what you know to do, and if you build according to that which is good for you, then you open yourself to be a channel for the Spirit of God to come forth. But it is you who commands the Spirit. You direct it according to your righteousness, your honor, your truth."

"Do you think I am very righteous?" Abigale asks sincerely. "I saw lots of golden light around my hand. Does that mean that I am quite righteous?"

"Do you think it does?"

"I think it must. I have never seen the golden light around anyone who did not have a great deal of righteousness." She glances around to see her friends all nodding.

"Then it must be true. For remember, that which you see from which you can take goodness, *is* goodness. It is as the tiny seed which grows into a mighty tree bearing good fruit ... If the fruit is good, then the seed must also be good. As it is above, so is it below. That fruit borne from whatever is rooted in the Spirit of God is the product of your intention. It is the answer to the request that comes to you."

There is a long silence.

Little Theresa raises her hand. "Why do some people who have very bad dis-eases get healed and then get the sickness again? Some of them came back to our people over and over. Our holy ones would heal them, but in a fortnight or two, back they would come with the same problem. They would ask again, and the holy ones would just smile and give to them again. Why do they not stay well? Why do they get filled with dis-ease again?"

"Excellent question. Do you think it is that your holy ones have not done a very good work?"

Abigale shakes her head, "Oh, no. Our holy ones do very good work. When they give healings to our people, that is it. The dis-ease is gone. They have no need to come back again and again like the outsiders."

"Well then, what do you think is the difference?"

Hannah smiles. "I have an idea. My idea is that they do not know God. They do not know that if they ask God, God will give it. So they come to our holy ones and ask them. And our holy ones give them, like you said, the Spirit of God. But they do not know the Spirit of God. It has no place to live in them because they do not know about their sacred place, the holy place inside of them. So our holy ones have to give them the Spirit of God again and again. They always come back because they do not make a house for God and the Spirit of God inside themselves like we do."

Mary nods an emphatic approval. They smile at one another for a prolonged moment, and then Hannah turns to look at the adept, who has moved around to sit next to Anna.

"Your sisters can speak more on this for you, but for now I must depart. We have our ceremonies coming very shortly, and before the call I should like to be ready. But thank you, children, for the many gifts you have given me."

A hand comes up, and a little voice says, "It would seem to me that it is you who have given the gifts to us. What have we given to you, sweet sister?"

"You have given me an opportunity to serve God by serving you. And you know that the more you serve God, the greater does God's light pour into you. If you had not given me this opportunity to serve, I might not be overflowing with the Spirit of God right now." The adept raises her outstretched hands, curls her arms towards the top of her head, placing her fingertips side by side in the center of the crown of her head, closes her eyes, and emits a soft, single tone.

The children gasp, as brilliant colors flow from the adept, dancing out as though they were living lights reaching out to touch them. Some of the children look down to see where a shaft of beautiful color seems to be touching them, and then quickly look up, smiling, as they feel and see the effect of the adept's loving intent.

"You see?" She brings her hands back down. "Thank

you for your gift. Now I must depart and share it with my brothers and sisters in our twilight ceremony. But I leave my love with you, as always." She emulates the Essene maidens' gesture of love, rises, and turns to walk up through the outcroppings to meet her colleagues.

"What did she mean, Anna? What was it that you would tell us?" asks one.

"Well, about the meaning of building a house for God within, and ways to build your place of holiness within through your intention ... the will that goes before you."

"Tell us about this, Anna," asks Eloise, and the children snuggle in close to their beloved teacher.

"If one comes to you who is in need, ask of them, 'Are you willing to dwell in the house of God?' If they answer 'Yes,' then speak to them this way, 'Then I shall build it for you, but it is you who must maintain it.'

"And if they say, 'Yes, build it,' then do so. But if, being healed, they rise up and go away and ask not how to maintain the house of God, then breathe the breath of the Spirit of God to them and release them. For to build a house in which the Spirit of God can dwell in your life is only the beginning. For then you must nourish it. It is the *dwelling* in the house of God that makes all aright, that creates a state of ease.

"Those who return again and again to our holy ones for healing do not know how to make their life a house for God. Some might try by going to the temples and purchasing this or that for sacrifice or asking for blessings. But in order to nourish the house of God, one must have a joyful intent. One must be the vessel, the cup, from which they give of that which has been given to them. Then the Spirit of God can flow into and through them, filling God's house as His Spirit passes through to fulfill their intent for others. Do you understand this?"

The children look at one another.

"I think it is like this ..." Hannah responds. "With some

people, you can feel the warmth of the Spirit of God quite a ways from their house, I mean from their body." The children smile at this. "But with other people, it is difficult to feel it even when you get your hand real close. I have not seen any like that for a long time. Only the outsiders seem to have cold houses."

"Maybe they do not have a house at all," interjects Abigale.

"Well, would they not die if they did not have a house to live in? The adept said that the Spirit of God gives us life, like a sort of house in which we live, and that the Spirit of God lives in it with us. So I guess if someone did not have a house like this, they would not have any spirit of life. And if they did not have any spirit of life, first they would get real sick and then I guess they would leave."

"There is much truth in what you say, Hannah." Rising and glancing around at all the children, Anna adds, "Well, you have another house, too, sweet children," and they look at one another. "It is the one that walks and talks ... and gets hungry and is about to get some food."

The children all laugh and clap their hands and jump to their feet, brushing themselves off in preparation for their return. The sisters arrange them so that they are three abreast, flanked on either side by sisters and elder maidens. As they move along, the children begin a little song about the wonder of God in the call of the birds, and in the beauty of this land and one another.

ଛଠ୧ଓ

"Are they established? Have they been well received, or have there been any troubles, Jason?" questions Elob.

"No, nothing significant. A few little challenges here and there, but these are commonplace even among those who have been resident for many, many years."

"Are they at work in their various trades?" asks Ruth.

"They are, indeed, and for the most part, doing quite well ... accepted, and their skills being sought after."

Judy nods, "These are all good things to hear."

"We have seen this, too," Benjamin glances over at Zelotese, and receives a smile of affirmation. "But the invocation of the power needs to be manifested slowly, that there is no reaction, no discovery of our people."

"Do you think it is possible for them to begin to gather and build the power yet?" questions Judy.

Jason nods, his face serious. "Yes, but slowly. For some of these villagers are ... Well, they have nothing better to do than to meddle and make accusations."

"Then we shall send emissaries to visit as relatives from distant lands. And we shall gather on the holy times and help them build the power."

"Very good," responds Jason.

As the discussion continues, they begin to talk about sending some of the children, particularly the boys, home to their parents.

"Do they have their foundations strongly in place that when they are called, their consciousnesses will know and see Him as the Christ?"

"Yes," Ruth responds, and Anna, as well. "They are well prepared. It is time for at least some of them to begin to be a part of their family again. Not all of them at once, of course. Randomly here and there, that one of the overseers does not note that many children have returned from visits with family and relatives all at once."

Judy and several of her sisters begin to select and record names.

As the discussions diminish and the fires ebb, some of the Essene elders and some of the seers and healers return to their own works and focus.

Of the small group remaining, Zelotese leans over close to Judy. "What is the method that you and your people use to build the power?"

Glancing up, somewhat startled to see his beautiful penetrating gaze so close to her own, she momentarily hesitates as she remembers her experience with the two seers when they called the storm. Her mind races, and she recognizes that entities such as this one, Zelotese, see her and her brothers as equals, see her energy as a uniqueness to be admired, revered, and to be at one with, warmly, lovingly.

In the seconds wherein these thoughts pass through her, she sees Zelotese' eyes soften, and he begins to smile. Apparently, he has sensed her reaction. "We use our ceremonies and our sacred works to build the power. We do this as you have seen them done many times here during the several years we have been with you."

"To what end do you build the power, if I might ask?" he continues, probing gently.

"That we can preserve and open the consciousnesses of those who will be at the ready when He comes; that we can anticipate and if need be make changes, make preparations, alter things, that the Promise can manifest."

Zelotese nods. "We will help you."

"Oh, we so hoped you would."

"We invite you to join us in some of our works, for we know you have the sight, and we know you have the power. Your seers have spoken of the event, as well. So be at ease with my invitation. Perhaps bring Anna, and any of the others you deem appropriate. We will share the gifts of the magi, which are one with the spirit of your own truths.

"Together we can strengthen that power to make the Promise move easily, joyfully, that He can manifest all that He is, and that the gifts your young Maidens will reflect back to Him may be given to those He knows are worthy. Do come soon. The time approaches quickly that these things must be made ready."

"That we shall," Judy whispers. "May the blessings of the

One God ever surround and embrace you all throughout your journeys."

"And you, as well." Zelotese smiles, and he reaches his hand up to place it upon her shoulder. His eyes flicker and close, and he utters beautiful lyrical words in his native tongue. Judy can feel the flood of energy rushing into her body. His eyes flicker open. "I shall repeat to you in your words, that which I said to our God, that you can know of the blessing I offer you. 'Hear me, Lord God. I, Zelotese, Thy son, offer the grace and love of my being unto this, your daughter, Judy. Let it flow between us ever, that wheresoever the need might arise, she may take of it and honor your Word, and embrace the Promise.'"

Her eyes do not waver, but a tear begins to form in the corner of one, for she has experienced the power of this beautiful being's intentions to her.

Gazing at her warmly, lovingly, Zelotese removes his hand, nods, rises, and departs.

Judy bows her head, alone now beside the small embers from whence earlier the flames had illuminated all who had gathered about.

"Lord God," we hear her pray, "my spirit knows You have blessed this one called Zelotese, and all those who are with him who hold the light and hopefulness of Your Word, as do we. As it is mine to give, I give it unto him, and his brothers and sisters. This is my intention. I direct my spirit to open itself, that You, Lord God, shall flow through same, bearing the loving intention as I have asked of Thee."

Her hands come up in closure to her prayer, and she straightens herself and gazes into the embers. Her vision dims and fogs.

The colors of the embers blend with the night's darkness and swirl about.

There is a brief flash of brilliant light, and before her is a vision.

She sees a small village and in it many children are laughing and playing. She sees her sisters, older now, and she sees the Maidens grown and joyful, filled with an abundant wonder of life.

And she sees one, the light illuminating Him, as He laughs with His friends, playing games. Her heart leaps with joy as the vision ends, and she whispers, "He comes."

Look you unto your own house of God, as was taught to the children, and give unto it thy sustenance. Fill it with the joy, the hopefulness, the love, of God, and bring these forth from within you, that you become the vessel through which all things are possible.

You will hear in coming times upon your Earth of turmoil and strife, and you will hear that contests between brothers and sisters grow more tenacious. Do not fall prey to the call of the illusion and contribute to that energy. Rather, build your intention all the stronger. Place your love and your grace with them. Breathe the Spirit of God unto their need.

Above all else, however, nourish thine own house aplenty. Be expectant. Be joyful ... and that shall be the harvest which will be gathered.

We are your brethren, your brothers and sisters, and we call to you ...

Join us.

The Way opens.
The Promise comes.

ABOUT LAMA SING

More than thirty years ago for our convenience, the one through whom this information flows accepted the name Lama Sing, though it was stated that they, themselves, have no need for names or titles.

"We identify ourselves only as servants of God, dedicated to you, our brothers and sisters in the Earth."

–Lama Sing

☙

ABOUT THIS CHANNEL

"Channel is that term given generally to those who enable themselves to be, as much as possible, open and passable in terms of information that can pass through them from the Universal Consciousness, or other such which are not associated in the direct sense with their finite consciousness of the current incarnation."

–Lama Sing

Books by Al Miner & Lama Sing

The Promise: *Book I of The Essene Legacy*
The Awakening: *Book II of The Essene Legacy*
The Path: *Book III of The Essene Legacy*

In Realms Beyond: *Book I of The Peter Chronicles*
Awakening Hope: *Book II of The Peter Chronicles*

Death, Dying, and Beyond: *How to Prepare for The Journey* Vol I
The Sea of Faces: *How to Prepare for The Journey* Vol II

Jesus: *Book I*
Jesus: *Book II*

The Course in Mastery

Watch for ...

Sacred City

The complete books of The Peter Chronicles

The Peter Chronicles Study Guides:
    Companion Guides to the Peter Chronicles
    consisting of questions from study groups
    about the Peter Chronicles
    with answers from Lama Sing

The movie based on The Peter Project

For a comprehensive list of readings transcripts available, visit the
Lama Sing library at www.lamasing.net

ABOUT AL MINER

A chance hypnosis session in 1973 began Al's tenure as the channel for Lama Sing. Since then, nearly 10,000 readings have been given in a trance state answering technical and personal questions on such topics as science, health and disease, history, geophysics, spirituality, philosophy, metaphysics, past and future times, and much more. The validity of the information has been substantiated and documented by research institutions and individuals. Those receiving personal readings continue to refer others to Al's work based on the accuracy and integrity of the information in their readings. In 1984, St. Johns University awarded Al an honorary doctoral degree in parapsychology.

Al conducts a variety of field research projects, as well as occasional workshops and lectures. He occasionally accepts requests for personal readings, but is mostly devoting his remaining time to works intended to be good for all. Much of his current research is dedicated to the concept that the best of all guidance is that which comes from within.

Al lives with his family in the mountains of Western North Carolina.

9 780979 126222